Praise for *Living the Cl*

D0901835

"Beautiful in its gentleness and humility, this
communions and denominations, for it deals with our beginnings and the
originating, sacred rhythms from which we all come. Only Bobby Gross could
have so gracefully opened the church's liturgical calendar to all who wish to
see, and only he could have laid so rich a feast of devotion as this for those who
yearn to enter."

Phyllis Tickle, author of *The Divine Hours*

"Many devout Christian believers are unaware of the richness to be found in the
Christian calendar year, with its high and low points, its celebrations, its times
of self-examination and repentance, and even what is known as 'ordinary time.'
Bobby Gross, who began to live the seasons of the Christian year as an adult,
celebrates the story of Jesus' life through liturgy. This is a bountiful resource,
thought-provoking, informative and motivational, showing how liturgy can help
us in our deep need to pursue God and a holy life."

Luci Shaw, writer-in-residence, Regent College, and author of *Water My Soul* and
Breath for the Bones

"The Scriptures of the Christian faith are two great stories to be savored. There
is the outer story, running from creation (Genesis 1—2) through to the consummation (Revelation 21—22). Within this expanse there is the crucial and climactic inner story, that of the birth, ministry, passion, death, resurrection, ascension and reign of Jesus. Yet some Christians seem uninterested or unable to
make the most of these accounts of the holy in our midst. . . . How tragic! But
Bobby Gross comes to the rescue, interpreting forgotten meanings in the biblical
accounts and giving practical suggestions that enable us to organize our daily
devotions (our own faith stories) around the biblical narratives the church uses
to shape the new identity we are given by God in Christ.

"If you have been a part of a church that observes seasons such as Advent and
Lent, this book will greatly deepen your grasp of what you may have observed
without much understanding. If you have been influenced by those who have
jettisoned such observances, here you will be introduced to time-honored spiritual practices in ways that can form you in newness of life, thereby causing you
to be more conformed to the fullness of the gospel."

Laurence Hull Stookey, Professor Emeritus, Wesley Theological Seminary,
and author of *Calendar: Christ's Time for the Church*

"Whether we know and believe it or not, we live in sacred time. The only time that is is created, given, sustained and re-created by God—time that God will one day fulfill. *Living the Christian Year* beckons us to lay hold of this reality, to richly dwell in the story that holds time together, and as we do so to practice the communion that holds God's people together in grace across time and around the globe. This is the biblical story out of which comes all true worship and justice."

Mark Labberton, author of *The Dangerous Act of Worship*

"Culture's daily story of noise, busyness, consumerism and competition is often the loudest shaping voice of our lives. It can influence choices more than a weekly or monthly dose of churchgoing does. Bobby Gross opens the possibility for another voice and another story to shape us on a daily basis. *Living the Christian Year* invites believers to live by the rhythms of God's redemption story. This lovely book hooks our daily life into the extraordinary beauty and usefulness of the liturgical year—a year spent in following the life of Jesus. I delight in a book that reveals how Advent, Christmas, Epiphany, Lent, Holy Week, Pentecost and Ordinary Time place our ordinary lives in the context of the most amazing story ever—the story that can guide us at all times and in all places."

Adele Calhoun, copastor, Redeemer Community Church, and author of *Spiritual Disciplines Handbook*

"Only occasionally does a book come along which will become a steady companion in my own journey of discipleship. Bobby Gross has engagingly written that kind of book. It both points the way to a fuller understanding of God's great story in Christ, and simultaneously provides guidance and tools to help me weave my life into God's story as I enter the steady rhythms of the Christian calendar. I have never seen a book quite like this."

Dr. Stephen A. Hayner, professor of evangelism and church growth, Columbia Theological Seminary

"Bobby Gross has written a jewel of a book about the depth and riches of observing the Christian year. Christians in nonliturgical settings will be touched by his understanding, not to mention those who are already living the Christian feasts and seasons in liturgical churches. They, too, will gain insight to match their customary practice. This is a book to dip into and enjoy."

Emilie Griffin, author of *Clinging* and *Doors into Prayer*

LIVING THE CHRISTIAN YEAR

Time to Inhabit the Story of God

AN INTRODUCTION
AND DEVOTIONAL GUIDE

BOBBY GROSS

FOREWORD BY LAUREN WINNER

IVP Books

An imprint of InterVarsity Press
Downers Grove, Illinois

InterVarsity Press
P.O. Box 1400, Downers Grove, IL 60515-1426
World Wide Web: www.ivpress.com
E-mail: email@ivpress.com

InterVarsity Press® is the book-publishing division of InterVarsity Christian Fellowship/USA®, a
movement of students and faculty active on campus at hundreds of universities, colleges and schools of
nursing in the United States of America, and a member movement of the International Fellowship of
Evangelical Students. For information about local and regional activities, write Public Relations Dept.,
InterVarsity Christian Fellowship/USA, 6400 Schroeder Rd., P.O. Box 7895, Madison, WI
53707-7895, or visit the IVCF website at <www.intervarsity.org>.

Scripture quotations, unless otherwise noted, are from the New Revised Standard Version of the Bible,
copyright 1989 by the Division of Christian Education of the National Council of the Churches of
Christ in the USA. Used by permission. All rights reserved.

The poem on page 47, titled "Annunciation" by Denise Levertov, is from The Stream and the Sapphire,
copyright ©1984 by Denise Levertov. Reprinted by permission of New Directions Publishing Corp.

For the poem on pages 196-97: Copyright © 1999 by Wendell Berry from A Timbered Choir: The
Sabbath Poems 1979-1997. Reprinted by permission of Counterpoint.

Design: Cindy Kiple
Cover image: Mosaics of ceiling with Chi Rho symbol, 6th C.E., at Baptistry, Albenga, Italy. Scala/Art
                Resource, NY
Interior image: Dorling Kindersley/Getty Images

ISBN 978-0-8308-3520-1

Printed in the United States of America ∞

Library of Congress Cataloging-in-Publication Data

Gross, Bobby.
   Living the Christian year: time to inhabit the story of God / Bobby
Gross.
       p. cm.
   Includes bibliographical references.
   ISBN 978-0-8308-3520-1 (pbk.: alk. paper)
   1. Church year meditations. I. Title.
   BV30.G83 2009
   242'.3—dc22

                                                                    2009021525

| P | 18 | 17 | 16 | 15 | 14 | 13 | 12 | 11 | 10 | 9 | 8 | 7 | 6 | 5 | 4 |
| Y | 24 | 23 | 22 | 21 | 20 | 19 | 18 | 17 | 16 | 15 | 14 | 13 | 12 | 11 |

To the priests who taught me
to live the Christian year:

Clifford Horvath
Church of the Resurrection,
Biscayne Park, Florida

Colin Goode
Milind Sojwal
All Angels' Church,
New York City

Contents

The Cycles of Love

Foreword

What time is it?

That's a trickier question than it appears at first blush, for in our world there are so many different calendars giving competing answers.

Take, for example, the problem of the new year. There are so many days we might designate as the beginning of the new year. January 1, of course, is one answer. If, like me, you have logged so many years in school that the academic calendar remains the fundamental calendar of your life, September, with its new lunch boxes and sharp pencils, may be the truest new year in your life. Or, if you're Jewish, the new year is Rosh Hashana (actually, there are four new years in the Jewish calendar, but that's a topic for another day . . .).

And then there's Advent—according to the church calendar, the first day of Advent is the first day of the year.

One of my goals in life is to inhabit the Christian story so fully that Advent will be the instinctive beginning of my year. One of my goals is to inhabit church even more fully than I inhabit school, so that Advent hymns, rather than pencil tips, signal the beginning of the year.

Why is this so important to me, this living into the church's calendar?

Well, for many reasons.

First, I want the Christian story to shape everything I do, even how I reckon time. I want it to be truer and more essential to me than school's calendar, or Hallmark's calendar, or the calendar set by the IRS. I want the rhythms of Advent, Christmas, Epiphany, Lent, Easter, Pentecost to be more basic to my life than the days on which my quarterly estimated taxes are due.

Second, I have found that inhabiting the church calendar is powerfully evangelistic. Quite simply, if you really live into Advent—rather than starting Christmas the day after Thanksgiving—and if you really live into a season of Easter that lasts long after the Peeps are gone from the grocery store shelves, you will be doing something so countercultural that it will not escape the notice of your friends and neighbors—and they will ask you why you are doing the things you are doing—and you will have a chance to tell them something about Jesus.

And third, most important: almost more than anything else I've done since becoming a Christian, trying to live inside church time has formed me in the Christian story. Which is to say, almost more than anything else, living inside church time has formed me in Jesus' story. Jesus drew my attention to himself, and the church calendar has kept it fixed there—on him. Church time has offered me the chance to reprise and reiterate Jesus' life every year. Church time has invited me to wait expectantly for Jesus during the days of Advent—even though, on some of those days, I feel like Jesus will never come back (and some of those days, I'm not sure if I want him to). Church time has invited me, during Epiphany, to meditate on who Jesus is and what he came to do, and how I might shine forth his light in the world—even though, on some of those Epiphany days, my attention more naturally wandered to matters like winter weight loss.

But it's hard to do, living inside the church calendar. Our surrounding society gives us so many different calendrical cues. It tells us that the opening day of baseball season, not Easter, is the most important day of spring. It tells us that the days on which stores have great sales are the real red-letter days. Ironically, we don't always get a lot of help living into the calendar that the early church developed.

Several books have especially helped me in this quest to live fully into the church's calendar—among them, my church's prayerbook, the Book of Common Prayer; Frederica Mathewes-Greens's memoir, *Facing East;* and this book, which I have been privileged to read and use even before its publication.

Living the Christian Year will guide you through the seasons of the church's calendar. It will connect you with Jesus' life, and it will connect you with a calendar that has been inhabited by faithful Christians for many centuries. It will supply you with quite an answer to the question "What time is it?" In short, *Living the Christian Year* will help you deepen your acquaintance with Jesus.

* * *

Book forewords are supposed to be about the book, but I hope you, kind reader, will indulge me one word about the author.

Bobby Gross and I had a first real conversation at a restaurant on the Upper West Side of Manhattan about a decade ago. I had recently started attending the church where Bobby was a lay leader—the church that taught both of us so much about the rhythms of the calendar, All Angels' Church in New York City. This book has been a gift to me, but Bobby's friendship and wisdom have been the greater gift. But, of course, what's so fundamentally wonderful about books is that through these pages, you get to encounter a bit of Bobby's wisdom, even if you don't meet him in person until the heavenly banquet.

I am so very excited that Bobby wrote this book. I have been after him to do so for years.

* * *

Oh, and one final note: sometimes books like this one can be intimidating, because (if you're like me) you think you're supposed to use them every day or every week, and then, if you fall out of the habit, you think you're somehow not allowed to open the book again later in the year and pick up there in the middle. Like in June. Or September. So, the final note is: don't feel bad if you don't use the book exactly as it was intended. Bobby—knowing my neuroses well—has already assured me that if I set the book down, I am welcome back in July, or whenever. I look forward to praying with you then.

Lauren F. Winner

1

Discovering Sacred Time

When we submit our lives to what we read in Scripture, we find that
we are not being led to see God in our stories but our stories in God's.
God is the larger context and plot in which our stories find themselves.

EUGENE PETERSON

I'm interested in the experience of sacred time, in our ability to feel the intersec-
tion of time and eternity at special places in the year. . . . Sacred time is what
makes the Church Year a genuinely transformative practice.

CHRISTOPHER HILL

It was our ritual. Every night around 8:30, our family would gather in the den for devotions. Only we didn't call it that; for us, it was simply time for "the story." Dad would sit in his big chair and one of my younger siblings would snuggle in his lap. The others would sprawl on the floor. Mom would settle into her spot and I would claim the rocker. Dad would find where we had left off the night before and then begin reading.

The story might be from *Little Visits with God* or The Chronicles of Narnia or *Pilgrim's Progress*. Or, of course, from the Bible. Maybe it was about Jesus. Or Samson. Or Esther. Or Shadrach, Meshach and "To-bed-we-go." If Mom and Dad were out for the evening, we made the babysitter read and one of us would pray at the end. (When I was old enough to watch my siblings, I'd take the lead and, well, some of those evenings didn't go so well.) This was our habit, year after year, until my youngest brother reached his teens. We spent twenty or so minutes nightly learning about God—sometimes it was magical, sometimes it fell apart in fussing and tears, most often it was simply routine. But over time, sharing in "the story" imperceptibly stitched our family together and wove into each of us threads of spiritual truth.

This book is about sharing in the Story. It's about keeping a centuries-old tradition with the family of God. It's about participating in the life of Jesus so that we can be transformed. It's about taking our place in the great drama of God's love and redemption of the world. It's about taking time to inhabit—to dwell inside, to be at home in—God's Story through living the Christian year and keeping its spiritual rhythms.

GOD'S STORY, OUR STORIES

I love stories. I love how they can unlock something inside of us. How they can make us laugh or cry or go silent with awe. How they can lift our spirits and break our hearts. How they can make us think. How they can take us into another world and in so doing illuminate our own. I love how they can move us to live more truly. All the great stories do this.

Take J. R. R. Tolkien's trilogy *The Lord of the Rings*. If you've read it, you know what I mean. If you've only seen Peter Jackson's movies, you still have a pretty good idea. The story takes place over the course of only two years, but for the four little hobbits, what a two years: an impossible quest to destroy a magic ring, a cataclysmic war between good and evil, encounters with elves and orcs, wizards and wraiths, deeds of courage and acts of betrayal, the making of friends and the grieving of deaths, the shadow of despair and the strength of hope. And Tolkien has set this story inside something even larger: the vast world of Middle Earth in its Third Age, complete with its own cosmology, mythology, languages and millennia of history.

This sense of small people becoming part of a large story is conveyed in the final chapter, in which the unlikely hobbit hero Frodo settles on a title for the book he's written to tell the tale. His uncle Bilbo, whose wanderings had gotten everything started, had named his part of the account *My Diary*, but this was a far cry from Frodo's final choice of title: *The*

Downfall of the Lord of the Rings and the Return of the King (as seen by the Little People; being the memoirs of Bilbo and Frodo of the Shire, supplemented by the accounts of their friends and the learning of the Wise).

Without even reading the book, you already get the picture: common folk from an out-of-the-way place are caught up in a huge adventure of momentous import. What starts as a simple diary ends as a grand epic.

Most of us think of ourselves as ordinary people living quiet lives in unremarkable places. We are merely hobbits in our shires. But listen! We may not be caught up in a dangerous drama like Frodo and his loyal companion, Sam, but we nonetheless live inside a big story, one that started long before our birth and that will go on long after our death, one that's as wide as the universe and as old as eternity: the Story of God as centered in Jesus the Christ.

Our personal narratives take their fullest shape and deepest meaning in relation to God's purposes for us and for the world. As Eugene Peterson puts it, "God is the larger context and plot in which our stories find themselves." A very large context and very long plot indeed.

In the beginning, the triune God creates the cosmos out of gratuitous love and sheer delight. He makes human beings in his image to know and love him and to know and love one another. He entrusts them with responsibility to care for creation and develop its cultural potential. Foolishly, they assert themselves against God's loving authority with woeful consequences for themselves and the earth. But God in his great mercy enacts his plan to rescue humanity and to right what is wrong. At first, he reveals himself to one nation by which he intends to bless all nations. Eventually he incarnates himself in one person by whom he intends to save all people.

Thus unfolds the drama of Jesus Christ: the prophecies and his miraculous birth, his compassion and teaching, his healings and actions against evil, his unjust suffering and atoning death, his triumphant resurrection and ascent into heaven, after which God gives his very Spirit to indwell Christ's followers and empower them as witnesses and servants in the world. And so the Story continues right to our day, and on it will go until the end of days, when Jesus will return in power to judge all of humanity and history. This long saga of redemption will culminate in the creation of a new heaven and earth in which God's people, resurrected and transformed, will enjoy his presence and share in his glory forever.

This is the Great Story. This is the gospel. It centers on Jesus Christ, but at its heart, amazingly, we also find ourselves. The Book of Common Prayer distills the Story in this Eucharistic affirmation:

Holy and gracious Father: In your infinite love you made us for yourself; and, when we had fallen into sin and become subject to evil and death, you, in your mercy, sent Jesus Christ, your only and eternal Son, to share our human nature, to live and die as one of us, to reconcile us to you, the God and Father of all.

To embrace Jesus is to be reconciled to God and to consciously step into his Story. And to follow Jesus is to have the shape and purpose of our lives conformed to the shape and purpose of his. So we choose to deny ourselves, to no longer live centered on ourselves as our culture urges but to live in allegiance to him who died for us. We choose to take on his character, live by his teachings and pursue his mission in the world. We seek to do our part in God's reconciliation to himself of all things. We seek to love God with our whole being and to love our neighbors as ourselves. And we are prepared to suffer and even to die in living this way. Nonetheless, we live in great hope.

In other words, we want to inhabit the still-unfolding Story of God and have it inhabit and change us. And this is exactly what the ancient liturgical habit of living the Christian year helps us to do.

OPENING TO LITURGY

It never would have occurred to my parents to select readings for our family story time that reflected the Christian year. They were unfamiliar with it, as was I for many years. For example, in my senior year of college, my literary-minded apartment-mate proposed throwing a Twelfth Night party à la Shakespeare. Well, I knew about the play but had never connected its title with the twelve days of the holiday song, nor did I realize that January fifth was the eve of a feast called Epiphany. Once, in ignorance, I pointed out to a Catholic friend that he had some kind of smudge on his forehead he just might want to take care of. Only later, to my embarrassment, did I realize it had been Ash Wednesday. I knew almost nothing about this holy day of fasting observed by Christians around the world.

When I was growing up, my family attended a Southern Baptist church. We celebrated Christmas and Easter, of course, but these were special Sundays, not special seasons. Well, in a way, Christmas was a season. In December there would be festive decorations in the sanctuary and extra performances by the choir, maybe a Christmas cantata or a more extravagant production, say, of "The Living Christmas Tree" (the choir arrayed on a seven-tiered, triangular structure). But apart from those children's calendars with the little paper windows you open one a day until the twenty-fifth, I didn't learn about Advent, much less the additional days of Christmas or the celebration of Epiphany.

It was much the same at Easter time. Palm Sunday was noted and a noon service held on Good Friday. To be sure, Easter worship was rousing, with lilies and brass and Handel's "Hallelujah Chorus." But we knew nothing of the weeks of Lent or the Great Fifty Days or Pentecost Sunday. Similarly, I knew about Mardi Gras as a big party night, especially in New Orleans, but not about its relation to Ash Wednesday. Nor was I aware that Halloween—All Hallows Eve—preceded All Saints Day.

My church paid little or no attention to the Christian year, as is still the case in so many churches. Baptists, like other Free churches arising from the Protestant Reformation, had discarded the long-standing observance of the liturgical calendar so central to the Orthodox, Catholic, Anglican and Lutheran traditions. This unawareness was to change for me.

When I met my wife, Charlene, I was a young campus minister with InterVarsity and she a college student. Although she had grown up Catholic and I Baptist, we had both been drawn to a college-oriented Evangelical Free church. There was strong biblical teaching there, but nothing of the Christian year. After marrying, we moved to Miami where we settled together on a small Episcopal church. It was multiethnic, mildly charismatic and missions-oriented. And also liturgical.

With her Catholic upbringing, Charlene felt right at home. Not me. I was lost for months. I'd never been in a church like this: they used a prayer book and a lectionary, they took Communion—with real wine— at an altar every week, they stood and knelt and crossed themselves, and the pastor—priest, actually—wore colors that coordinated with seasons of some sort. I had no idea what was going on. It all seemed very "Catholic" to me, which was not particularly positive given my uninformed stereotypes and inherited suspicions. I had concerns about empty rituals, rote prayers and outdated traditions. Didn't it all add up to religion rather than relationship, formality rather than faith, aesthetics rather than authenticity? But I stuck it out, and two choices proved important.

First, I determined to learn more by asking questions and reading. About the history of the Episcopal church and the Anglican tradition. About the shape and meaning of the services. About the nature of sacraments and the reasons for ritual. About the holy days and church calendar. Second, I decided to participate with an open heart. I chose to trust that there was something valuable in all of it. I prayed for God to guide me and guard me. I tried to be patient.

Slowly, over time, I began to experience the beauty and power of the liturgy. I remember the moment when I knew I had truly absorbed this form of worship. I was attending an InterVarsity staff conference. At that time there was little knowledge or appreciation of liturgy in our evangelical ranks. Our guest Bible expositor was a local Episcopal priest, and in our closing meeting he led us in a simple celebration of the Eucharist using the Episcopal liturgy.

As I heard and recited the now familiar words of worship in that very different setting, I was flooded unexpectedly with joy and gratitude. Maybe I was surprised that the liturgy "worked" in an InterVarsity context. I'm not sure. But suddenly I felt united to all the Christians throughout the world who would be saying the same pattern of words in worship that week and to all who had said them over the centuries of the church. A pattern of words that, I now realized, inhabited me and drew me close to God. I was experiencing what C. S. Lewis wrote in explaining liturgical worship:

> Every service is a structure of acts and words through which we receive a sacrament, or repent, or supplicate, or adore. And it enables us to do these things best—if you like, it "works" best— when, through familiarity, we don't have to think about it. As long

as you notice, and have to count, the steps, you are not yet dancing but only learning to dance.

I had learned the steps and now I was freely dancing with my eyes on Jesus. Eventually, I would learn the steps of keeping the liturgical year as well.

The word "liturgy," formed from the Greek words *laos* ("the people") and *ergon* ("to work"), means the "work of the people." In Scripture it refers to the service of sacrifices in the temple; hence, Jesus "has obtained a more excellent *liturgy*" (Heb 8:6). Today we apply the term to a variety of communal acts of worship and devotion, from the monastic practice of fixed-hour prayer to the weekly service of Communion to the annual "calendar of celebration." Each of these provides an ordered means of engaging with God, a graceful dance, if you will.

This book will acquaint you with the movements of this liturgical calendar so that you can use them in your own devotion to God. I want to teach you the steps so you can enjoy the dance.

SACRED TIME

I was living in New York City on 9/11.

This simple statement comes loaded with meaning. For example, the date needs no explanation. It doesn't even need a specific year. It is seared into our consciousness and fused with images: collapsing towers in Manhattan, a gaping hole in the Pentagon, charred ground in Pennsylvania. It still elicits emotion. Those too young in 2001 to remember the day will nonetheless absorb the date.

The statement also tells you something about me. Without knowing any details, you already know that my life was surely caught up in the story of 9/11 to one degree of intensity or another.

In fact, I was in New Jersey that morning, about two hours west of New York, meeting with a small group of colleagues. It was hours before I could phone through to Charlene and Evan, my wife and seventh-grade son, and the next day before I could return to the temporarily closed city. I will never forget my first sight of downtown as I traveled in. I later wrote about it:

The day blooms cruelly beautiful.

On the PATH from Newark we see
the towers . . . gone . . . as if
extracted, and bleeding profusely.

The smoke drifts and coagulates darkly downwind.

No one speaks on the uptown A,
all thoughts running downtown.

Home. I hold my wife, then snap
at my too boisterous boy of twelve,
both of us bandaging our fear.

Yes, the small story of my life was caught up in the huge and cata-
strophic story of 9/11. Not marked to the extent of those who lost family
and friends that day or who were downtown at the time of the attack or
who directly responded in the rescue efforts, but marked nonetheless. As
were millions of others.

A year later, with a three-day meeting scheduled with those same colleagues over September 11, I realized that I simply could not go about
routine work on that first anniversary. Graciously, my supervisor agreed
to reschedule. Three years later on the date, sensitivities seemingly less-
ened, I led a team of coworkers in a brief time of remembrance and
prayer, but I found myself unexpectedly dissolving into tears. The date,
the memories, the emotions, all were irreversibly linked.

My experience illustrates how an ordinary day in our common calendar can become charged with memory and meaning, can become, in a
way, hallowed. In this country, September 11 is now a day set apart, an
anniversary of historical significance and, for many, solemn remembrance. It is a date of cultural importance shared by a nation.

Other dates carry individual significance for us, occasions both happy
and somber. Our birthdays and those of people we love. Wedding anni-
versaries. Baptisms and confirmations. The date of a dear one's death.
The anniversary of some larger tragedy like Hurricane Katrina or a private trauma such as an auto accident. We choose to mark such dates
because in some way they have marked us. So we set them apart to re-

member and, as appropriate, to grieve or celebrate or give thanks. Such days for us are no longer ordinary.

In addition, we observe various holidays—Martin Luther King Jr. Day, Memorial Day, July Fourth, Thanksgiving—and these distinctive days in the calendar give at least a modicum of shape to our civic awareness and family traditions. Christians, of course, celebrate certain spiritually important days, most notably Christmas and Easter, and these become additional high points in the year.

But we can go much further! We can go beyond scattered celebrations, memorials and holidays. We can go beyond the heartfelt but brief attention we give Christmas and Easter. We can go beyond keeping the year's special occasions to regarding the entire calendar as sacred. We can, in effect, sacralize time itself.

To sacralize something, according to Merriam-Webster, is to "imbue [it] with sacred character, especially through ritualized devotion." We find compelling examples of sacralized time in Scripture when God declares the sabbath holy, when he ordains annual festivals for Israel and when the early Christians, in light of the resurrection, shift worship to the first day of the week. Over the centuries, the church has fittingly sacralized time by means of the liturgical calendar with its practices and celebrations, and we can fruitfully appropriate this pattern in our personal discipleship and devotion.

The Christian year consists of more than a sequence of holy days; it contains, in fact, whole seasons of spiritual meaning. Perhaps you are somewhat familiar with Advent and Lent, but, as was my case, you may not think of Christmas and Easter as seasons or know much about the periods after Epiphany and Pentecost. How can a season of time—four, six, even twenty-six weeks—become full of spiritual significance?

Think for a moment about your own experience with various seasons. Perhaps tax season if you're an accountant or tourist season if you own a shop at the beach. Maybe Opening Day in April if you're a baseball fan or March Madness if you love college basketball. Maybe deer season if you're a hunter or migration time if a birder. It could be planting season on the farm or picking time in the groves. Such times take on individual significance for us, providing satisfaction or stress as the case may be.

And then we experience the cycle of natural seasons. Does the transition from one to the next affect you? Does springtime bring you joy and energy for new endeavors? Do you grow wistful as autumn comes on? Do you relish snowy winter or find it dispiriting? The seasonal rhythms of creation both impinge on and invigorate our creaturely existence. So we have always invested these seasons with some measure of spiritual or cultural or personal meaning. In fact, the natural seasons can add texture to the Christian year, as we will see later.

For many of us, our childhood experience of Christmastime may supply the best intuitive sense of how an extended period can be invested with significance. I remember the mounting enchantment when I was a boy: the upbeat holiday music, the colorful neighborhood lights, the evening we decorated our tree. Then school would let out, presents would accumulate, anticipation for Santa would grow. And finally the commotion and thrill of Christmas morning! Plus, I knew there was a marvelous story behind it all, the birth of Jesus in a stable with angels and shepherds and all the rest. All of this made December a time like no other for me as a child. So, despite a profound tension in this case between sacralizing and commercializing, we grasp the idea: a whole season can become charged with meaning.

THE LITURGICAL CALENDAR

The Christian year entails a sequence of seven seasons built around the holy days that correspond to the major events in the life of Jesus. The beginnings of the liturgical calendar date back to the earliest centuries of the church. First, a cycle of preparation and celebration developed in remembrance of the death and resurrection of Jesus, the central events of the gospel. Later, a second cycle took shape around the commemoration of Jesus' birth. The six-month period between these two cycles is called Ordinary Time and lasts from Pentecost until the first Sunday of Advent.

Here is an overview of the calendar and how it helps us to rehearse the Christ Story, especially over the course of the two main cycles.

The Cycle of Light. The symbol of light ties the first three seasons together beautifully. First, with all who live in a world of darkness, we anticipate "a great light" (Is 9:2); then, we celebrate the "true light . . .

coming into the world" (Jn 1:9); finally, we proclaim Jesus as the "light of the world" (Jn 8:12). These are seasons of revelation: God makes himself known to us in Jesus.

Advent. The liturgical year begins four Sundays before Christmas Day. Over these three to four weeks, we prepare for Christ's advent, that is, his "coming." This is a time of anticipation, for in it we identify with the ancient Jews in their longing for the Messiah as foretold by the prophets. John the Baptist echoes these prophets as a forerunner to Jesus. Like them, we open our eyes to the darkness around us and lament the suffering in the world. We cry out for God to come and put the world right. Thus we are looking for the second advent of Christ, his return in glory. Also in these days, we identify with expectant Mary waiting for her time of deliverance. While our culture mounts its consuming frenzy, we wait quietly for the coming of the Christ.

Christmas. On the Feast of the Nativity of Our Lord, we rejoice with angels and shepherds that "a Savior is born." And we extend this celebration for twelve days! This is a time to contemplate the mystery of the incarnation: "The Word became flesh and lived among us" (Jn 1:14). It is a time to open our hearts anew to the presence of Christ. It is a season of fulfillment and wonder.

Epiphany. On January 6, the Feast of the Epiphany, we recall Jesus' manifestation to the Gentiles in the visit of the Magi (*epiphany* means "manifestation"). We also remember his first miraculous sign, the turning of water to wine. On the next Sunday, we focus on Christ's baptism, which inaugurates his public ministry and confirms his identity as the Spirit-anointed Son of God. Over the weeks of this season, we give attention as Jesus reveals himself through his teaching, healing and miracles, culminating on the last Sunday when we contemplate his transfiguration. Epiphany is a season of light, the light of Christ as manifested in history and now mediated through our witness.

The Cycle of Life. The same pattern—preparation, fulfillment, proclamation—characterizes the second set of seasons, but here the unifying theme is *life*. First, we follow Jesus as he serves and eventually "give[s] his life a ransom for many" (Mk 10:45); then we relive the stunning drama of his resurrection; finally, we bask in the promise of sharing in his new life, now and forever. These are the seasons of redemption: God rescues us from death through Jesus.

Lent. Ash Wednesday marks the beginning of Lent, the forty days (excluding Sundays) that lead up to Easter. By fasting on this day, conscious of our human sinfulness and finitude, we set a tone for Lent as a season of humility and self-examination. We continue to follow the life of Jesus, remembering his temptation in the wilderness and his journey toward Jerusalem to undergo suffering and death. We consider what it means to "deny ourselves, take up our cross, and follow him." Palm (or Passion) Sunday begins the final week of Lent or Holy Week, during which we contemplate the last days of Jesus' life with increasing intensity.

The Paschal Triduum. Pascha means "Passover" and *triduum* (pronounced tri´·juh·wum or tri´·dyuh·wum) means "three days." These are the final three days of Holy Week when "our paschal lamb *[pascha]*, Christ, has been sacrificed" (1 Cor 5:7). On the evening of Maundy Thursday, we focus on his Last Supper and final words to his disciples. On Good Friday, we fast and contemplate his betrayal, torture and cruel crucifixion. We seek to plumb the spiritual and theological mystery of our redemption in Christ. On Holy Saturday, quietly aware of his entombment, we wait for the light of Easter Sunday. This Friday-Saturday-Sunday is the heart of the Christian year.

Easter. We celebrate with amazement and joy the Feast of the Resurrection of Our Lord. But this only marks the beginning of the Easter season. The celebration continues for forty-nine days, a "week of weeks." During this festive period, the Great Fifty Days, we trace Jesus' post-resurrection appearances, which lead up to his ascension. We concentrate on what it means to be "made new" in Christ. We renew our hope in the promise of our own resurrection. The season culminates on the fiftieth day, Pentecost, when we celebrate the outpouring of the Holy Spirit on the nascent church in Jerusalem. This great feast sets the stage for the rest of the year.

The Cycles of Love. I have coined the phrase "cycles of love" as a means of thematically animating the lengthy period from Pentecost to the next Advent. We live our Christian lives in rhythms: shared love for God (worship) and sacrificial love for his world (mission), appropriate love of self and self-giving love of neighbor, love of fruitful work and love of renewing rest. This is the extended season to walk in Christ's light, to grow in Christ's life and to embody Christ's love.

Pentecost and Ordinary Time. We call this long stretch of the Christian calendar *ordinary* because the Sundays are ordinal, or simply "numbered." Yet our usual sense of the word also applies, since this is the nonfestal part of the year. But it is *not* ordinary from a spiritual point of view. Pentecost sets the overall theme: the presence of Christ in the world through the Spirit, transforming the individual Christian and empowering the church for mission. In this season we renew our commitment to love God with our whole being and our neighbors as ourselves.

Full circle. After the summer months, as we move into autumn, our desire for a new festal cycle grows. Ordinary time concludes in late November with Reign of Christ Sunday when we celebrate our Lord enthroned in glory and pray for his "kingdom to come on earth as it is in heaven." Thus, as we start a new Advent, we find ourselves again lamenting our broken world and anticipating the final coming of our Lord, which leads us back to the prophets who foretold both comings. The circle of the year—and the Story of Christ—begins for us anew.

DEVOTIONS IN LITURGICAL TIME

"Within each [liturgical] season," writes Dorothy Bass in *Receiving the Day: Christian Practices for Opening the Gift of Time,* "specific days make manifest the mystery of God's active presence with and for the world, with and for us, as each fast or feast invites us into this mystery in a different way." In this book I not only explicate the Christian year with its thematic dynamism but also invite you, whether a new learner or a liturgical veteran, to let the year give shape to your personal practice of Bible reflection and prayer. We can inhabit God's Story, with all of its mysteries, by habits of devotion—those disciplines by which we focus our attention on God and respond to his presence and promptings.

Each chapter of this book includes a body of devotional material appropriate for the season being presented. With only a few exceptions, I've designed the units by the week rather than the day. In all there are fifty-nine units of material, enough for a full year. In each unit I introduce the theme for the week, which ties into the season and anticipates the Scripture readings. Next I offer opening prayers. Most often the wording of these prayers derives from one or more of the Scriptures for that week. The four to seven biblical texts for the week, which will always include a psalm and a Gospel reading, and often a selection from the Old Testament and the Epistles, are each followed by a brief commentary supplying background information, initial insights and a question or two for reflection. For each week overall, I suggest one practical way that we might respond to the Scriptures. Finally, I provide a closing prayer. These devotions are composed around a simple fourfold pattern for our personal encounters with God:

Approaching God. We begin by getting quiet, not just externally but also internally. As we direct our attention toward God, we assume an inner posture of gratitude for his love and humility before his holiness. We enter his presence without fear but with much reverence.

Presenting Myself. Secure in his grace, we uncover our hearts before God. We acknowledge our weaknesses and admit our recent wrongs. Then we rehearse his mercy and remember our forgiveness in Christ. We may have things to give thanks for. We may have needs to place before him or deep concerns to express. We may have friends in trouble, prompting our intercession. Or we may have a great sense of contentment and joy. Whatever our state or situation, we come and God welcomes us.

Inviting God's Presence. Now we are ready to listen to God and respond. God can speak and reveal himself in many ways, but primarily he speaks through his Scriptures and his Spirit, usually in combination. We take in Scripture, as we do food, in three stages. First, we put it in our mouths and chew it, using our *minds* to carefully read, study and interpret texts in their context before appropriating their meaning for our own time and situation. Second, we inwardly digest it, using our *hearts* to mull it over and absorb its implications. Third, we metabolize it, using our *bodies*, literally, to act on what we hear. And our first response will be in prayer. If God exposes our sin, we confess and repent. If God displays his glory, we fall on our knees in praise. If God shows his goodness, we voice our thanksgiving. If God reveals his justice, we lament our broken world and our part in that brokenness. If God makes known his compassion, we pray for those in need. If God pours his love into our hearts, we sing with joy.

Responding to God and Closing Prayer. Our departure is not from the presence of God but from the place of prayer. We end our devotional time with the intent to embody his Word with the help of his Spirit. We have a renewed awareness of God's greatness, which makes us confident, and a fresh assurance of his blessing, which makes us joyful. Whether we are starting in to the activities of our day or turning out our lights for sleep, we do so in the peace that comes from the ongoing presence and grace of God.

By offering these devotional resources in a weekly rather than daily format and by using an approach that is more suggestive than prescriptive, I am leaving room for you to compose your own devotions. Think music: I provide the key and the melody, but you set the rhythm and add harmony as the Spirit leads. You can use the prayers I have provided to open and close your devotions during each week. Of course, you can riff on these prayers—or you can disregard them altogether. It is not necessary to use all of the passages suggested for each week. You may choose to focus on only a few; indeed, you might spend the whole week immersed in one text. It's up to you and the Spirit. I have put in bold type the texts I consider most important for the week, so if you have to choose, start with these. Finally, my reflections are purposefully succinct. I am assuming that you will use these promptings as an impetus to "chew, digest and metabolize" the Scriptures for yourself. My thoughts are merely appetizer; the Scripture itself is the main course.

The titles of the chapters point to the sweeping actions of our triune God: his *waiting* until the fullness of time, his *giving* of his Son to be born of a virgin, that Son's *telling* of the good news of the kingdom of God, his resolute *turning* toward the cross, his *dying* for us and for our salvation, his *rising* from the grave and ascension to the Father, his *pouring out* of the Spirit on the church in anticipation of the renewal of all things. Week by week, we immerse ourselves in the narrative of these divine actions.

Each season also suggests a spiritual choreography for our own lives.

We perform movements that mirror God's: waiting, giving, telling, turning, dying, rising and pouring out. Furthermore, a set of spiritual graces accompanies this dance: we are enlarged, enriched and enlightened, we are humbled, healed and heartened, and, lastly, we are empowered. During each season, especially the longer ones, our habits of devotion will rehearse us in these movements and lead us into these graces.

HONORING THE CHURCH TRADITIONS

My goal has been to write a book that is useful to a wide range of Christians. This turns out to be tricky because of the significant differences between the major church traditions. First, there is the divide between churches that are deeply liturgical and those that aren't at all. Then there are the centuries-old divergences in belief and practice between the oldest traditions of Roman Catholicism and Eastern Orthodoxy. If we look at the older Protestant traditions—Lutheran, Anglican and Reformed—we see additional distinctions. Add in the dizzying variations among mainline, evangelical, Pentecostal and emergent churches, and it becomes tricky indeed.

My own tradition is mostly evangelical and Episcopal, but I have learned much about other traditions as well. Certainly my limited research and brief exposures cannot substitute for the understanding gained by full participation over a long period of time, but I have tried to acknowledge liturgical traditions familiar to Christians from many churches in the pages that follow. Even so, it has been necessary to shape my treatment of the year in a way that will appeal to a wide audience, particularly those who are discovering the Christian year for the first time. The relationship of this book to three core traditions that vary among the traditions requires brief comment here.

Use of the lectionary. I have selected the devotional texts for this book with one eye on the overall Christian story and one eye on the Revised Common Lectionary, the cycle of Scripture readings prescribed for public worship and used by many traditions. Readers from liturgical churches will discover a degree of resonance with the passages featured in their worship services. But my first priority is for all readers to experience a coherent rehearsal of the Christ Story, so my use of the lectionary is intentionally selective. For most weeks in the first half of the year, I have included at least one selection (and often several) from one of the three annual cycles of readings of the lectionary. I have marked these texts A, B or C to represent Year A, Year B or Year C accordingly. In the selections for Epiphany and Ordinary Time, however, I have for the most part departed from the lectionary in order to present a particular thematic scheme.

Getting the dates straight. Easter is a "moveable feast," and this makes the liturgical calendar a bit complicated. Since the date of Easter shifts each year, so do all the dates for the Lent-Easter cycle. So each year one needs to determine the date of Easter and from there mark out the dates for Ash Wednesday (the beginning of Lent) and Pentecost Sunday (the end of Easter) and each of the feast and fast days in between. If Easter comes early, Epiphany will be shorter and Ordinary Time longer; if Easter comes late, it's the reverse. Easter can fall as early as March 22 and as late as April 25. Note that I have provided devotional material for the maximum number of Sundays in Epiphany: nine. Since the last Sunday of Epiphany should always be Transfiguration Sunday, in years when Epiphany is shorter than nine weeks, it will be necessary to skip ahead to the Transfiguration, leaving off those weeks that won't fit that particular year. For the dates of Easter and the related moveable feasts and fasts through the year 2025, see the appendix. Also, notice that the Eastern Orthodox churches set the date for Easter differently.

The sanctoral calendar. The word *sanctoral* comes from the same linguistic root as *holy, sacred* and *sanctified*. The sanctoral calendar "sets apart" a series of days for commemorating important events in the life of Christ or remembering the exemplary lives of saints, both biblical and historical. The recognition and celebration of saints is one of those significant differences between traditions. "That's right, Protestants don't have saints," some will quickly aver. But that is not quite true. In fact there are many men and women whose godly and courageous lives we admire and honor—and whom we name churches and schools after. Whether we call them saints or heroes or role models, there is value in focusing our attention on such persons in order to be instructed and inspired. In celebrating these lives we are actually giving praise to God for his work in and through them, which is why near the end of the liturgical year, on November 1, we celebrate All Saints Day. I am not emphasizing the sanctoral calendar in this book other than the holy days which fall naturally within the course of the liturgical seasons.

THE INTERSECTION OF TIME
AND ETERNITY

But how does inhabiting the Story of God in liturgical time actually shape our lives? Here is the simple answer: by remembering and anticipating. But this turns out to be more theologically profound and spiritually mysterious than it sounds. Scholars sometimes employ the Greek words *anamnesis* and *prolepsis* to describe these spiritual transactions.

As you might suspect, the first of these terms relates to the familiar idea of amnesia, the loss of memory. *Anamnesis* means the opposite: remembrance, recalling to mind, or literally "the drawing near of memory." Jesus at his Last Supper said, "This is my body, which is given for you. Do this in *anamnesis* of me" (Lk 22:19). When we take part in Communion, we do more than simply remember; in some spiritual way we bring the past into our present experience. Laurence Stookey describes this type of ritual as "an active kind of remembrance," one "by doing rather than by cognition." We identify with Jesus and vicariously participate in his life in a way that brings spiritual dividends to our own.

If anamnesis brings the past to bear in the present, prolepsis does something similar with the future. The literal meaning of the word is "to take beforehand," and we use it to represent a future event as if it had already been accomplished. For example, I might put away a signed copy of Madeleine L'Engle's *A Wrinkle in Time* to give to my proleptic grandchild, who is not yet born. The experience of prolepsis is perhaps more mysterious than anamnesis, but in those acts that anticipate "the hope to which he has called you," we receive a kind of spiritual down payment, as Paul puts it: a "pledge of our inheritance toward redemption as God's own people" (Eph 1:14, 18). The future comes into our present experience. Eugene Peterson describes his personal realization of this truth:

I finally got it: end time influences present, ordinary time, not by diminishing or denigrating it but by charging it, filling it with purpose and significance. The end time is not a future we wait for but the gift of the fullness of time that we receive in adoration and obedience as it flows into the present.

This bringing of the past and the future into the present is a work of the Holy Spirit. In the Eucharist we experience this process intensively as we remember Christ's death in history and anticipate his feast in the age to come. In the liturgical year we experience it extensively over time, as Laurence Stookey describes:

> The great festivals of the church celebrate in our present experience what has occurred or what we resolutely believe will happen: The birth, ministry, suffering, death, and resurrection of Jesus; the reign of Christ in glory and the final sovereignty of God over all things. . . . We keep these occasions in order that God may work in us through them and in our world through us.

The power that overshadowed Mary and raised Jesus from the dead also guarantees the final redemption of all things in Christ. That same power is at work in us now (Eph 1:15-23). Living the Christian year opens us further to this power as week by week, year after year, we rehearse the eternal Story.

Like the hobbits Frodo and Sam, we come to realize that we are part of a great and ongoing tale. This occurs to Sam one night at the edge of Mordor, the evil realm that the two hobbits are set to enter to their almost certain doom. The two are musing about the nature of adventurous tales, how the ones caught up in them do not know the outcome, for if they did, they might turn back. Then Sam remembers one of the great tales:

> "Beren now, he never thought he was going to get that Silmaril [jewel] from the Iron Crown in Thangorodrim, and yet he did, and that was a worse place and a blacker danger than ours. But that's a long tale, of course, and goes on past the happiness and into grief and beyond it—and the Silmaril went on and came to Eärendil. And why, sir, I never thought of that before! We've got—you've got

some of the light of it in that star-glass that the Lady gave you! Why, to think of it, we're in the same tale still! It's going on. Don't the great tales never end?"

"No they never end as tales," said Frodo. "But the people in them come, and go when their part's ended."

Then the two begin to imagine some family by a fireside, years in the future, and the children clamoring for the story of Frodo and the Ring. It makes Frodo laugh aloud on the desolate crag. "Why Sam," he says, "to hear you somehow makes me as merry as if the story was already written."

You see, it dawns on Sam at that dark moment that the crystal vial given to Frodo contains a bit of ancient light, the light of life, the light of the bright Evening Star. A part of the past was available to them, with power, in their present situation. Frodo, too, experiences a kind of grace. His laughter "as if the story was already written" lifts him in his present moment. And so it is for us. By some mysterious grace, the *light* of the Christ who lived in history comes into our present experience with spiritual power, and the *hope* of the Christ who will return in glory to renew all things also brings power into our lives. Eternity intersects Time.

Keeping the Christian year helps us to live at that intersection.

The Cycle of Light

ADVENT

CHRISTMAS

EPIPHANY

2

Advent
Enlarged in the Waiting

*I've learned how much the Advent season holds,
how it breaks into our lives with images of light and dark,
first and last things, watchfulness and longing, origin and destiny.*

KATHLEEN NORRIS

*All around us we observe a pregnant creation. The difficult times
of pain throughout the world are simply birth pangs.
But it's not only around us; it's within us. The Spirit of God
is arousing us within. We're also feeling the birth pangs. These sterile
and barren bodies of ours are yearning for full deliverance.
That is why waiting does not diminish us, any more than waiting
diminishes a pregnant mother. We are enlarged in the waiting.
We, of course, don't see what is enlarging us. But the longer we wait,
the larger we become, and the more joyful our expectancy.*

ROMANS 8:22-25 THE MESSAGE

For four years my wife and I were eager to have a baby. At first, naturally, we tried like everyone else. After some time, we had tests. Then we tried drugs—as prescribed by my urologist. At one point we considered artificial means and later looked into adoption. We were praying and trying and waiting and hoping, all a bit anxiously, no doubt.

One spring Sunday at our church in Miami, at a point in the service open for worshipers to speak words of testimony or encouragement as led by the Spirit, a young man said something that caught my attention. André was a rotund, deep-voiced Jamaican temporarily among us as a participant in the Youth with a Mission program hosted by our church. "I sense from the Lord that a couple here today has been trying to have children, but unsuccessfully; the Lord is saying: trust in me and you will receive the desires of your heart."

I was generally open-minded about the charismatic workings of the Spirit, but more as an observer than a practitioner. Was this a prophecy of some sort? Was it meant for us? That's what our priest suggested when André asked him who might be the subject of this pronouncement. Father Cliff pointed him to us. We listened, neither dismissing his words with skepticism nor seizing on them with enthusiasm; rather, we tucked them away to ponder quietly in our hearts. And we waited.

André returned to Jamaica. We went off that summer to Vancouver for study. Our friends John and Martha Zimmerman lived there and we sought their pastoral counsel. They prayed earnestly with us about our situation and the idea of adoption. The months passed. In December, while Charlene went to see a specialist in her hometown of Clearwater, I stayed in Miami to host a missionary friend and spiritual mentor visiting from Mexico. Doug listened to my confused questions: Adopt? Remain without children? What were our desires, really? And he prayed with me. It was one of those times of prayer that seemed charged.

Shortly after Christmas, out of the blue, we received a brief note from André in Jamaica: "Have been praying for you and wondered what was up." I was startled. I had not thought of him for months. A trace of hope rose within me. I was even more startled when only days later Charlene learned that she was pregnant.

Then, two weeks after that, the Zimmermans flew in to visit and we picked them up at Miami International. Back at the house we shared our exciting news, whereupon Martha, wide-eyed, blurted out, "Oh, Charlene, when I saw you at the airport, the Lord told me you were pregnant, but I couldn't bring myself to say it aloud." It was our turn to be stunned. Signs from God before and after!

Nine months later, Evan was born.

I am mindful just now of the innumerable stories of couples seeking to have children. Many are wildly successful and others deeply disappointed. Some joyfully adopt. Some of those adoptions become painful down the road. Some give birth to babies with Down syndrome or other heartbreaking conditions. And many others are disheartened by miscarriages. So many stories, such a wide range of emotions.

Just this week, a friend gave birth to triplets. Bits of e-mail from these past months tell Diana and Joel's story:

> Good news: we are expecting! . . . Counting our blessings: twins! . . . Recounting our blessings: triplets! . . . Urgent prayer needed: babies missing membrane to separate them in the womb, chances of survival low. . . . Against the odds, we made it to week 24, so Diana can enter the hospital to wait the next two months. . . . Woohoo! We will be delivering Logan, Hope and Lilli this Friday. I just can't believe our time has come. . . . They are here at 9:35, 9:36, and 9:37 a.m.! All three came out pink and screaming and look wonderful. Amazingly, Dr. P said that the power of prayer was proved to him today! PTL.

Such long and arduous and prayerful waiting followed by such joy!

Wendy Wright, in her book of reflections on "keeping watch in the season of Christ's coming," suggests, "Of all types of waiting, the waiting of pregnancy is most like the waiting that we do during Advent. The waiting of pregnancy is like the waiting we do for God."

Advent is a season for waiting; we wait for the coming of God. We need him to come. Our world is messed up and we are messed up. We lament our condition and long for God to set things right, to make us better. So we pray and watch for signs of his presence. We do all we know to do so that we are open and ready. In the midst of hardship and disappointment, we continue to wait. We wait in hope. We believe that something is happening in our world, something is taking shape in our lives, something large, light-filled and life-giving. Even in December's lengthening darkness, this seed of joyful hope grows within us. We are pregnant with it. In our waiting, we are enlarged. God is coming!

THE HEART OF ADVENT

In Advent we focus on three "comings" of Christ: his arrival in history as a baby born of Mary, his return in fearsome glory at the end of time and his intermediate entrance into our own lives. During Advent we are engaged by the prophets of Israel—Isaiah, Zephaniah, Micah, Malachi—and their messianic visions. We are confronted by John the Baptist's stern call to prepare for Jesus by repenting. We are beckoned to walk with Mary and Joseph in their anxiety and expectation. We are sobered by the teachings of Jesus and his apostles on the judgment to come at the end of the age.

But to seriously attend to things both eschatological and historical in a few short weeks (Advent lasts twenty-two to twenty-eight days, depending on the year) is not easy, especially when these weeks are for many of us the busiest and most demanding of the year. How can we experience Christ coming anew into our already full lives? How can we be absorbed in hope when we are so harried? How can our lives be enlarged in so brief a time?

Clearly it takes some work, some wrestling against the culture and our own proclivities. But making it happen isn't all on us. A grace is also at work in this season. Think again of a pregnant woman. Yes, she must pay attention to her body and take care of herself, but the life within her mysteriously takes shape and steadily grows of its own accord. As Luci Shaw encourages:

> During the waiting times God is vibrantly at work within us. And if through the Spirit of God we have been united with the Father in dynamic relationship, if God has sown his gospel seed in us, then Jesus is being formed within us, little by little, day by day. But we have to wait if the Word is to become flesh in us. And that kind of waiting feels like work.

The paradoxical work of waiting. The prophets and psalmists can help us. Old Elizabeth and Zechariah can help us. Their son John can help us. Young, expectant Mary can help us. We can enter their stories, listen to their words and pray their prayers over these weeks. By so doing, we deepen our longing and heighten our hope for God's coming. By so doing, we become more attuned to the joyous wonder of Christ's incarnation and better prepared for the fierce glory of his return. By so doing, year after year, we will be changed as Word becomes flesh in us.

ADVENT IN CHURCH AND CULTURAL TRADITION

In the early centuries, churches in the East celebrated both the birth and the baptism of Jesus on January 6. Not surprisingly, the day became a major occasion for performing baptisms, which led to a preparatory period of fasting and catechesis (instruction). During the fourth century, the Eastern churches followed the West's lead and adopted December 25 for the Feast of the Nativity. Even though this was no longer a day for baptisms, Eastern churches retained their tradition of penitential preparation. This practice spread to the northern and western regions of the church, where it fit well with the greater emphasis there on the final coming and judgment of Christ, which called for self-examination and spiritual readiness. Today, Orthodox Christians still observe a nativity fast from meat November 15 through December 24.

In the church centered in Rome, it was a different story. There, Advent entailed a festive preparation for the birth of Christ from the start. In the sixth century Pope Gregory the Great established the forerunner of our Advent by creating special masses for the four Sundays preceding Christmas Day. After seesawing over the ensuing centuries, these two traditions, the "warm Latin joy" and the "ascetic northern preparation," eventually merged into the synthesis that characterizes Advent today. While fasting has largely fallen away in the West, we still feel a subtle and fruitful tension. As Christopher Hill puts it, "The pull between the affectionate backward look and the anxious forward look—both situated in the world of human time" opens up the present moment for Christ to come in our hearts.

Obviously, Advent and Christmas are closely linked, and many cultural customs apply to both seasons. For example, the Feast of St. Nicholas, from which we get our idea of Santa Claus, falls on December 6 in Advent (for more on "St. Nick," see chapter three). Three Advent traditions—the Christmas tree, the Advent wreath and the "O" Antiphons—

open for us respectively the themes of death and life, darkness and light, doubt and longing.

The Christmas tree. Encroaching winter, with its growing cold and darkness, provides the seasonal context for Advent, at least in the northern hemisphere. The "dead of winter," as we say, invokes images of fallow fields, barren trees, hard ground, absent birds and lowering skies. From as far back as we have record, people in northern Europe decorated their dwellings at midwinter with evergreens such as holly, ivy, laurel and yew. "The strange survival of summer greens in the snows had always been a sacrament of the hope for new life through the winter," explains Hill. In fact, Gregory the Great instructed missionaries to tolerate such customs and dedicate them to Christ. So, for example, holly can remind us of Christ with its prickly leaves (crown of thorns) and red berries (blood).

The decorated Christmas tree derives from this ancient tradition. The custom flourished in Germany as far back as the fifteen hundreds (Martin Luther is said to have decorated a tree indoors), although it did not spread widely in Europe until the nineteenth century. Interestingly, Christmas trees may have reached Revolutionary America by way of German settlers even before they appeared in England! But not until the early twentieth century did Christmas trees became more widely popular in the United States.

The Christmas tree, then, with its dark green branches and forest fragrance, its garlands and lights and bright adornments, comes into our homes in the dead of winter as a symbol of life and a sign of hope.

The Advent wreath. This simple arrangement consists of four candles set equidistant in a circle of evergreens, with a larger fifth candle placed in the middle. On the first Sunday of Advent, one candle is lit, on the second Sunday, two candles, and so on. Finally, on Christmas Eve, we light the Christ candle in the middle. Usually, three of the outer candles are purple, the liturgical color of Advent that signifies both penitence and royalty, but the candle for the third Sunday is rose-colored, denoting the theme of joy. The Christ candle is white. The circle suggests eternity, the greens symbolize life, and the cross of lighted candles points to Christ.

In ancient northern cultures, the lighting of bonfires and yule logs was meant to ward off the midwinter darkness and its sinister denizens. So it is easy to see how Christians combined the greenery of life and the candles of light into the Advent wreath. By lighting a new candle each week, by accumulating the brightness, we signify our hope in the coming light of Christ, even as daylight diminishes and darkness rises with the approach of the winter solstice. Lighting the Advent wreath in our homes and churches enacts our faith in John's testimony: "The light shines in the darkness, and the darkness did not overcome it" (Jn 1:5).

The minor feast day of St. Lucy, or Lucia, on December 13 provides another opportunity to celebrate the coming light of Christ during Advent. Lucia, whose name derives from *lux* (Latin for "light"), was martyred in Italy in 304. Devoted to Christ, she gave all of her dowry to the poor, infuriating the man she was to marry by arrangement. He denounced her to the governor, who had her killed by the sword after attempts to burn her failed. Lucy is especially honored in Scandinavia as the Queen of Light. The custom is for a daughter in the home to wear a crown of candles and go from room to room awakening the family from their deep midwinter sleep and bringing them Lucia buns baked with saffron.

The "O" Antiphons. Since the seventh century, this set of seven prayer texts has been sung or recited over the final days of Advent during the daily service of vespers, or evening prayer. They are voiced in response to the Magnificat (Lk 1:46-55). Each antiphonal prayer addresses God with "O" and a biblical name and concludes with a call for him to come. The phrases of the prayers derive from Scripture. You may be familiar with them from the verses of the well-known Advent hymn "O Come, O Come, Emmanuel." They may be used devotionally, one a day, from December 17 to 23. Here are the traditional texts of the "Great O's."

O Wisdom, O holy word of God, you govern all creation with your strong yet tender care: Come and show your people the way to salvation.

O Sacred Lord of ancient Israel, who showed yourself to Moses in the burning bush, who gave him the holy law on Sinai mountain:

Come, stretch out your mighty hand to set us free.

O Flower of Jesse's stem, you have been raised up as a sign for all peoples; rulers stand silent in your presence; the nations bow down in worship before you. Come, let nothing keep you from coming to our aid.

O Key of David, O royal power of Israel, controlling at your will the gate of heaven: Come, break down the prison walls of death for those who dwell in darkness and the shadow of death, and lead your captive people into freedom.

O Radiant Dawn, splendor of eternal light, sun of justice: Come, shine on those who dwell in darkness and the shadow of death.

O Ruler of all the nations, the only joy of every human heart, O keystone of the mighty arch of humankind: Come and save the creature you fashioned from the dust.

O Emmanuel, ruler and lawgiver, desire of the nations, savior of all people: Come and set us free, Lord our God.

On December 21, the church remembers St. Thomas, the apostle famously known as Doubting Thomas for his refusal to believe in Jesus' resurrection until he had fingered the nail marks and felt the spear wound. After Jesus graciously accommodated his doubt, Thomas declared, "My Lord and my God!" (Jn 20:28). According to tradition, he is credited with taking the light of the gospel to India. As his feast day falls in the week of the "O" Antiphons, these meditative prayers can be for us affirmations of faith and longing in the face of doubts that we, like Thomas, may experience.

THE CHRIST STORY IN ADVENT

The biblical scope of Advent stretches from the garden in Genesis to the New Jerusalem in Revelation. Advent concerns first and last things. It involves looking back and leaning forward. In Advent we ponder the promises of God from beginning to end.

In one sense, the whole of the Old Testament is text for Advent: the creation of the world and the fall of humankind, the choosing of one family to bless all families and one nation to bless all nations, the exodus of that nation from captivity, the giving of the law and settling of the land, the choosing of kings and building of a temple, the sins of the people and cries of the prophets, the exile in Babylon and the return to live under Persians, then Greeks, then Romans, and the long, long wait for the one anointed to come and deliver. This is the history—the story—that leads up to Jesus.

The Old Testament not only tells the story that Jesus completes, argues Christopher Wright, "it declares the promise that Jesus fulfills." The prophets, in addition to denouncing sin and calling for repentance, reveal God's multilayered promise of mercy and redemption. But we must discern the different horizons in these prophetic visions: the immediate historical, the intermediate messianic and the ultimate eschatological. For example, the prophets foretell the restoration of Israel, the blessing of all nations and the renewal of creation itself, but distinguishing these horizons can be difficult.

Likewise, unraveling different prophetic strands about the Messiah can be confusing. Would he be a kingly "Son of David" bringing about political liberation and social justice, as in Isaiah 9? Would he be a lowly "Servant of the Lord" saving many through suffering and sacrifice, as in Isaiah 53? Or would he be a godlike "Son of Man" coming in the clouds to receive glory and everlasting dominion, as in Daniel 7? Expectations in Jesus' day centered on the first of these: deliverance from Roman rule and restoration of national greatness. This is the backdrop as we read of God breaking into the lives of Zechariah and Elizabeth, Mary and Joseph, and John the Baptizer. These individuals are filled with expectation, yet they barely know what to expect.

From our perspective now, we see that these vast promises were all fulfilled in Jesus—and yet not fully fulfilled. He announced a kingdom at hand and yet spoke of a reign to come. He gave his life as a ransom for many and yet pointed to a day of salvation in the future. He rose from the dead and ascended to heaven yet pledged to return one day on the clouds. We who belong to him are a new creation (2 Cor 5:17), yet we groan for the day when the whole cosmos will obtain with us the freedom of glory

(Rom 8:21). So we find ourselves in this time of now and yet to come.

Advent dramatizes this tension for us. The hopes of ancient Israel resonate in us and amplify our own hopes as we wait for the full redemption to come. The great symphony of Christ begins in this season and the strains of the overture already anticipate the soaring crescendo.

INHABITING ADVENT

If Advent is a time of watching for signs of hope and waiting for the light of Christ, a time for God to enlarge us with his quiet presence, how can we enter into this season and let it enter into us? The approach I've embraced is to give myself two permissions, practice two disciplines and cultivate two postures.

Permission to sing, permission to groan. Our experience of the weeks of December can vary widely, depending on our disposition and situation. Some of us are readily caught up in the festive atmosphere. Kids are released from school, lights and decorations sparkle, gifts and cards arrive, friends throw parties, we gather with extended family and a generous impulse rises in us. We do want peace on earth and feel good will toward others. All this makes us want to sing.

Some of us, however, readily feel the weight of these days—the obligations, the drift into depression, the pull of temptation, the anxiety of difficult family relationships, the resurfacing grief over those we have lost, the discouragement from daily headlines. We feel cynical in the midst of all the holiday hoopla and superficiality. It makes us want to groan.

The dual nature of Advent invites both songs and groans.

Imagine, with Isaiah's help, life in the world to come, the new Jerusalem: a place with no wrenching losses, tearful memories or cries of despair, a place where every baby grows up healthy and every person lives a long and fruitful life, a place where all work is meaningful and the economics are always just, a place where the environment is unspoiled and its creatures unthreatened, a place where each of us knows a joyful intimacy with God (Is 65:17-25). Imagine . . . and let your heart sing! Then open your eyes to every contemporary sign of such shalom, such full-orbed peace and well-being, in the world around you and in your own life. We see and sing for joy.

Paul, too, speaks of a "glory about to be revealed" but not without acknowledging "the sufferings of this present time" (see Rom 8:18-25). The whole creation, the very cosmos, groans as if in labor. There will be the birth of a new order, free from the decay and devastation and disease we see now. And not only creation; we ourselves groan. We see the corruption of our world and we know the corruption within ourselves, our own moral flaws and our own part in what is wrong. We see and groan in lament.

So in your Advent prayers, give yourself permission to sing and permission to groan. Remember that the sweet taste of shalom during Advent is only that, a taste; it is not the full feast yet to come. And the groans induced by our sufferings are not the final sounds; one day they will be subsumed into a chorus of glory. So sing and let your songs be joyful longings; groan and let your cries be hopeful laments.

Practice restraint, practice retreat. "My struggle boils down to this," bemoaned my friend Courtney. "You can't be Mary and Martha at the same time; someone has to do the cooking!" She vented this frustration after a dinner party where the conversation had turned to the tension between Advent as a spiritual season and December as a month of cultural craziness. "Your description of Advent requires Mary time," she said in a later e-mail,

> yet of all the times of the year—especially for a woman with children and a conscience—Advent is the most impossible to be Mary-like. The Christmas machine (church, school, family, neighborhood, office, charitable activities) is so giant that it would require radical steps to extricate oneself. Steps that could send a message to one's community of being uncharitable and that could feed resentment in one's own family.

Point taken. To keep Advent as a season of spiritual reflection and waiting does require us to be countercultural. It is fitting then for the proclamation of John the Baptist (Lk 3:1-18) to be an Advent text, since he calls us to examine our patterns of behavior—resource sharing, business practices, uses of power—over against what is common in our culture. It is also fitting for Courtney to bring up the domestic episode involving Jesus and the two sisters of Bethany in Luke 10:38-42. (I suspect Martha would agree with Courtney's complaint.) Indeed, we *should* take Mary of Bethany as our model: she went against cultural expectations in giving her attention to Jesus, and Jesus praised her choice and shielded her from Martha's disapproval.

Our culture says, "Buy! Buy! Buy!" and starts saying it right after Halloween. We live year round in a consumer society, but Christmastime is consumerism gone nuts. The cacophony of advertising, the appropriation of religious themes for commercial gain, the secularizing and sentimentalizing of the sacred, all of this disturbs us. Still, it's not easy to resist the pressures.

So we must choose to practice restraint. Although fasting in Advent is no longer emphasized, a variation of this discipline can benefit us spiritually. When we fast, we abstain from something that at other times and in appropriate measures is good. What good thing could we forgo or cut back as an Advent discipline? Could we skip mailing Christmas cards and send greetings at Easter instead? Or simplify gift-buying by making charitable donations in loved ones' names as an alternative? Could we decline a holiday party or two? Or cut back on baking goodies—and on eating them? There is no right answer, of course, and we'll likely take different steps in different years. The point is to practice restraint as a countercultural act that opens up space in our lives for God.

We can also practice retreat. Again, our culture says, "Go! Go! Go!" and "Do! Do! Do!" We can easily feel that our social reputation depends on our obedience to these impulses. Or our self-image. Or even our sense of spiritual worth. But these imperatives lure us into a trap, and we unthinkingly heed them to our spiritual detriment. If we practice restraint from activity, we can use some of the time gained to be alone, quiet and reflective. Even if the time is meager, even at the risk of criticism, we can follow Mary in her choice to stop and sit for a time at the feet of Jesus.

Alert posture, open posture. One day the old man Zechariah is on duty at the temple with his fellow priests. It falls to him to light the incense in the inner sanctuary. He enters, properly reverent. But then he sees the angel and is terrified. He hears the words about his many prayers being answered, his aging wife becoming pregnant and his son growing up to be a prophet; but he can't quite absorb them. His skepticism kicks in and he challenges the Being before him: "How will I know that this is so?" So Gabriel gives him nine months to think it over (Lk 1:5-25)!

How hard to stay alert to the presence and workings of God, even when our lives are patterned around worship and service. As a season of anticipation, Advent calls us to a posture of alertness. Be watchful and ready, Jesus repeatedly urged, because he could come at any time, like a burglar breaking into our home. So in these weeks of Advent we ask God to heighten our awareness of his presence, to open our eyes to what he is doing—in us and in the world. He may speak to us through the words of others, he may show himself in the face of someone in need, he may care for us through the kindness of friends, he may move us when we gather for worship, he may stir us through art or music, or he may whisper inwardly by his Spirit. Stay alert.

Young Mary stands in contrast to Zechariah (Lk 1:26-38). She too is caught off-guard by the same angel and hears words she can scarcely take in. She too questions, but from a different posture; hers is a more humble perplexity. Gabriel's reply only pushes deeper into mystery. She has a choice, as Denise Levertov insightfully considers in her poem "Annunciation." Levertov muses on the typical painting of this biblical scene with its "angelic ambassador" arriving "on solemn grandeur of great wings" and then writes:

> But we are told of meek obedience. No one mentions
> courage.
>   The engendering Spirit
> did not enter her without consent.
>   God waited,
>
> She was free
> to accept or to refuse, choice
> integral to humanness.

Yes, so very human. Just like us. Mary chooses a posture of openness: I am wholly yours, I am fully open to your Word, I believe, let it be so with me. A humble stance, a courageous *yes*. She is our model. By her

posture she makes room for God. She too will have nine months to ponder the workings of God and to wait for his arrival. Advent invites us to
do the same. Stay open.

THE FULLNESS OF TIME

"By patient watchful attendance, the mystery will, 'in the fullness of
time,' make itself known. Time will come to term and deliver eternity,"
writes Hill. And so we start a new liturgical year by entering this complex season of mystery. We turn once again to the beginning of the great
Story but with its glorious end very much in mind. With ancient Israel,
we long for the one who will come to set us free. We try to get ready. We
watch for his arrival with expectancy. We let hope gestate within us.
Something good is happening to us and to our world. The days are dark
but the light is growing. Sometimes we sing, sometimes we groan. We
resist the cultural frenzy with chosen restraint and moments of retreat.
That's how we remain alert, how we stay open to God's presence. We
wait for Christ to come, and in our waiting, we are enlarged.

*   *   *

Preview of devotions in Advent. The four weeks can train us in hopeful waiting. In week one, we frame the story of God's redemption within
its widest margins: the beginning in Genesis and the culmination in Revelation. Weeks one and two awaken our longing for Christ to return and
put the world right. Weeks three and four focus more on Jesus' entry into
human history by the womb of Mary. Each week features texts from the
prophet Isaiah and the Evangelist Luke.

Come, Lord Jesus!

At the start of a new Christian year, it is fitting to contemplate both the beginning of time and the end of time, the creation of the cosmos and the promised new heavens and earth. We live between these two horizons in an age and world in which something is terribly wrong. Yet we know that God has been acting in history to redeem this brokenness, to put all things right, and that he will one day complete this redemptive work as promised through the writings of the prophets, the teachings of Jesus and the letters of the apostles. We have a picture of our ultimate home, a glimpse into our final destiny. So in this season of hope, we imagine what is promised and intensify our longing for that future. We cry, "Come, Lord Jesus!"

Approaching God. Jesus, you are the Alpha and the Omega, the first and the last, the beginning and the end. You are the root and descendant of David, the bright morning star: I believe you are coming soon.

Presenting Myself. Today, O Lord, I come to your mountain, to the place of your presence, so that you may teach me your ways and I may walk in your paths. Amen.

Inviting God's Presence. You, O Lord, have promised to come and make all things new, to dwell among us as our God and embrace us as your people, to wipe every tear from our eyes, and remove from us all pain, so that we may live forever in peace and security—O Lord Jesus, come!

LISTENING TO GOD

Genesis 1—2; Isaiah 2:1-5 (A); Psalm 122 (A);
Isaiah 11:1-10 (A); Revelation 21—22; Luke 21:25-36 (C)

[Note: In each week's list the texts in bold should be given priority.
The letters in parentheses indicate Year A, B or C
in the Revised Common Lectionary.]

Genesis 1—2 tells the story of creation with poetic beauty and theological profundity. As you reflect on this familiar text, give rein to your imagination. Ponder the cosmos: its incomprehensible infinity, its mysterious quantum particles, the intricate web of life on earth. The eternal triune God spoke all this into being. And it was good. Imagine Eden: the fecundity, the sweet fruitfulness, the astounding biodiversity, the beauty of sight and sound. And think about the humans: unimpeded in their intimacy, unbounded in discovery and cultivation, unhampered in spiritual communion with the Creator. Yes, let yourself long for what was lost, that beauty, that innocence, that freedom, that joy.

Isaiah 2 is the great prophet of messianic hope. He preached in the eighth century B.C.E., the tumultuous era in which the northern kingdom of Israel fell to the Assyrians and the southern kingdom of Judah lurched toward Babylonian exile. Here he prophesies impending judgment but also future restoration to national and spiritual greatness. Isaiah 2:1-5 (this poem is also found in Mic 4:1-3) envisions the day when the people of the earth will be drawn to the dwelling place of God—to learn his truths and to walk in his ways. The result? International justice and universal peace. "Come, let us walk in this light."

Psalm 122 calls us to worship. One of fifteen Songs of Ascents (Ps 120—134) most likely sung by ancient Jews on their annual festival pilgrimages, this psalm celebrates the moment of arrival in beloved Jerusalem. Here the architecture metaphorically suggests a vision for the people in their tribal diversity. Why do they come to worship? What do they expect to find? This psalm teaches us how to pray for communities of God's people today: for prosperity, peace and security. Reread the psalm in the eschatological light of Isaiah 2:1-5 and Hebrews 12:22-24.

Isaiah 11 envisions a David-like political leader of spiritual wisdom who will rule justly over a peaceable realm in which there is no danger, conflict or destruction. Our natures will be transformed. All the earth will be God's glorious home, and knowledge of him will saturate the entire human community. Let your longing for such a future fuel your prayers for our present world.

It is easy to spot the echoes of Genesis and Isaiah in **Revelation 21—22.** As you read these visions of the future, allow the images and symbols to convey their powerful meanings. This is what our ultimate home will be like. No roiling sea-like chaos. No pain or cancer or depression. No death or wrenching losses. No crime, racism, hunger or poverty. No wars between nations or clashes of cultures. The cultural achievements of all nations will be incorporated. Why so glorious? Because the God of glory will make his home among us and we will enjoy once again that unrestricted intimacy with our loving Creator. We will drink deeply from the river of life and eat freely from the tree of life. The Lamb of God will be our king. And in some fashion we will reign with him. Imagine! Imagine, and long for that day.

As Jesus teaches in **Luke 21,** surely the day of redemption is drawing near. Surely he is coming with power and great glory. Be alert. Live wisely. Keep watching.

RESPONDING TO GOD

The more we let the Scriptures fuel our imagination and intensify our longing for the gracious rule of God, his just and peaceful realm, the more robust will be our frequent prayer: Let your kingdom come on earth as it is in heaven. This week, pray this vision repeatedly. Be alert for opportunities to embody the prayer in your own small actions.

Closing Prayer. Renew in me this day, O Lord, the hope of the new heaven and earth in which you will reign in light and we will live in peace; meanwhile, may your kingdom come and your will be done, on earth as it is in heaven; through Jesus Christ our coming King. Amen.

WEEK TWO OF ADVENT

Beginning the Sunday
between December 4 and 10

How Long, O Lord?

If last week awakened our longing for the universal shalom of God with all its contentment and joy, this week moves in the other direction. Now we let ourselves see and feel all that is wrong and woeful in our world and in our lives. For many, this festive season accentuates our losses, our struggles, our disappointments. Around us we see greed and drivenness. In the news during these days of "peace on earth, good will to all," the ironies abound: war, poverty, violence, political machinations and disease. Our own vulnerabilities and temptations are heightened as well: loneliness, depression, addiction, materialism. So we groan within ourselves, "How long, O Lord, is life going to be like this?" Even as we cry out we remember that evil in the world—and in us—merits God's judgment. His coming will bring a fearsome but welcome justice. But also glory, a glory greater than our current suffering. So we lament the darkness in the world, the sin in ourselves and the judgment that will fall. But we do not succumb to despair. Ours is a hopeful lament as we prepare for the glory to be revealed.

Approaching God. O Lord, you God of vengeance, you God of vengeance, shine forth! Rise up, O Judge of the earth; give to the proud what they deserve! O Lord, how long shall the wicked, how long shall the wicked exult?

Presenting Myself. As is true for all people, O Lord, I am like grass and my constancy like the flower of the field; grass withers, flowers fade, but your Word, O God, will stand forever. In your mercy, dear Lord, breathe on me this day. Amen.

Inviting God's Presence. How long, Almighty King? Come and bring justice with your ruling hand. How long, Good Shepherd? Gather your flock in your gentle arms. How long, O Sun of Righteousness? Rise with healing in your rays. Amen.

LISTENING TO GOD

Habakkuk 1:1-4; Psalm 94; **Isaiah 40:1-11 (B);**
Malachi 3—4 (C); **Luke 3:1-18 (C); Romans 8:18-25**

The prophet **Habakkuk** baldly complains to God about the state of his society. He decries the violence, the strife, the injustice and the exploitation, and he all but accuses God of not caring. Reading on we learn that God does care and stands poised to bring about judgment, but the way he will do it shocks and dismays Habakkuk. A fascinating prophetic dialogue ensues.

Starkly, the writer of **Psalm 94** acknowledges God as the judge who exacts vengeance against the wicked and warns us not to misinterpret the apparent immunity of the arrogant as a sign of God's ambivalence. God sees, hears and disciplines. As you survey contemporary society or the global scene, what makes you angry? What causes you to weep or ache? What in your local community upsets you? And more personally, how have you suffered because of the mistreatment of others, the unfairness of a system or the plain misfortune of circumstance? Advent is a season for seeing the wrongs and feeling the pain. We lament the darkness and look for the light; we cry out, "How long, O Lord?"

Isaiah announces comfort to God's people at the end of a period of punishment. A call goes out to prepare the way of the Lord: straighten the highway! Smooth out the road! Announce his coming! The glory of the Lord, the Creator of the universe, will be revealed. By contrast, we mortal, inconstant humans are like mere grass in a field. If God breathed on us, we would wither away. But Isaiah announces good news: the mighty God will treat us as a shepherd tends his flock—with gentleness and care.

Malachi 3—4, the last chapters of the Old Testament, echo the theme of a messenger who prepares for the coming Lord. But, like Isaiah's grass, who can endure his coming? He will refine and purify, he will cut down and burn up. Pay attention to what Malachi condemns. What can we do? Return to God! For Malachi's audience, this meant resuming tithes and ceasing cynicism. What about us? Ponder God's response to those who revere him and encourage one another in such reverence.

Traditionally, we highlight John the Baptist during Advent because he is the messenger spoken of by Isaiah and Malachi, the voice crying out, "Get ready!" In **Luke 3,** this means not only remorse for our moral failings but change that brings fruit, such as sharing with needy neighbors, conducting business with fairness and exercising power justly. If John were preaching today and you were to ask him what you should do, what might he say?

We lament the sin and suffering in the world. We repent of any part we play in it. And then we exercise hope. In **Romans 8,** the apostle Paul speaks of a glory to be revealed. The whole creation waits for it, groaning to be released from a kind of bondage. We ourselves wait for it, groaning to be redeemed in our very bodies. Like the prophet and the psalmist, we may not see it right now, but in hope, patiently, we wait for it.

RESPONDING TO GOD

This week, even in this season of distractions, take in the news and listen to people around you. Pay attention with head and heart. In your prayers, voice your groans and fears and disappointments to God. But don't just lament; seek an opportunity to respond concretely to someone in need.

Closing Prayer. How long, O Lord, must we suffer under evil and darkness? Shine your light on me this day, that my life would point to your coming glory, by which the world will be healed and your people set free through Jesus Christ, the Light of the World. Amen.

You Will Have Joy!

Having fueled our longing for God's universal shalom and voiced our lament over our broken and to-be-judged world, in this third week we begin to anticipate joy. We are growing more aware of Christmas Day approaching, with all its bright celebration. Still we must wait, and this is good practice. Like the faithful of Israel in their day, we wait for the earth-shattering advent of God, believing that his second arrival in history will put the world right and heal our lives. But we also watch for signs of his coming in our present experience. Whenever we see social justice or human flourishing or personal renewal, whether large in scale or small, we experience joy—a foretaste of that everlasting jubilation that will be ours on the day we "come singing into Zion."

Approaching God. Blessed be you, Lord God of Israel, for you have looked favorably on your people and redeemed them; you have raised up a mighty Savior for us, just as you spoke through your holy prophets of old.

Presenting Myself. O Lord, mindful of your great mercy, grant that I might serve you without fear, in holiness and righteousness, this day and all of my days. Amen.

Inviting God's Presence. Break upon me like the dawn, O Lord, to give me your light this day and to guide my feet into the way of peace. Amen.

LISTENING TO GOD

Psalm 126 (B); Zephaniah 3:14-20 (C); **Isaiah 35:1-10 (A);**
Luke 1:5-25, 57-80 (C); 1 Thessalonians 5:16-24 (B)

Another of the Songs of Ascents, **Psalm 126** speaks of a joyful restoration of fortunes. It is an apt Advent psalm because it both remembers and anticipates. The first stanza recalls past times of dreamlike joy when God did great things for the people. The second half pleads for God to act once again so that seeds planted with bitter tears may be harvested with joyful shouts. Think back to times when you have experienced God's hand in your life and remember the joy. Then think about your life now. Are there desert places where you long for the rains to come and fill the watercourses? Ask God for this and let yourself anticipate the return of joy.

The prophecy of **Zephaniah** concludes with a psalm, which we can read through the same Advent lens as Psalm 126: restoration, homecoming and joy.

Once again **Isaiah,** the great prophet of Advent, paints a vivid picture of the joyous realm to come: the barren wilderness blossoms, people observe the glory of the Lord, salvation comes to the fearful and the disabled find healing. The highway to God lies wide open and God's people come singing home in safety. Let yourself soak in this poetry.

Luke 1:5-25 gives us Zechariah's story. As you read, put yourself into it, perhaps as a neighbor or relative, perhaps as Elizabeth or even Old Zech himself. This aging couple has lived with spiritual integrity and faithful service for many years, all the while bearing the perplexity, disappointment and subtle shame of childlessness. On an ordinary day, as Zechariah performs his customary lot and duty as a priest, God suddenly, dramatically intersects his life. He is shocked; fear overwhelms him, as it would us. Pay close attention to the dialogue. The angel reassures him and—this is encouraging—acknowledges his years of prayer. Then comes the extraordinary announcement, resonant with prophecy. What do you make of the old man's reply? Honest curiosity? Doubtful uncertainty? Gabriel's fierce rejoinder makes it clear. Poor Zechariah, stunned into silence and given nine months to think things over. Improbably pregnant, Elizabeth spends the first five months in seclusion. Imagine the reaction when she reappears during her middle trimester!

The account in **Luke 1:57-80** of John's birth and naming always moves me. Zechariah insists on the name John, countering the expectations of everyone around him. It is his redemptive moment: he obeys and his speech is restored. Fear comes over the neighbors—they had already adjusted themselves to his muteness—but not Zechariah; joy comes over him! He is full of praise and full of the Holy Spirit. He blesses the Lord and speaks a prophecy. Now he understands—he believes!—that hope draws close, that what has been long promised is at hand, that the Most High is coming with salvation and forgiveness. He looks for the light to dawn on all who wait in darkness and the shadow of death. As do we.

Paul writes to the **Thessalonians** about the coming of the Lord (see 1 Thess 4—5). He highlights the resurrection of the dead and the transformation of the living; he calls us to "wakefulness" and wise living. With this eschatological backdrop, read each of the closing exhortations in 1 Thessalonians 5:16-24. How much do they characterize your own life: prevailing joyfulness, constant prayerfulness, consistent thankfulness, spiritual openness, moral steadiness? How does a vivid hope in Christ's coming enable such postures in us?

RESPONDING TO GOD

How prepared—ready, alert, watchful—are we to encounter God as we simply go about our devotional practices and daily business? This week, during the times you've set aside for God, don't just go through the motions. Make this a season for active listening! Be willing to reiterate, like Zechariah and Elizabeth, prayers for the darkened world or prayers for yourself and those close to you. Put your trust in God, even at your points of greatest disappointment and doubt.

Closing Prayer. O God of peace, sanctify me entirely; may you keep my spirit, soul and body sound and blameless at the coming of our Lord Jesus Christ. Because you have called me and you are faithful, I believe you will do this. Amen.

Blessed Is She Who Believed

The fourth "week" of Advent (anywhere from one to seven days, depending on the year) will likely be full, what with all the purchases, the preparations, the parties. So much to get ready. Spiritually, the goal is the same—getting ready—but the approach runs counter to our external busyness. We must find a way to inwardly settle and center ourselves, to become open to the momentous. Our model is Mary. Despite her own stress from late-pregnancy travel and overcrowded accommodations, she is ready. She's certainly ready to "be delivered," but more profoundly, she is ready to encounter God in a new way. Since that startling day when Elizabeth declared to her by the Spirit that she was blessed in believing, Mary has been waiting expectantly. For us too, as the time draws close, we believe and wait in quiet readiness.

Approaching God. O Mighty One, you have done great things and holy is your name; your mercy is for those who fear you from generation to generation.

Presenting Myself. Here I am, O Lord, your servant; let it be with me according to your word.

Inviting God's Presence. Come Holy Spirit and enlarge your presence in me this day, that I may bring into the world more of your life and more of your love. Amen.

LISTENING TO GOD

Micah 5:2-5 (C); Psalm 123; Luke 1:26-38 (B); Luke 1:39-56 (C); Matthew 1:18-25 (A); Romans 16:25-27 (B)

The prophet **Micah** was contemporary with Isaiah. In the middle of a foreboding situation that would lead to Israel's collapse before the Assyrians, Micah speaks a prophecy about a Messiah to be born in lowly Bethlehem. This shepherd-king in the mold of David would bring security and peace to the ends of the earth. How does this prophecy apply to Jesus?

Psalm 123 places us in a humble posture before God in response to the overbearing arrogance of some around us. When we experience unremitting scorn from the wealthy or contempt from the powerful, we turn to God for mercy. He sits enthroned above the proud and will exercise his power against oppressors. We patiently wait before God until we receive mercy; we stand ready to do whatever he asks. This is the very posture of the young virgin Mary.

Luke skillfully parallels the birth narratives of John and Jesus. Compare the angelic announcements in 1:5-25 and 1:26-38. How does Mary's question to the angel differ from Zechariah's? The clue lies in Gabriel's response to each. To Mary's honest confusion, he offers an explanation—of sorts. And the news of elderly Elizabeth's pregnancy gives her something to go on, or rather, someone to go to. This is both a sign and a provision. Elizabeth, six months into her miraculous pregnancy, will offer refuge and counsel for this unmarried, overwhelmed teen. Together they will ponder the mysterious grace of God. How caring of God to give each to the other. What signs has God given you of late? Whom has he woven into your life as a source of encouragement and care? But it is Mary's final response to the angel—to God—that deserves our deepest reflection. If you can, imagine your way into Mary's experience: the fear, the perplexity, the exhilaration, the wonder. What would you say to such a being as Gabriel? Mary responds, I am wholly yours, I am fully open to your Word, I believe, let it be so with me. Extraordinary for being chosen and exemplary in saying yes, Mary is the spiritual mother of us all.

As described in **Luke 1:39-56**, picture Mary's arrival at Zechariah's house in the hill country of Judea. At her greeting, Elizabeth's baby Spirit-kicks in utero and she herself is jolted by the same Spirit into a shout of blessing! And Mary, also full of God, breaks into a prophetic outburst of praise, what we call the Magnificat, after the opening word in Latin. It is a song of good news for the poor and lowly, of warning to the rich and proud and of mercy for all who believe the ancient promises. Do you hear the echoes of the prophets we have been reading? Compare Mary's praise with the prayer of the formerly barren Hannah in dedicating her son, Samuel, to God (1 Sam 2:1-10).

We turn to **Matthew 1** for a glimpse of Joseph and his reaction when his wife-to-be becomes pregnant by another. Try to put yourself in his shoes. Joseph too encounters the angel, hears the impossible explanation, learns of the messianic destiny and receives explicit instructions. Exemplary in his own way, he does just as the angel of the Lord says. He too is ready for God's mysterious coming and blessed in his believing.

Paul concludes **Romans** with a doxology praising God and his wisdom as revealed in Jesus Christ. God is able to strengthen us according to what three things? As we imaginatively place ourselves on the verge of Christ's birth, this doxology helps us to recall the prophetic writings that preceded his life and to anticipate the profound glory that proceeds from it.

RESPONDING TO GOD

Try to emulate Mary in her humble openness to God. As God knocked on the door of her womb, as it were, so he knocks on the door of our lives (Rev 3:20). Is there some new way that he might want to enter into your life? Mary believed and said yes. Then she waited for the fulfillment of what had been promised to her, for the birth of what had been growing in her. In your own quiet moments this week, open yourself to God and listen. May you have courage to say yes. And may you be blessed in believing.

Closing Prayer. Like Mary our exemplar, I believe this day that there will be fulfillment of all that you have spoken, O Lord, and I say to you again: I am your servant, let it be with me according to your word. Amen.

3

Christmas
Enriched in the Giving

For Christmas is not merely a day like every other day.
It is a day made holy and special by a sacred mystery.
It is not merely another day in the weary round of time.
Today, eternity enters into time, and time, sanctified,
is caught up into eternity.

THOMAS MERTON

For you know the generous act of our Lord Jesus Christ,
that though he was rich, yet for your sakes he became poor,
so that by his poverty you might become rich.

2 CORINTHIANS 8:9

In telling the story of Christ's birth in his Gospel, Luke matter-of-factly records the political context at the time, explains the travel down to crowded Bethlehem for census registration and then simply reports that Mary went into labor and "gave birth to her firstborn son" in some sort of shed or stable (Lk 2:1-7). We are free, of course, to imagine the scene: the anxious young couple far from family and friends, the dark barn given warmth and smell by the cattle, the long night of contractions on a makeshift bed, the baby finally pushed out wet and wrinkled, then cleaned, wrapped and nestled into a well-worn manger, and finally the joyful exhaustion of Mary and her husband. Such a bodily experience—painful, messy, emotional—and such a commonplace human event.

But the apostle John tells it differently: "The Word became flesh and lived among us" (Jn 1:14).

This is a mystery, a great and wondrous mystery. As John spells out in the prologue to his Gospel, in speaking of the Word he is speaking of God, the Creator of all that is, the source of light and life, the one full of glory. This Word took on flesh, this God became human. How do we apprehend such a mystery? How do we articulate it?

We can certainly use theological and philosophical discourse. But better, perhaps, is the language of poetry by which we "break the confines of ordinary meaning," as David Impastato puts it in his introduction to an anthology of contemporary Christian poetry aptly titled *Upholding Mystery*. Throughout the centuries, beginning with John, writers have explored the mystery and paradox of this divine enfleshment, this incarnation, through the language of poetry. Consider these five excerpts from poems:

> Him who dwells beyond the worlds
> The Virgin bore today.
> Him who bounds the universe,
> Earth shelters in a cave.
> (St. Romanos, "The Melodist," Syrian, sixth century)

> Blessed mother, by God's gift,
> the One who is the highest of all powers,
> the One who holds the world in his hand,
> was cloistered in your womb.
> (Hymn from *The Prymer*, European, fifteenth century)

> Today you see in a stable
> the Word speechless,
> Greatness in smallness,
> Immensity in blankets.

Such wonders! . . .

He who had no beginning,
his being of Time begins;
the Creator, as a creature,
is now subject to our griefs.
Such wonders!
(Sor Juana Ines de la Cruz, "Carol 3," Mexican, seventeenth century)

This air . . .
Minds me in many ways
Of her who not only
Gave God's infinity
Dwindled to infancy
Welcome in womb and breast,
Birth, milk, and all the rest . . .
(Gerard Manley Hopkins, "The Blessed Virgin Compared to the Air
     We Breathe," English, nineteenth century)

     After
The white-hot beam of annunciation
fused heaven with dark earth,
his searing, sharply focused light
went out for a while,
eclipsed in amniotic gloom:
his cool immensity of splendor,
his universal grace,
small-folded in a warm, dim
female space—
the Word stern-sentenced to be
nine months' dumb—
infinity walled in a womb,
until the next enormity—
the Mighty One, after submission
to a woman's pains,

helpless on a barn's bare floor,
first-tasting bitter earth.
(Luci Shaw, "Made Flesh," naturalized American, twentieth century)

For all their longing and waiting for a messiah to come, the Jews had little notion of what would actually take place in the plan of God. How could they? Certainly God could choose and by his Spirit anoint some person to set his people free, but for God himself to become human, for Spirit to be embodied? It was inconceivable. Only in light of the resurrection does the enormity of the incarnation begin to be clear. The apostles wrote gropingly of it. The earliest theologians wrestled to formulate it. The first liturgists wove it into rituals of worship. Poet after poet has sought to say it. But even with our long retrospective view, this mystery borders on inconceivable to us. And well it should.

Ah, but humble Mary did conceive the impossible and bear the mystery and deliver for us a gift beyond reckoning.

Christmas—not just the single day but the festival of twelve days—offers us anew this gift and draws us again into this mystery: Word-become-flesh, Creator-turned-creature, immensity-contained, fullness-poured-out, power-made-vulnerable, eternity-subject-to-time. All this self-giving by God for our sakes—a gift immeasurable, a love incomprehensible.

THE HEART OF CHRISTMAS

In Advent we aligned ourselves with ancient Israel in her long anticipation of a messiah; now the waiting is over, the promised Savior is here. Likewise we identified with Mary in her auspicious pregnancy; now the waiting is over, the Holy One is born. And during darkening December we lit candles in hope, mindful of the brokenness around us; now the waiting is over, the light of the world dawns.

If Advent is a season of waiting, Christmas is a season of wonder.

But in this we face impediments. The first is overfamiliarity. We're seeing the little crèche for the hundredth time, we sing the old carols from memory and by rote, we can practically recite the Christmas story from Luke and December sermons sound wearily familiar. The second obstacle is closely related: sentimentality. The clichéd greeting cards, the nostalgic music, the sweet manger scenes, all of this mingled with a watered-down holiday ethos. The third problem is the commercial eclipse of Advent compounded by the reduction of Christmas to a single day (albeit, for many of us, a joyful and satisfying day). As Gabe Huck puts it, "We take our Christmas with lots of sugar. And we take it in a day."

Even the phrase "the true meaning of Christmas" has become a cliché. We are in danger of skating over the glistening surface of the season and forgetting the depth of its truth and meaning.

Christmas invites us to inhabit the beginning of the Christ Story more vividly. Stepping into these scenes as narrated by Matthew and Luke, we are provoked to awe and perhaps to action. We anxiously pace the birthing floor with Joseph. Our hearts pound with the stunned shepherds reeling on the hillside. We wince as the baby is circumcised and nod as he's given a name destined to excel all names. When old Simeon takes the child in his arms and prophesies, we listen intently. We marvel at the Magi arriving with their portentous gifts. We cringe in angry dismay as Herod's soldiers slaughter the innocent toddlers of Bethlehem. Trudging with the refugee family, we escape into exile with all its inherent difficulties. And sitting with Mary quietly at night, we ponder all these things in our hearts.

The Christmas season also bids us to explore the story's theological mysteries more deeply. What does the incarnation tell us about God? What does it say about the physical creation, about our biological bodies? What does it mean for our being as humans? Or, for that matter, for Jesus' being as a human? What does it teach us about life? About love? How does incarnation connect with redemption?

And Christmas draws us into spiritual life more profoundly. The incarnation is God's great gift to us, or at least the beginning of the gift that culminates in the death and resurrection of Jesus. For God so loved the world—so loved us—that he gave his only Son. God's mind was to empty himself for us. God took on our poverty so that we might gain his riches. This is what the medieval Christians called the *admirabile commercium*, the wonderful exchange. Here is how Laurence Stookey puts it:

Christmas is the enfleshment of God, the humiliation of the Most High and divine participation in all that is painful, ugly, frustrating, and limited. Divinity takes on humanity, to restore the image of God implanted at creation but sullied by sin. Here is the great exchange Christmas ponders, that God became like us that we might become like God. God accepted death that the world might accept life. The Creator assumed temporality to redeem creation from futility.

So we open ourselves anew to this gift. We say yes to the marvelous exchange by which we are changed. As he gave all of himself for us, so we give generously of ourselves for others. And in this giving, his and ours, we are spiritually enriched.

CHRISTMAS IN CHURCH
AND CULTURAL TRADITION

Here we will consider the origins of the Feast of the Nativity, the saint who lies behind Santa Claus and the special significance of the days of Christmas.

December 25. The earliest Christians apparently gave little thought to the celebration of Christ's birth. For one thing, these believers were intently focused on the spread of the gospel and the imminent return of Jesus. For another, no one knew the actual date of his birth, hence the evolution of dates in various parts of the church over six centuries. Scholars are divided between two theories on the reason for the date that gained eventual consensus. One approach identifies March 25 (the spring equinox, in ancient reckoning) as the date for both Christ's death and his conception and then calculates nine months forward to December 25. The other theory postulates that Christians chose December 25 in response to pagan festivals in Rome.

Worship of the sun has a long history in ancient cultures. The Roman emperor Aurelian, who apparently wanted to unite the empire around a common religion, instituted the cult of *Sol Invictus*, the "Unconquered Sun," in 274 and declared the day of the winter solstice, December 25, as the birthday and feast of the sun-god. The earliest evidence of Christians in Rome celebrating Christ's nativity on December 25 appears later in 336. Many scholars conclude that the church purposefully countered the pagan festival by adopting its date for their celebration of the birth of "the sun of righteousness" (Mal 4:2). This cultural appropriation became an implicit witness to the truly unconquerable light.

In addition to *Sol Invictus*, the Romans celebrated the seven-day feast of Saturnalia from December 17 to 23 in honor of the fertility god Saturn. These were days of drinking and feasting, of game playing and role swapping, of parading and giving presents. Roman Christians rejected the raucous revelry, but as was the case with similar pagan customs in the northern and western regions of Europe, a festive element persisted in uneasy association with the midwinter celebration of Christmas.

In fact, the celebration of Christmas has been vociferously opposed at various times in church history, including our own. Christmas did not fare well during the Reformation. The Calvinists condemned it, as did John Knox in Scotland. The English Puritans opposed the excessive entertainments promoted by the Tudor and Stuart monarchs. The British Parliament under Oliver Cromwell declared December 25 a fast day and forbade all decorations and festivities and even services at church. It was a mixed picture in Colonial America, with austere restrictions in Puritan New England and more festive activities in Anglican Virginia. Christmas became a legal holiday in various states only in the nineteenth century, beginning with Louisiana in 1837 while the New England states held out until late in the century.

The gift giver. What about Santa Claus? Christians are divided on the jolly old fellow. Some worry about telling their kids a "story"; others delight to create a sense of enchantment that feeds the imagination; and many object to Santa as part of the commercial conspiracy that encourages children's greed. Regardless of our stance, the story of "St. Nick" is worth knowing.

The actual St. Nicholas was born in the late third century in Asia Minor (modern Turkey) and served as bishop in the port city of Myra. He died around 343. A cult of veneration developed in Myra and his legend spread widely in the Middle Ages. Tradition focuses on his great generosity, especially toward children in need. One story tells of his compassion for a shipping merchant who, having lost all his ships at sea, could not provide dowries for his three unmarried daughters. Thrice Nicholas secretly intervened by dropping bags of gold over a window sill, with at least one falling, it is told, into a stocking hung up to dry. He became a patron saint of children and also sailors. The feast day of this Middle Eastern saint is December 6.

In America the tradition evolved. The Dutch who settled in New York—originally New Amsterdam—in the 1600s knew this saint as Sante Klaas. (Dutch children still put their shoes by the fireplace on the eve of December 6 to receive gifts from him.) In 1809 Washington Irving augmented the figure into a man with a flying horse who dropped gifts down chimneys. Clement Clarke Moore's 1823 poem, "The Visit of Saint Nicholas" (or "The Night before Christmas"), introduced the fanciful sleigh and reindeer and moved the visit to Christmas Eve. Emerging entrepreneurs such as F. W. Woolworth reinforced this image with enthusiasm. A series of Thomas Nast illustrations for *Harper's Weekly* beginning in 1863 made Santa rotund and white-bearded, dressed him in red and white, and gave him a North Pole address. A 1921 advertisement by Coca-Cola completed the modern image.

Strands of the gift-giver legend appear in many countries. In Germany, an elfish girl called the Christ-child (*Christkindl*, from which we get our slurred Kriss Kringle) is guided from home to home by candles in the windows. In Great Britain, the ancient bearded figure of Father Christmas, perhaps a holdover from Saturnalia, has fused with Santa. In Brazil, Papa Noel brings gifts from the South Pole. In Italy, the good witch Befana fills stockings on the Eve of Epiphany (January 5) and looks into the faces of sleeping children in search of Jesus. In Russia, she is called Babushka and helps St. Nicholas leave gifts beneath the tree. Whatever the culture, the tradition points to the great Gift Giver who gave his only Son for all humanity.

The twelve days of Christmas. As the church sorted out the dates for Christmas and Epiphany in the fourth century, eventually the whole period between the two feasts was proclaimed sacred and festive. Liturgical churches will speak of the first eight days (December 25 to January 1) as the octave of Christmas, which echoes the Jewish pattern of an extended feast (see 2 Chron 7:9). Within the octave fall several other holy days or feasts, and these add meaningful notes to the chord of Christmas.

December 24 and 25: Christmas Eve and Day. "So hallow'd and so gracious is the time," goes a line in Shakespeare's *Hamlet* that reflects a longstanding belief in the spiritual potency of this night, especially the midnight hour when Christ was thought to have been born. "All is calm, all is bright," we sing in the treasured carol "Silent Night, Holy Night." T. S. Eliot called Christmas Eve "the still point of the turning world . . . where past and future are gathered." In the fifth century, following a practice that started in Jerusalem, the church added a midnight mass on Christmas Eve alongside the one on Christmas morning. In England this came to be called "Christ's mass," from which we get *Christmas.*

December 26: Feast of St. Stephen. It may come as a surprise that the church remembers the first Christian martyr immediately after Christmas Day. But the connection reminds us that the child in the crib will one day die on the cross, and that many who have followed him have given their lives in witness to his light.

December 27: Feast of St. John. On December 27 we remember the apostle who wrote of the Word become flesh, the disciple "beloved" by Jesus, the Evangelist who, according to tradition, received the Revelation while exiled on the island of Patmos.

December 28: Commemoration of the Holy Innocents. These were the infant boys slaughtered in Bethlehem on Herod's paranoid orders (Mt 2). With Stephen and John they are called *comites Christi,* or "companions of Christ," a medieval designation that recognizes their suffering. The above three days correspond, in order, to the three types of martyrdom: voluntary and executed (Stephen), voluntary but not executed (John) and executed but not voluntary (the Bethlehem children). To remember Herod's atrocity is to strip sentimentality from the birth of Christ. On this day we confront the evil in our world, the violence of the powerful against the weak, the sorrow of those who suffer injustice and the very real darkness into which the light shines.

January 1: Feast of the Holy Name. On the eighth day after his birth Jesus was circumcised and named, in keeping with Jewish law. So the church marks this octave day, previously called the Feast of the Circumcision and also, in the Roman church, the Feast of Mary. It reminds us of the Jewishness of Jesus. But also on this day we celebrate with the wider culture the beginning of a new calendar year. (Julius Caesar in A.D. 46 first designated January 1 as the start of the new year.) It is fitting that we begin a new secular year by meditating on the names given to the Christ child: Jesus (the Lord saves) and Immanuel (God with us).

THE CHRIST STORY IN CHRISTMAS

John speaks of the Word made flesh in terms of light and glory, or, to use Peterson's words, "brightness radiating from God as he moves into our neighborhood." We know the bright aspects of this story—annunciations, glorias, Magi—but the light also casts shadows, and these darker elements of the story cause us to shake our heads in a different kind of wonder.

Mary had encountered the angel of God, opened herself to the engendering Spirit and taken courage from her miraculously pregnant cousin, all amazing and reassuring experiences. But now, after the difficult late-term journey to Bethlehem and the dishearteningly crude accommodations, young Mary must feel quite alone as labor comes on. Who besides her new husband and perhaps a local midwife knows where she lies this night? Jesus is born in utter obscurity.

Well God knows, of course, and he chooses to make it known also to a handful of country shepherds whom he sends as ambassadors of his care. Keeping sheep was a lowly job, so these shepherds represent the poor and disregarded of the world. Mary had prophesied that God would lift the lowly (Lk 1:52), and now a band of shepherds receive their own angelic annunciation, a "gospel of great joy" accompanied by a vast glorifying chorus. Like Mary and Zechariah after their annunciations, the shepherds have a choice: would they believe and act on that belief? They do, and in so doing, they are blessed. They are the first after Joseph and Mary to witness God in the flesh and the first to bear witness to others. Their experience suggests a pattern for us: they hear, they act, they see, they tell and they praise. The poor see Jesus, born in humble poverty.

But the rich and powerful can also find the Savior, as seen in the story of the Magi (Mt 2). God communicates to these foreigners and they too come, bearing their extravagant gifts. But Matthew entwines the account of their homage with that of the malevolent actions of King Herod. Again we think of Mary's Magnificat: "He has brought down the powerful from their thrones," and we want to respond, "Yes, Lord, do just that." The slaughter of the children, the anguish of the parents, the flight to Egypt—these dramatize that Jesus was born into a situation of great vulnerability.

These shadows—obscurity, poverty and vulnerability—only heighten the paradox and wonder of Christ's coming: the omnipresent God forgoes fame, the majestic one forfeits wealth, the Almighty relinquishes power. This is exactly what Paul stresses in Philippians 2: Jesus empties himself ("did not regard equality with God as something to be exploited") and humbles himself ("became obedient to the point of death"). Something incomprehensible takes place within the triune God: costly, extravagant, self-giving love for us, his wayward creatures living in darkness.

Thus, the Word becomes human, fully human: Jesus is part of a family and belongs to a village; he goes to school and plays games and learns a craft; he suffers injuries and tastes grief; he jokes with friends and feels sexual attraction; he engages in business and talks politics; he studies Torah and sings at synagogue and spends hours in prayer; he makes spiritual discoveries and wrestles with doubts; he embarks by faith on a visionary and controversial mission; he takes the risk of going public with his preaching and healing; he feels the pull toward fame and power but stays his humble course; and in the end he faces betrayal and endures death. "He had to enter into every detail of human life" (Heb 2:17 *The Message*). We can identify with him because he so fully identified with us. God with us!

INHABITING CHRISTMAS

Even if we follow the suggestions in the previous chapter for keeping Advent, the weeks leading up to Christmas can be crazy, sapping our energies and emotions. With Christmas Day over, we may feel more than ready for a return to "normal." The culture around us will quickly move on, but we can treat these twelve days differently. We can live as if we have arrived on a spiritual island after a long and arduous trip. Take a deep breath now and settle in for the time being. Let yourself relish where you are in the year—and in the Story. Four simple suggestions may help you.

Stay in the Christmas mode. Even though your friends and neighbors may find it puzzling, you can choose some concrete ways to linger in the season. For example, you could:

- Keep your tree and decorations up until the end of the season on January 6.
- Continue to light candles each night.
- Host a leftovers party on December 26 for friends or neighbors.
- Save some of your gift-giving for the twelve days, especially the Feast of the Epiphany.
- Plan one or two special activities with your children or friends.
- Get outdoors to enjoy the creation hallowed by Christ's incarnation.
- Host a gathering of friends in association with one of the lesser feasts.
- Write the cards or notes that by choice or circumstance you did not send earlier.
- Rehearse Scriptures, read writings, say prayers and play music fit for Christmas.
- Hold a Twelfth Night party on the eve of Epiphany.

Engage in spiritual reflection. Schedule for yourself some times of quiet and solitude, perhaps some early morning moments or sabbath afternoon hours or even a retreat day if you are off from work or school. Re-immerse yourself in the infancy narratives of Matthew and Luke. Study them as texts. Imagine them as stories. Pray the prayers within them. Also, plumb the theological depths of the season with help from the New Testament Epistles or the writings of theologians ancient and contemporary. Give your attention to the artistic response of musicians or visual artists. Write your own reflections in a journal. One way or another, make space over the dozen days for quiet wonder and thankful joy. The devotional material that follows is meant to help you in this.

Practice self-giving love. God emptied himself and entered the world for us. We are to have the same mindset and demonstrate the same love (Phil 2). The lead-up to Christmas prompts many good works—clothing for the homeless, gifts for children of prisoners, visits to the elderly, dollars in the Salvation Army kettle—but the deeds fall off conspicuously after December 25. How fitting for us to choose a concrete means to embody Christ's compassion during these twelve days. Serving the poor, working for justice and preserving the environment should not be symbolic gestures or rhetorical sentiments in a month of heightened good will; they should be part of our ongoing pattern of life.

Identify with Jesus. The conjunction of New Year's Day with the Feast of the Holy Name provides us a lovely opportunity to dwell on who Jesus is and who we are in him. The baby is circumcised whose flesh will later be torn so that we can be "circumcised in heart." The child is called Jesus, the name assigned by the angel as a sign of our salvation, the name at which every knee is destined to bend, the name we take on ourselves as "Christ-ones." Sometime on January 1, take a few moments to meditate on that name. Pray that it be hallowed, speak or sing it in praise or perhaps mark yourself with it by making the sign of the cross. In the Eastern tradition, apropos to this season, this physical gesture—forehead to heart, shoulder to shoulder, return to heart—is made with the thumb and first two fingertips touching, symbolizing the Trinity, and the last two fingers pressed to the palm, representing the two natures of Christ and his coming down to earth. In so doing this day, you renew your intention to live the new calendar year in a manner worth of the holy name.

WORDS ABOUT THE WORD

The first poem in response to the mystery of the incarnation was uttered by Mary. Full of grace and full of God, she burst into praise:

> My soul magnifies the Lord,
>   and my spirit rejoices in God my Savior,
>   for he has looked with favor on the lowliness of his servant. (Lk 1:47-48)

The angels arrayed above the shepherds later echoed her song:

Glory to God in the highest heaven,
  and on earth peace among those whom he favors! (Lk 2:14)

This is the season of wonder: the Highest gave up glory to be born of the lowly, the Logos and Light became body and blood, the government of God began in a barn, and the angels of heaven sang the hope of all humanity. Wonder fills us with joy and moves us to self-giving love, for wonder is the posture of the humble, the grateful. As Oscar Romero, the martyred archbishop of El Salvador, taught, "Without poverty of spirit, there can be no abundance of God."

So in this season we come once more to Bethlehem in the poverty of the shepherds and humility of the Magi. We bow before the feedbox which holds the Bread of Life, the gift by which we're enriched. We find our words, even our poetry, failing us, as Dietrich Bonheoffer so eloquently discerned:

> Our words rush out at the sight of the divine child; we try to put into language what is implied in the one name: Jesus. But at the bottom these words are nothing except a wordless silence of adoration before the ineffable, before the presence of God in the shape of a human child.

*   *   *

Preview of devotions in Christmas. The material for this twelve-day season is divided into two "weeks." For Christmas Day and the six days afterward, we focus on the narrative of Christ's birth with its paradoxes and wonders. Beginning on New Year's Day, we shift to a more theological reflection on the mystery of God's incarnation. The Scripture selections heighten our wonder and joy over God's gift of himself to us.

Feast of the Nativity of the Lord
Beginning December 25

Good News of Great Joy!

After weeks of patient expectation, now we celebrate with boisterous joy and wide-eyed amazement the actual arrival of the "Savior, who is the Messiah, the Lord." Something utterly glorious! But, surprisingly, he arrives in virtual obscurity: born a helpless infant to an unattended peasant girl in a crude cowshed unbeknown to all but a handful of scruffy strangers. Like those lowly shepherds, their darkness suddenly dispelled by an ensemble of angels, we are given to know this almost hidden glory and to revel in this good news of great joy.

Approaching God. Praise the Lord! Praise the Lord from the heavens, praise the Lord from the earth. Glory to you, Lord God, in the highest heaven, and on earth, peace among those whom you favor. Amen.

Presenting Myself. Like the shepherds who hurried to Bethlehem, I want to see this day with spiritual eyes the amazing thing that has taken place in history, which you, O Lord, have made known to us.

Inviting God's Presence. Let your great light shine on me today and on all who walk in darkness. Amen.

LISTENING TO GOD

Isaiah 9:2-7 (ABC); Hebrews 1:1-4 (ABC);
Luke 2:1-20 (ABC); Psalm 148 (ABC); Matthew 2:13-18 (A)

Isaiah's prophecy sheds light, from our vantage point, on the meaning of the birth in Bethlehem. Note the familiar themes: light shining on those in darkness, communal joy as at harvest time, alleviation of oppression and cessation of war, establishment of justice and pervasive peace. Reflect on the simple pair of prepositions in "A child born *for* us, a son given *to* us." God so loved us that he gave his Son. Finally, reflect on the fourfold name of the child and how it speaks of wisdom, power, love and shalom.

The opening verses of **Hebrews** put the whole business in grand perspective. In all of history, God has spoken to us most decisively and dramatically "by a Son." The one who uttered the cosmos into being, who sustains it now by his powerful word, who is destined to inherit it when remade, this one entered the very creation to reflect God's glory to humanity and to rescue us from our sin and its consequences. This is who was born in that barn.

Luke tells the story. He sets it in political and geographical context. He explains how Joseph and Mary came to be in the crowded village. Almost matter-of-factly he reports the birth and the use of a feed trough for a cradle. But the real drama takes place in the nearby grazing fields. Shepherds were not the most reputable of folk, so it was to those at the social margin that the angel appears in luminous glory. Terrified at first, they hear the announcement of "good news of great joy" and then the chorus of angelic chanting. With these herdsmen God makes the first move, one of sheer grace; the next move is theirs. And they make it! Wanting more of God they go to find the baby. Thus they become the first witnesses, in both senses of the word. Oh, the joy they experienced as they returned to their fields! What do you make of the way God orchestrates this whole story? Where do you find yourself in it? Has God made a move toward you of late that invites your response? Do you want to see more?

If you are filled with fresh wonder, **Psalm 148** will help you join with all creation in celebration and praise. Join the psalmist in glorifying God but with this paradox in mind: God's glory was once wrapped in bands of cloth and laid on the straw of a feed box. As you call on the heavens to praise him, remember the choir of angels over Bethlehem. As you call on the earth to praise him, remember the animals around the crib, the shepherds in the field and the Magi bearing their gifts. Praise God for raising up a horn—a deliverer—for us all (see Lk 1:69).

Matthew gives the grim account of the holy innocents, the male babies in Bethlehem two years and younger who were slaughtered on the orders of King Herod, a ruler ruthless in eliminating any threat to his power. During this time of festivity it is useful to meditate on this brutal act of infanticide and the devastation it brought to so many families. The scene offsets our sentimental leanings. The darkness into which Christ came is no mere metaphor. Nor is the darkness of our time. Then again, the light of Christ is no mere metaphor either! Even as you rejoice in the light, continue to intercede for the evil-darkened world of our day.

RESPONDING TO GOD

Given the predominant pattern in our culture of ending Christmas with December 25, it may be response enough to deliberately continue, however quietly, your wonder and celebration of the glory hidden first in the womb and then the stable and even now in your own life. Immanuel—God is with us! Keep rejoicing.

Closing Prayer. Wonderful Counselor, Mighty God, Everlasting Father, Prince of Peace: by your zeal may you establish your throne with justice and righteousness and bring about endless peace on the earth. Amen.

The Word Became Flesh

In a fitting conjunction, we celebrate January 1 as New Year's Day and also as the Feast of the Holy Name, commemorating the naming of Jesus eight days after birth. The Word who spoke the world into being is assigned a linguistic configuration of sounds and symbols within that world. He is named Jesus, as the angel had instructed. The Word becomes flesh. The divine takes on the human. The ineffable is named. This is the mystery of the incarnation. Yet the marvel goes even deeper. "He was made man that we might become god," wrote St. Athanasius in the fourth century. A great exchange! He becomes like us that we might become like him. In these remaining days of Christmastide we contemplate this deep mystery.

Approaching God. Jesus, you are the Word. You are with God and you are God. You were in the beginning with God and all things came into being through you. In you is life and this life is the light of all people. The darkness cannot overcome your light.

Presenting Myself. At your name, Jesus, I bend my knee this day and confess with my tongue that you are Lord, to the glory of God the Father. Amen.

Inviting God's Presence. O God, send the Spirit of your Son into my heart so that I may cry, "Abba! Father!" Amen.

LISTENING TO GOD

Luke 2:21-40 (ABC); John 1:1-18 (ABC);
Philippians 2:5-11 (ABC); Galatians 4:4-7 (ABC);
Psalm 8 (ABC); Numbers 6:22-27 (ABC)

Luke reports the circumcision and naming of Jesus on the eighth day as the law required (Lev 12:2-7). The name Jesus, given by the angel, is the Greek equivalent of Joshua, "God saves." Luke next recounts the visit to Jerusalem forty days after the birth for the purpose of Mary's purification and Jesus' presentation in the temple, again as the law required (Ex 22:29; Num 3:13). They encounter two elderly prophets, Simeon and Anna. Both are devout and attuned to the Holy Spirit. They exemplify those who wait and watch for the coming of the Lord. Once again God orchestrates a remarkable encouragement for the young couple, yet Simeon's blessing is laced with the ominous. Simeon's canticle is prayed by millions each night as part of compline prayer; we entrust ourselves to God before sleep with a sense of security and contentment, for we too have seen the Messiah, the Lord's salvation.

Whereas Luke and Matthew start their Gospels with the birth of Jesus, **John** begins his with a profound theological prologue. Note the echoes of Genesis. Note the symbol of light. What do you make of John's designation of Jesus as the Word? The Greek word *logos* entails "idea, wisdom, truth, coherence"; *logos* means "meaning." But this transcendent "being-ness" of God does not remain inaccessible in the spiritual realm. No, the Word becomes flesh and lives among us: he enters our history, he shares our creaturely experience, he completely identifies with us. He is like us—fully human—but not like us. John summarizes his firsthand experience: We saw his glory and it was full of grace and truth. Take time to reflect on this powerful and beautiful combination, grace and truth present in equal fullness, love and righteousness fully conjoined. What would this look like in your life? Further, how do you experience both grace and truth in your own relationship with Jesus?

Paul's christological hymn in **Philippians 2** captures the incarnation in a succinct but compelling fashion. It deserves extended meditation. Jesus chooses to let go of his divine nature and prerogatives, as it were, and to empty himself in becoming human. A great descent! And not simply human in some privileged way, but he came all the way down to the point of tortuous execution. And it is right to anticipate the death of Jesus even in this Christmas season—and his resurrection and great ascent! For God gives him a name above every conceivable name in heaven and earth, one that ultimately will command the allegiance of every creature in existence. It certainly commands ours.

For the **Galatians,** Paul stresses that Christ became the child of a woman that we might become children of the Spirit. He identifies with us so that we can identify with him—children of the same "Abba" and heirs of the same inheritance.

Psalm 8 is always read during the Feast of the Holy Name. It celebrates the paradox that we humans, while small and inconsequential compared with the majestic glory of our Creator, have been accorded remarkable responsibility within his creation. But deeper theological reflection (aided by New Testament citations of the psalm in Heb 2:5-9; 1 Cor 15:24-27 and Eph 1:19-22) points to the incarnate Word by whom this human role is ultimately fulfilled.

In **Numbers 6,** God gives a blessing for the priests of the Israelites to say over the people, and in so doing, to "put God's name on them." The blessing of God accompanies the bearing of his name. Reaffirm to God your willingness to hallow and bear his name in this new calendar year, and let yourself freely ask his blessing for yourself and for those you love.

RESPONDING TO GOD

This is a week for deep wonder at the mystery of the incarnation and a week for dwelling in this prayer: let your name be treated as holy, in my life and throughout the world. Amen.

Closing Prayer. In this new year, O Lord, bless me and keep me, along with those I love; make your face to shine upon us and be gracious to us; lift up your countenance upon us and give us peace; I ask this in your holy name. Amen.

4

Epiphany
Enlightened in the Telling

I am the light of the world. . . . You are the light of the world.

JESUS

We who have seen the light of Christ are obliged,
by the greatness of the grace that has been given us,
to make known the presence of the Savior to the ends of the earth . . .
not only by preaching the glad tidings of His coming;
but above all by revealing Him in our lives. . . .
Every day of our mortal lives must be His manifestation,
His divine Epiphany, in the world which He has created and redeemed.

THOMAS MERTON

Pay attention.
Be astonished.
Tell about it.

MARY OLIVER

I claimed a space in the line already meandering through Central Park one early July morning in 1999, grateful that my spot was shaded as we were headed toward 100 degrees for a second straight day. It would be a few hours before the distribution of tickets for that night's Shakespeare in the Park production, *The Taming of the Shrew*. At dusk Charlene and I returned to the open-air theater for a raucous and, shall I say, warmly received evening of comical gender-clashing on stage. Around eleven, as we were driving home to our apartment in Washington Heights, I exited the Westside Highway at the George Washington Bridge as usual. But then I sensed that something was not quite right. What was it? I turned several corners and headed up Fort Washington Avenue, still vaguely unsettled.

Suddenly I saw it—or, rather, didn't see it. Except for the beams of a few oncoming headlights and those of my own car, there was no light. No humming streetlamps, no orange glow from the bridge, no fluorescent storefronts. And no traffic signals either, I noticed. Dead black.

As any urban dweller knows—and this is especially true in New York—it's never completely dark in the city. Moon or no moon, there is always some light, usually enough to read by. So this was eerie. Improbably we found a parking place two blocks from home. We crept nervously down the sidewalk, hearing the voices of people we could not see. A waving flashlight here or there provided bearings enough to reach our building. Carefully we shuffled up the walkway to the lobby door and fumbled with our key. Inside we felt our way along the walls to our first-floor apartment, awkwardly let ourselves in, then groped our way to the pantry, finally finding candles and matches. In the small merciful glow we began to breathe easier, anxiety giving way to a sense of adventure.

The blackout persisted into the next day, affecting some two hundred thousand people in northern Manhattan. With the coming of daylight, hordes of people spilled out into the neighborhood sidewalks and parks. As the day wore on without power, folks grilled meat and shared food that would go bad in the rising heat. Radios blared, kids played in the fire hydrants and neighbors chatted in what amounted to a huge block party. The shared experience created a kind of camaraderie. Around five o'clock the power came back on and, with it, lights, refrigerators and air conditioners. Then everyone went back inside.

This experience became for me a kind of parable about how dark our darkness can be and, in contrast, what a relief when light is restored. The night without power was disorienting and dangerous; the coming of daylight brought order and safety and even joy. To state the obvious spiritual point: without light, we cannot see.

During Advent and Christmas the metaphors of light and darkness infuse our spiritual reflections. In Advent we heard Isaiah cry out prophetically,

> The people who walked in darkness
>   have seen a great light;
> those who lived in a land of deep darkness—
>   on them light has shined. (Is 9:2)

During Christmas we joyfully celebrated the coming of that light in the birth of Jesus. Now the Feast of the Epiphany on January 6 brings this theme to culmination—the light of Christ made manifest to the whole world as symbolized by the Gentile Magi from the East. Thus the day of Epiphany and the season that follows complete what is sometimes called in the liturgical year the Cycle of Light.

THE HEART OF EPIPHANY

Three events in the life of Christ are associated with the Feast of the Epiphany: the visit of the wise men from the East, the baptism by John in the Jordan River and the turning of water into wine at Cana. The common theme is manifestation: what has been largely hidden is made more widely known. A star guides Gentiles to a future king, a voice identifies Jesus as the beloved Son and a set of wine-brimming pots reveals miraculous power. Epiphanies!

Epiphany comes from the Greek verb *phainein*, which means "to cause to appear" or "to bring to light." The word can refer to the visible manifestation of a deity (also, in ancient writings, the arrival of a ruler honored like a god) or to an experience of sudden insight or revelation: those "aha" moments when we "see the light." Churches in the Orthodox tradition use a slightly different word, *theophany*, which places even greater emphasis on the idea of *God* shining forth.

Epiphany is a season of enlightenment. In these five to nine weeks (depending on the date of Easter) that follow January 6, we focus our attention on Jesus and the unfolding manifestation of his glory "full of grace and truth" (Jn 1:14). We watch him bring healing to the sick and desperate. We witness his confrontations with the powers of darkness. We listen as he teaches the eager crowds. We observe him patiently training his disciples. We behold him transfigured on the mountainside. We say, like those unnamed Greeks who seek him out during a festival, "We wish to see Jesus" (Jn 12:21). To which Jesus replies, as he often did, "Come and see" (Jn 1:39).

But later Jesus will also say to his followers, "Go and tell." The one who summons us to himself sends us out on his behalf. The one who shows himself to us asks us to make him known to others. The one who declares, "I am the light of the world," says to us, "You are the light of the world."

On more than one occasion Jesus sends his followers out to various villages to heal the sick and preach the kingdom of God. When one group of seventy returns, full of joy and amazement, they can't wait to tell Jesus what happened, how even the demons had submitted to them. Jesus rejoices with them over the success of their mission but even more over what was revealed to them along the way. They have seen something firsthand and have been changed (Lk 10:1-24). They've experienced small epiphanies.

So it is for us. Epiphany is a season for seeing more of Christ's glory by focusing on his life and mission. Simultaneously, it's a time for making that glory better known to those around us. We bear witness to what we have seen and learned and experienced. Herein lies a spiritual paradox: not only do we say what we see, we also see as we say. Epiphany, then, is a time both to inhabit the Story and to tell the Story, for in the telling itself we are further enlightened.

EPIPHANY IN CHURCH
AND CULTURAL TRADITION

The first indications of an Epiphany feast come from Alexandria in the early third century. Some scholars postulate that the celebration was inaugurated to counter the Egyptian festival for the birthday of Aion, god of time, which included the ceremonial drawing of water from the Nile. Some Egyptian legends even speak of springs whose water turned to wine. So perhaps Alexandrian Christians wanted to proclaim Christ's baptism, in which the water is made sacred by *his* presence rather than he by its, and his miracle at Cana, in which he transforms water to wine by his own power. To this day in Orthodox churches the priest, besides performing baptisms on Holy Theophany, also conducts the great blessing of the waters, first sanctifying a supply of water for the church to use in the next year and often also leading a procession to bless the nearest body of water.

While the whole church settled on December 25 for the birth of Christ, the East and West varied as to when they celebrated subsequent events. Thus today the East includes the visit of the Magi in the nativity celebration and emphasizes Christ's baptism on January 6, while the West recognizes the Magi on January 6 and commemorates the baptism on the first Sunday afterward.

Epiphany is also known as the Feast of the Three Holy Kings, or Three Kings' Day, especially in Latin America. In Matthew's account, however, the Magi are neither numbered as three nor described as kings. It's the third-century theologian Origen who first speaks of three Magi, presumably extrapolating from the three gifts. The designation of the Magi as kings first occurs in the sixth century, as do the traditional names of Caspar (Gaspar), Melchior and Balthasar. In the eighth century the Venerable Bede, an English monastic scholar, proposed that the kings represented the three parts of the known world—Asia, Europe and Africa, respectively—and thus have the wise men often been depicted racially in art and verse.

One Epiphany tradition, the blessing of the homes using holy water and incense, has been practiced since the end of the Middle Ages. The letters *C*, *M* and *B* are usually traced on the doors as a reference to the names of the Magi, although Adolf Adam reports an alternative interpretation: the initials stand for *Christus mansionem benedicat*, or "May Christ bless the dwelling." Frederica Mathewes-Green describes the use of newly blessed water in her church on Epiphany: "The holy water represents baptism, and during the period between Theophany and Lent each year, every Orthodox home is to be visited by the priest and sprinkled with the water, carrying our baptism home."

The thinking about the weeks between Epiphany and Lent varies among churches. In the Roman Catholic and much of the Anglican tradition, the period after the Baptism of the Lord is designated as either Ordinary Time or simply the Season after Epiphany. In this approach, Ordinary Time falls into two blocks, the five to nine weeks after Epiphany and leading up to Lent, and the remaining twenty-five to twenty-nine weeks after Pentecost and leading up to Advent. But many Protestant churches regard the weeks after January 6 as the Season of Epiphany and continue to emphasize the manifestation of Christ to the world, which is the approach I have followed in this book.

How fitting then for the final Sunday of Epiphany, which immediately precedes Ash Wednesday, to be designated in the Revised Common Lectionary as Transfiguration Sunday. Thus two profound events in the life of Christ frame the season of Epiphany: his baptism in the river, during which the heavens open, the voice speaks and the Spirit descends, and his transfiguration on the mountain, during which the light dazzles, the prophets appear and the voice calls from the encompassing cloud. Scenes of glory and moments of revelation—epiphanies!

THE CHRIST STORY IN EPIPHANY

Who were the Magi and where did they come from? There are no definitive answers. Scholars surmise that they were astrologers, perhaps Zoroastrian, probably from Persia or Babylon or possibly Arabia. Whom these wise men represent, however, is fairly clear in Matthew's narrative: the Gentiles, which is to say, the nations of the world. The Magi receive and respond to a revelation from God through nature (a star or conjunction of planets), which is then augmented by revelation through the Hebrew Scriptures (cited by the priests and scribes). They complete a long pilgrimage to Bethlehem to pay homage to the newborn king. Light shines in the darkness.

By contrast, the Jewish ruler Herod the Great rejects this "good news" and, foiled by the dream-warned Magi, implements his ruthless extermination plan. This atrocity echoes the slaughtering of male babies at the time of Moses' birth, as recounted in Exodus 1. Darkness opposes the light.

Guided by a dream, Joseph flees with his family to Egypt and waits until they can return home in relative safety. These incidents reinforce the allusion to the Israelites' long sojourn in Egypt. The light is not overcome.

In this one story of the Magi, then, Matthew refers to the two greatest salvation episodes in the history of the Israelites: their exodus from slavery in Egypt and their return from exile in the East. The implication? The Messiah's redemption will extend throughout the world to all people, even to the historic enemies of Israel, even to their contemporary oppressor, Rome.

This same theme emerges in the encounter with Simeon and Anna in the temple (Lk 2:22-40). Joseph and Mary go to Jerusalem to fulfill two expectations of the law: the consecration of their firstborn son to the Lord (Ex 13) and the purification of Mary on the fortieth day after childbirth (Lev 12). Guided by the Holy Spirit, Simeon finds them, blesses them and prophesies. Like a watchman who's finally spotted what he's long sought, or an aged man ready to die in peace, Simeon rejoices. His prayer, called the *Nunc Dimittis* (Latin for "Now you are dismissing [your servant]"), speaks of "seeing salvation," of "light for revelation to the Gentiles" and of "glory for the people Israel," all epiphany motifs. The elderly widow Anna, also a prophet, likewise shares in this temple epiphany. She sets an example for us by praising God and speaking about the child to all who share her longing for redemption.

Except for attention to the above episode on the Feast of the Presentation, February 2, the focus of Epiphany shifts to the adult Jesus and how his identity and purpose are gradually revealed to those who respond to him, beginning with his baptism. Other than the interesting episode of Jesus in the temple at age twelve (Lk 2:41-52), we are told nothing of his adolescent or young adult years. Nor are we told what his cousin John knew of him and his intentions. The public story begins when Jesus travels down from Galilee to the river region where John has been preaching repentance and baptizing for forgiveness. Jesus too enters the river and submits to baptism. But his baptism is unlike that of anyone else's.

As Jesus emerges from the water praying, three things happen: the heavens open to him, the Spirit descends on him and a voice reassures him. It is an epiphany for Jesus and also for John, presumably, and possibly for the bystanders. And, yes, for us too. His baptism points to both his divinity and his humanity. We do not know how in the years before this encounter his self-awareness has taken shape or his sense of mission has come into focus. But surely this is a decisive moment for him, a moment of confirmation, encouragement, empowerment—although this would soon be tested in the desert. Witnessing this event convinces John that Jesus is the Son of God. Some in the crowd experience heightened hunger and openness, and they soon give up everything to follow Jesus. And for us, seeing Jesus identify with us in baptism opens the way for us to identify with him in our baptism—as sons and daughters of God, beloved, accepted and Spirit-bathed.

When Jesus returns from the wilderness, he begins to preach about the kingdom of God now at hand. He performs miracles that enact the kingdom and calls men and women to follow him for the sake of the kingdom. His ideas, actions, conversations and miracles all progressively reveal him as the leader of this kingdom. They manifest his authority and power. They show his wisdom and love. They bring to light his unique relationship with God.

Jesus befriends the poor, heals the sick, touches the "unclean," defends the powerless, forgives the sinful, stills a storm, exorcises demons, raises a girl from death, feeds the hungry, makes the blind to see, and more. The people, amazed at his teaching and healing, flock to him—women and men, young and old, rich and poor, pious and pitiful—and he shepherds them with compassion. To them he shows himself a merciful king.

John refers to these manifestations as "signs." He structures his Gospel around a series of seven such signs: turning water to wine at Cana, healing an official's dying son, curing a long-term invalid, feeding five thousand, walking on water, giving sight to a man born blind and raising Lazarus from the dead. John intersperses these signs with a set of discourses in which Jesus both teaches about God and makes claims about himself. Jesus makes metaphorical statements that imply his divinity: I am the bread of life . . . the light of the world . . . the door . . . the good shepherd . . . the resurrection . . . the true vine . . . the way . . . the truth . . . the life. By his signs, his teachings and his claims, Jesus displays his

glory and discloses his identity. "These are written so that you may come
to believe that Jesus is the Messiah, the Son of God" explains John at the
end of his Gospel, "and that through believing you might have life in his
name" (Jn 20:31).

But this does not become clear to his disciples right away, not even to
the twelve. People follow Jesus with fascination and gratitude and rising
hope. Those closest to him receive his most extensive instruction, share
his public acclaim and risk the hostility of his opponents. Many of them
harbor visions of his political messiahship and their place in the coming
new order. Eventually Jesus calls the question: "Who do you say that I
am?" (Mk 8:29). In an epiphanic moment, Peter blurts out the words
"You are the Messiah"—and he is right, but he understands only par-
tially. When Jesus begins to explain his destiny of suffering and death,
Peter and the others cannot take it in.

Shortly thereafter Jesus takes Peter and the brothers John and James
with him to a mountain. While praying there he is transfigured—face
ablaze like the sun, clothes dazzling white—while Moses (representing
the law) and Elijah (representing the prophets) "appear in glory" to talk
with him about his imminent departure (literally "exodus") (Lk 9:28-36).
Peter and the others almost miss it because of drowsiness, but they do
see and hardly know how to react. Peter makes a hasty and awkward
proposal for prolonging the experience, but the enveloping cloud and
terrifying voice silence them into a listening posture. Like Moses on
Mount Sinai and Elijah on Mount Horeb, these three men experience
their own epiphany: an immersion in light, an overshadowing presence,
an encounter with glory.

Hans Urs von Balthasar, one of the greatest Catholic theologians of
the twentieth century, in his magisterial *The Glory of the Lord: A Theological Aesthetics*, explores the correlation between God's glory and his
beauty. He writes of the human encounter with beauty in words that
seem apt for the encounter of the disciples on the Mount of Transfiguration and, in one sense, the experience of Jesus himself:

> Before the beautiful—no, not really before but within the beauti-
> ful—the whole person quivers. He not only "finds" the beautiful

moving; rather, he experiences himself as being moved and possessed by it. . . . Such a person has been taken up wholesale into the reality of the beautiful and is now fully subordinate to it, determined by it, animated by it.

Paul says something like this in writing to the Corinthian church. He describes the freedom and opportunity given to each of us to gaze upon the face of Jesus Christ and be changed:

And all of us, with unveiled faces, seeing the glory of the Lord as though reflected in a mirror, are being transformed into the same image from one degree of glory to another; for this comes from the Lord, the Spirit. (2 Cor 3:18)

Whatever the unveiling on the mountain was like for Peter, John and James that day—"We had been eyewitnesses of his majesty," Peter would later write (2 Pet 1:16)—the greatest epiphany for them lay ahead: the death and resurrection of Jesus. Our reflections in Lent will move toward those climactic events. Meanwhile, in this season of seeing, our eyes are fixed on Jesus.

INHABITING EPIPHANY

We can inhabit Epiphany by responding to the twofold call of Jesus: come and see, and go and tell. Like the original disciples, we are "to be with him, and to be sent out" (Mk 3:14). Over these weeks, then, we give our attention to Christ's disarming invitation and to his challenging command.

Encountering Jesus. I have worked in campus ministry with InterVarsity for three decades. One of the best experiences we offer to students is the "Mark Study," which we sometimes call "Encountering Jesus." We want each participant to see Jesus with new eyes and to respond in faith. We facilitate this experience through communal Bible discovery using the "manuscript method."

Simply put, we print Mark's gospel double-spaced on 8-by-11-inch paper with no verse or chapter markings, no headings or explanatory notes, no red letters or gold edges. We sit around tables with nothing but the text, a pile of colored markers, a few basic reference resources such as a Bible dictionary and atlas, and, most important, minds and hearts illumined by the same Spirit who superintended Mark's writing. We first study individually, marking our pages to track repeated words, trace themes, note connections, detect literary structure, make observations and jot down our questions. Then we discuss in our table groups. Finally, a teacher facilitates a community conversation about our discoveries, questions, interpretations and personal responses.

By immersing ourselves in Mark's telling of the story, session after session, we see Jesus afresh. Over and over he surprises us, just as he did his disciples. We find ourselves captivated or puzzled or even irked by the things he says. We find ourselves disturbed or delighted by the things he does—or doesn't do. Always we are compelled by the person of Jesus.

Here's my first suggestion for inhabiting Epiphany: immerse yourself once more in the story of Jesus. You could use the devotional material that follows or choose some other approach. For example, you could read an entire Gospel one or more times from start to finish, absorbing the full narrative sweep of Christ's remarkable life. Or you could select a handful of episodes to explore more thoroughly, spending, say, a week on each one, reading and rereading, placing yourself imaginatively within them, quietly meditating on them (an approach called *lectio divina*, or "divine reading").

Of course, we encounter Christ in other ways besides engaging with Scripture. We can commune with him in prayer, we can sense his presence when gathered in worship, we can know him in the breaking of the Eucharistic bread and we can receive his love in the community of believers. In all these ways and more, Jesus invites us during Epiphany to come and see anew.

Exhibiting Jesus. Before he was the apostle Peter, he was just an ordinary fisherman named Simon. He first meets Jesus through his brother Andrew. And maybe he's in on the wine miracle in Cana. But as Luke tells it, Simon definitely gets to know Jesus when he first preaches in Capernaum (Lk 4:31—5:11). After an eventful synagogue service, Simon has everyone over to his house for dinner, even though his mother-in-law is sick with a fever. But Jesus heals her right there in the home. At dusk as the sabbath ends the whole town shows up at Simon's doorstep bringing the sick—the synagogue service had been quite an epiphany!—and Jesus lays hands on them for healing. Simon sees it all. He's thrilled, I imagine, to be associated with this amazing new rabbi. But his next experience with Jesus draws him in even deeper.

One day Jesus stands preaching on the shore of Lake Gennesaret as the crowd presses in. Simon sits nearby, cleaning his nets after a night of futile fishing. Jesus steps into Simon's beached boat and asks him to push out so as to create a floating pulpit. When he's done speaking Jesus proposes to Simon that they put out into deep water and try some fishing. Simon, tired and somewhat irritated by this request, reluctantly agrees. What does a preacher know about fishing? Soon he finds out. Struggling with the bulging nets, he calls to his partners for help. This moment reveals to him the power and authority of Jesus as well as his own smug sinfulness. But Jesus speaks kindly: "Don't be afraid; from now on you will be catching people." Simon and the others decide on the spot to follow him, convinced he will empower them for a new kind of fishing. Jesus catches them in his "net" only to turn them loose with the gospel.

And so it is for us. Jesus draws us to himself and then enlists us in his mission. But how do we bring others into the light of the kingdom? Our lives can point to Christ in many ways—our care for neighbors, our integrity at work, our hospitality at home, our generosity with money, our service to the poor, our concern for justice, our practice of forgiveness, our joy in worship, our hope in suffering. All of these reveal something of Christ's presence in our lives. Jesus stressed two things when he first sent out the twelve: proclaim the kingdom and heal the sick (Lk 9:2). In other words, communicate the message to others and respond to their needs with compassion.

The idea of purposefully talking about Jesus with our friends and acquaintances makes many of us uneasy. We live in a cultural moment when religious zeal is suspect, spiritual beliefs are considered strictly personal, tolerance is paramount, and anything resembling proselytizing is off-limits. The image of catching people in our nets may not be the most helpful these days. Actually, we would do well to imitate Andrew

(Jn 1:40-42): he simply said what he knew about Jesus—what he had seen and heard and experienced—and invited his brother Simon to come and see for himself. Jesus was able to take it from there.

In Epiphany we renew our willingness to let the light of Christ within us shine to those around us. Uncover the lamp, as Jesus put it. We want to reflect the luminous beauty of God in Christ so that our friends turn and see the source for themselves. This requires equal measures of compassion and courage. But here's where Simon's lesson comes in: Jesus is fully able to make us able as his representatives.

Here are some practical steps you could take.

- Ask Jesus to increase your compassion for those who are far from God. Ask for greater courage to speak to them.

- Read a book to sharpen your thinking about sharing your faith.

- Choose a few friends or coworkers or family members to pray for during Epiphany.

- Become alert to openings in your everyday conversations where you can mention Jesus in a natural and interesting way.

- If someone seems open, suggest going for coffee and some conversation about spiritual matters—be prepared to really listen to their experiences, beliefs and questions.

- Invite a few folks to take a look at Jesus with you through a four-to-six-week informal, investigative Bible study.

- Propose to a few friends that they serve with you in a volunteer opportunity like Habitat for Humanity.

- Invite a neighbor to come to a social activity or worship gathering at your church.

- Give a friend a thoughtful book on Jesus or the Christian faith.

We let the light of Christ shine through us, verbally in our conversations and visibly in our actions. It's not our responsibility to generate the response, only to say and to show what we ourselves have been given to see. As Paul reminded his audience in Corinth:

Remember, our Message is not about ourselves; we're proclaiming Jesus Christ, the Master. All we are is messengers, errand runners from Jesus. . . . It started when God said, "Light up the darkness!" and our lives filled up with light as we saw and understood God in the face of Christ, all bright and beautiful. (2 Cor 4:5-6 *The Message*)

A GLIMPSE OF HIS GLORY

Epiphany makes us think about darkness and light. How easily I can become complacent about spiritual darkness. But then I read the paper and listen to the news. I think about the struggles and pain of the people I know. I look within my own heart and find plenty of darkness. So I am drawn back to Jesus, eager to see him anew, like the Magi at the crib and John in the Jordan and Mary at the wedding and Simon in the boat and the disciples on the mountain. And each of these set out to tell others what they had seen. Having encountered the light, they exhibited the light.

So too for us during the weeks of Epiphany. We focus our gaze on Jesus in order to glimpse his glory, his transfigured beauty and power, his embodied grace and truth. And what we are given to see, we gladly speak of to our friends that they might share with us the light of Christ.

*   *   *

Preview of devotions in Epiphany. With the Feast of the Epiphany, the days of Christmas end but the Cycle of Light continues as the identity and glory of the adult Jesus come to light over the ensuing weeks. The first set of devotions centers on the feast and covers the days up to the first Sunday. The second week focuses on the baptism of Jesus. The final week features his transfiguration. The weeks between highlight a progression of signs and miracles that reveal Jesus as the Christ. The Gospel texts come from Mark and John and do not reflect the lectionary. Because the length of Epiphany varies annually, it will be necessary in most years to skip some devotional units in order to conclude with the transfiguration (see week nine) just before Ash Wednesday.

Feast of the Epiphany of the Lord

January 6 through the next Sunday

His Glory Will Appear

Isaiah prophesies a time when God will rise like the sun over Israel: his glory will appear and nations and kings will be drawn to the brightness of the light. The traditional texts for the Feast of the Epiphany explore this theme. Indeed, light is given to the kinglike Magi in the East who journey to Palestine to pay homage to a newborn king. Psalm 72 supplies words that can help us pay him homage ourselves. And Paul interprets the universality of this new kingdom. Christ came for people of every ethnicity and culture on the earth. He is the glory that appeared, revealing the wisdom and love of God; now God chooses to make this glory manifest through us, his church.

Approaching God. O Lord, may your name endure forever and your fame continue as long as the sun; may the people of every nation be blessed in you, and may they pronounce you blessed. Amen.

Presenting Myself. Like the Magi of old, O Father, I am overwhelmed with joy to enter the presence of Jesus, your incarnate Son, and like them I kneel before you this day to pay homage and to offer my gift, the gift of myself. Amen.

Inviting God's Presence. Let your light come, O Lord, let it shine on me this day; let your glory rise upon me like the sun appearing at dawn. Amen.

LISTENING TO GOD

Matthew 2:1-12 (ABC); Isaiah 60 (ABC); Psalm 72 (ABC); Ephesians 3:1-12 (ABC)

Matthew recounts the story of the "wise men from the East." It is likely that the visitors are seers or priests from Persia, or modern-day Iran. Tradition speaks of three men because the text identifies three gifts, which are generally taken to represent respectively his kingship, priesthood and sacrificial death. A God-given light guides the Magi to Jesus; a God-given dream steers them away from Herod and his despotic intrigues. What does this story mean for us? Certainly it points to Jesus as a universal Savior. Also it shows that Jesus deserves our gifts, the best of ourselves and of our cultures. To the foreign visitors—and to us—Jesus makes visible the glory of God.

Once more in our readings **Isaiah** sheds prophetic light on the gospel. The lectionary features Isaiah 60:1-6 for Epiphany, but the entire chapter celebrates the triumph of light over darkness. Again we can detect the multiple horizons of his poetry: the political, the messianic and the eternal. Isaiah envisions a time when the nations, as represented by their leaders, will be drawn to the transformed city of God and the redeemed community of his people. The light will draw them and they will bring the finest treasures of their cultures as gifts. Note yet again the hallmarks of this kingdom: peace, righteousness, salvation and praise. This pictures something far greater than the nationalistic triumph of the nation of Israel; this prophecy anticipates the visions of John's Revelation. The visit of the Magi harkens back to Isaiah's prophecy and prefigures the greater glory yet to be manifested. Take time today to bask in this vision of the day when the Lord will be our everlasting light and God will be our glory (Is 60:19).

Read **Psalm 72**, the appointed psalm for Epiphany, and mark its resonance with Isaiah 60 and Matthew 2. It is a prayer for a king, but it escalates into a vision beyond the political. Pray it with Jesus in mind. Picture not the conquest and political domination of other nations but the welcome of the world's cultures into the community of God. The glory is for everyone! Let this psalm shape your prayers in response to the world news that you read or hear this week.

Paul in his masterful letter to the **Ephesians** and other churches in Asia Minor lays out his theological perspective on Jesus. As a Jew, the great epiphany for him was that God intended the "promise in Christ Jesus" for Jew and Gentile alike. These far-apart peoples are now joined into one body, one community and one destiny. By an astounding plan, the "wisdom of God in its rich variety" is to be made manifest to the world through the church, and not only to the human world but to the spiritual "rulers and authorities in the heavenly realms" as well. We the people who bear the holy name of Christ are meant to show forth, to reveal, to make known the glory of God by our love for one another, our love for our neighbors and our loving proclamation of Jesus. With Paul we become servants of this gospel according to God's gift of grace.

RESPONDING TO GOD

The Feast of the Epiphany and the ensuing days invite our continued worship and celebration of Jesus. We might want to continue using candles or lights a bit longer as a reminder of the light that has come, the glory that has risen on us. Begin thinking about the opportunities you may have over the coming weeks to reflect that light to those God has placed in your life. Epiphany inaugurates a season for discovering Jesus afresh and renewing our commitment to bear him witness.

Closing Prayer. Blessed are you, O Lord, the God of your people, who alone does wondrous things; blessed be your glorious name forever; may your glory fill the whole earth. Amen and amen.

The Baptism of the Lord

In each Gospel the story of the adult Jesus begins with a portrayal of John the Baptist, the eccentric prophet who shows up in the river environs of Judea proclaiming the kingdom of God, baptizing the repentant and paving the way for a new spiritual leader. Then Jesus comes and, surprisingly, asks to be baptized. But what happens to him as he emerges from the water is unique. Jesus does not confess sins to God; rather, God himself bears witness to Jesus: the voice from heaven confirms his identity and the Spirit from heaven tangibly descends. For Jesus it's an epiphany, and for the people a glimpse of glory! In focusing this week on the baptism of the Lord, this "anointing" of the Christ, we have an opportunity to rehearse our own baptismal identity as beloved children of God who have received his very Spirit.

Approaching God. You spoke, O Lord, over the deep at creation; you roared, God of Glory, in the waters of the flood; you thundered, Mighty God, from the clouds on the mountain: your voice, O Lord, is powerful, your voice is full of majesty; all your people cry "Glory!"

Presenting Myself. With the heavenly beings I ascribe to you, O Lord, glory and strength, I ascribe to you the glory of your name; before your holy splendor, O Lord, I worship you.

Inviting God's Presence. As you spoke to your beloved Son at his baptism, let me hear your voice this day; as the heavens opened to reveal your descending Spirit, open my eyes to your heavenly glory. Amen.

LISTENING TO GOD
Psalm 29 (ABC); Isaiah 42:1-9 (ABC);
Mark 1:1-11 (B); John 1:29-34 (A); Romans 8:14-17

The lectionary always assigns **Psalm 29** for the Sunday we celebrate Jesus' baptism, most obviously because of the common elements of voice and water. But look for deeper resonances as you meditate. The psalm opens with heavenly beings and closes with human beings, moving from glory in the highest to peace on earth. The middle part features creation, comparing a thunderstorm in its fierce progression to the majestic voice of God. We hear echoes of God's voice at creation, in the flood and perhaps on Mount Sinai. The God enthroned as king who creates and judges and redeems is the same one who speaks to Jesus at his baptism and who speaks also to us.

Isaiah prophesies a servant whom God will give as a covenant to all peoples, a light to all nations and a liberator to all prisoners of darkness. What we anticipated during Advent begins to be revealed in this season of Epiphany. God is doing a new thing! He upholds and presents his servant Jesus, his chosen one in whom he delights, on whom he puts his Spirit and through whom he will bring justice to the nations.

Read the account of Jesus' baptism in **Mark** or one of its parallels in the other Synoptic (meaning "through the same lens") Gospels (Mt 3:13-17 or Lk 3:15-22). With imagination put yourself in those crowds. Why does Jesus want to be baptized, given that he has no sins to confess? If nothing else, in humility Jesus fully identifies with the people and thereby with us. Pause and consider that Jesus is now well into adulthood; over some thirty years he has grown from toddler to boy to teenager to young man. He is part of a family, a member of a village and a product of a culture. He is fully human. Yet his experience at the river also tells us—and him—that he is not like us. What do you think the voice and the vision meant for Jesus at this beginning point in his public life? What might it mean for you as you identify with him?

Rather than describing the scene at the river, **John** in his Gospel emphasizes the Baptist's testimony afterward. How does John understand his role? With humility he reveals Jesus to his community; with forthrightness he testifies to what he has seen. And what does he say of Jesus? Take some time to meditate on the implied meanings of John's testimony: "the Lamb of God" (atonement), "He was before me" (preexistence), "The Spirit . . . remain[ed]" (empowerment), "the Son of God" (divinity). While John the Baptist fulfilled a unique calling, what can we learn from his example for our own roles as witnesses?

This excerpt from **Romans 8** helps us connect our experience with that of Jesus. When we identify ourselves fully with the one who identified with us, we receive the same Spirit that descended on him at his baptism. By that Spirit we've been adopted as sons and daughters of God. By that Spirit we may utter the intimate cry to God, "Abba! Father!" By the voice of that Spirit we are affirmed as deeply beloved by God.

RESPONDING TO GOD

Two questions can usefully guide us during this season of revelation. First, as we see Jesus anew, how are we moved to respond to him? Through imitation? obedience? worship? Second, how can we, like John the Baptist, bear witness to what we are seeing?

This is a good week to renew the meaning inherent in your own baptism: your humble repentance, your dying to sin and self, your opening to God's life-giving Spirit, and your public expression of allegiance to Jesus. Listen this week for the voice that assures you of God's love, and look for the Spirit that strengthens you to point out the Lamb to those around you.

Closing Prayer. Heavenly Father—Abba, Papa—thank you for the assurance of your Spirit; thank you for embracing me as your beloved son/daughter; thank you for the grace of your approval in Jesus, my baptized Lord. Amen.

Come and See

After his baptism and his temptation in the desert, Jesus comes to Galilee proclaiming the good news that the kingdom of God has come near. Soon he begins to call men and women to follow him. Come and see, he says, and when they do they witness Jesus teaching with authority and doing extraordinary things. The first of these manifestations takes place when Jesus turns some one hundred gallons of water into good wine for a wedding feast. By this and other signs Jesus begins revealing his glory, and the nascent disciples see and believe. Likewise during this season, as we see Jesus afresh in the Gospels of Mark and John, our belief will be strengthened, our desire to follow him will deepen, and our eagerness to tell about him will grow.

Approaching God. How precious is your steadfast love, O God! All people may feast on the abundance of your house and drink from your river of delights, for with you is the fountain of life and in your light we see light.

Presenting Myself. Lord Jesus, Teacher, today I want to come and see what you are doing and hear what you are saying; and I will be quick this week to tell others what I am seeing and learning about you. Amen.

Inviting God's Presence. O continue your steadfast love to me and to all who know you; may we find refuge in the shadow of your wings and joy in your glorious presence. Amen.

LISTENING TO GOD
Mark 1:14-34 (B); John 1:35-51 (AB);
John 2:1-11 (C); Psalm 36 (C); 1 John 1:1-5

In **Mark 1,** note the condensed summary of Jesus' message: the ripening of time, the announced presence of the kingdom, the call to repent and the invitation to believe. The four fishermen respond to the seemingly abrupt call to join up with Jesus in a new vocation. (See Lk 5:1-11 for a more detailed account of how Jesus catches Simon.) Soon they see him in action in the Capernaum synagogue. Imagine yourself that day in the assembly, witnessing this public episode or in the house afterward as Jesus lifts up Simon's fevered mother-in-law. Then picture the scene after the sabbath sun sets as Jesus responds to the townsfolk with their procession of needs and tremors of amazement. What do you see?

John too tells how the first followers connect with Jesus. In **John 1:35-42,** two men spurred by John the Baptizer tentatively approach him. What do you make of their terse exchange? They spend the day with Jesus and Andrew is impressed enough to tell his brother that they'd found the Messiah. What does it mean that Jesus renames Simon on the spot? In **John 1:43-51,** two more become followers, but this time Jesus takes the initiative. Examine these encounters. What does Nathaniel conclude about Jesus? Notice how his declaration of faith prompts Jesus to reveal more of himself to him. Jesus depicts himself as the locus for the meeting of heaven and earth. What do we learn from this passage about the Epiphany themes of seeing and telling?

John 2:1-11 tells how three days later these new disciples go with Jesus and his family to Cana where, as John puts it, they witness their first sign that reveals his glory: turning water to wine. And they believe in him. Why this for his first miracle? If nothing else, it affirms Jesus' humanity—he revels with friends at a wedding—and underscores the earthy goodness of creation—wine to gladden the heart! What is Mary's role in this episode? What do you make of her exchange with Jesus? Put yourself in the shoes of other participants: the servants, the banquet master, the bridegroom, the disciples. This extravagant, gracious gesture foreshadows a greater glory—

a messianic abundance—yet to be revealed.

Psalm 36, with its picture of delightful feasting and drinking in verse 8, resonates with the Cana story; we find the overall theme of Epiphany in verse 9: "In your light we see light." Read the full psalm to put these verses in context. In the first part David characterizes the wicked. In the middle part he celebrates the grace of God: steadfast love, faithfulness, righteousness and justice. Notice the metaphors that amplify these attributes. In the final part David puts his trust in God's saving grace.

The preface of **1 John** interlaces the themes we explore during Epiphany: revelation (seeing) and testimony (saying), light and life, time and eternity. Trace how John relates these themes to one another. Why does John bear witness in his writing?

RESPONDING TO GOD

Jesus reveals his glory—his authority and power and love—in the place of worship, yes, but also inside a home, out in a front yard, down by the riverside and in the midst of a wedding. It's in these everyday contexts that he invites belief, at least enough to begin following him. This week come and see even more, and then tell somebody else.

Closing Prayer. Open my eyes, O God, that I might see more of your glory as revealed in your Son, and soften my heart that I might trust more deeply in the fullness of your grace and truth. Amen.

Be Made Clean

The connection between sickness and sin—hence between healing and forgiveness—is elusive. Upon passing a blind man one day Jesus' followers ask him about this connection, and Jesus makes clear that the man's physical affliction did not result from any moral failing (Jn 9:1-3). Yet on another occasion Jesus heals a man and then warns him to sin no more, lest something worse befall him (Jn 5:14). The readings for this week portray Jesus healing various infirmities in various ways, and they also include the next two of John's seven signs. These stories show Jesus' concern for the whole person: physical suffering, spiritual guilt, emotional shame and social alienation. Jesus heals, forgives, cleanses and restores. All of this is encompassed when he says, "Be made clean." This week let Jesus reveal to you anew his compassion and power to bring healing and forgiveness in response to your humility and faith.

Approaching God. Bless the Lord, O my soul, and all that is within me; bless his holy name. You have established your throne in the heavens, O Lord, and your kingdom rules over all. You are merciful and gracious, slow to anger and abounding in steadfast love; you will not always accuse, nor will you keep your anger forever.

Presenting Myself. Have compassion for me, O Lord, as a father has compassion for his children; for you know, O Lord, how I am made, you remember that I am dust.

Inviting God's Presence. I bless you, O Lord, as the one who forgives all my iniquity and heals all my diseases, who redeems my life from the pit and crowns me with steadfast love and mercy. Amen.

LISTENING TO GOD

Psalm 103 (B); **Mark 1:40-45; Mark 2:1-12 (B);**
2 Kings 5:1-19a (B); John 4:46-54; **John 5:1-18**

Psalm 103 bids us to rouse our souls into thanksgiving and praise. David guides us through a litany of reasons to bless the Lord, first among them our forgiveness and healing. God is generous with his acts of redemption, as we see in the stories of Israel and the church and our own lives. Consider reading this psalm during each of your times of reflection this week. With David rehearse what you know of God's character: his eternal love compared to our mortality, his forgiving mercy in light of our moral shortfall and his compassion to heal given our frailty. Recount the benefits you personally have received from him. Then bless him!

In reading **Mark 1,** recall that lepers were considered unclean. This designation conveyed far more than an indication of infection and quarantine. Such a person also came under moral suspicion and social stigma; he or she was forced to live "outside the camp" (see Lev 13—14). So Jesus risks his own "cleanness" when he reaches out in pity to touch the beseeching leper. He chooses to heal and he also chooses to physically embrace. Jesus makes him clean again, which is also why he insists that the man go through the formal process of reincorporation into the community as clean (see Lev 14). Can you identify with this leper in any way?

The next episode, in **Mark 2,** carries drama. Take time to imagine the scene from the different standpoints: first as a bystander crowded into the house, then as one of the four friends taking initiative, then as the paralyzed man placed, perhaps reluctantly, at center stage, and finally as Jesus, who surprises everyone with his response. It *is* easier, of course, to say to someone, "Your sins are forgiven," as this cannot be proved; to declare someone healed is another matter. Thus when Jesus accomplishes the healing, he confirms his authority to forgive as well. This week, whom can you "carry" to Jesus in prayer? Do you need to let friends carry you? And if you were set before Jesus today, what might he say to you?

2 Kings 5:1-19a is an interesting story of healing in the Old Testament. What parallels do you find with the episodes from Mark? Whose gracious initiative leads to this miracle? God generously heals a foreign military leader. Naaman believes and God is glorified. How does this story speak to you?

John 4:46-54 records Jesus' second sign. A father intercedes for his dying child and, amazingly, Jesus heals at a distance. John highlights the man's belief. The pleading father is not interested in a sign as such, only that his son will live. And Jesus cared not that the man worked for hated Herod.

In **John 5** we get the third sign. This time it is Jesus who takes the initiative, approaching a man who's been disabled for thirty-eight years. Why do you suppose Jesus asks if he wants to be made well? Jesus commands the man in faith to get up. He does! Notice how the man is buffeted afterward by sabbath fanatics. But Jesus finds him and offers reassurance; he also calls him to a grateful repentance (but surprisingly he turns around and betrays Jesus). Notice that John says nothing of anyone else at the Beth-zatha Pool being healed.

RESPONDING TO GOD

In the Gospel accounts, Jesus heals many but not all. The healing miracles demonstrate the in-breaking of the kingdom of God and reveal the glory of Jesus. It is the same for us. If you are suffering from physical or emotional affliction, dare to present yourself (or family members or friends) to God in faith, asking for healing. Ask too for the fortitude and grace needed to bear the suffering if it is not alleviated. But if healing is an intermittent sign of the kingdom, you can be sure of this: God's forgiveness is always available, and this too is foretaste of future glory.

Closing Prayer. Touch me, dear Jesus, and make me clean; heal me and forgive my sins so that my life will be a sign of your kingdom. Amen.

WEEK FIVE OF EPIPHANY
Beginning the Sunday between January 28 and February 3
(If the last Sunday of Epiphany, use week nine.)

Bread for the Hungry

The psalmist acknowledges God as the source of wine to gladden the heart and bread to strengthen it (Ps 104:15). Jesus implicitly reveals himself as God in the miracles of turning water to wine for the guests in Cana and multiplying loaves and fishes for the multitude in the countryside. These signs manifest his glory and show his compassion. Jesus provides bread for the hungry, as Moses did in the wilderness and Elisha did in the time of famine. But even more than food for physical sustenance, people hunger for that which brings eternal life. Jesus offers himself as the bread of life. This week we meditate on this true food and true drink by which we may live forever.

Approaching God. Bless the Lord, O my soul. O Lord my God, you are very great; you are clothed with honor and majesty and wrapped in light like a garment. O Lord, how manifold are your works! In wisdom you have made them all; the earth is full of your creatures—we all look to you to give us our food in due season; when you open your hand, we are filled with good things. Amen.

Presenting Myself. O Jesus, I am hungry not for the food that perishes but for the food that endures for eternal life, which only you can give.

Inviting God's Presence. O Jesus, feed me today with the bread of life, feed me with yourself. Amen.

LISTENING TO GOD
Psalm 104; 2 Kings 4:42-44;
Mark 6:30-44; John 6:1-15; John 6:22-59

Psalm 104 celebrates God's greatness as Creator and his goodness as sustainer of creation. We can read it as a companion poem to last week's Psalm 103—note the identical phrases that begin and end both. An interesting exercise: correlate the poetic progression in Psalm 104 to the days of creation in Genesis 1. But the relevance of this psalm to our Epiphany theme for this week is found in verses 14-30, where God is praised for providing for his creatures: he gives food to the wild animals and he enables humans to cultivate the earth (grapes, olives and grain to make wine, oil and bread). In his providence God feeds us; by his breath/ spirit he sustains us and all life. So with the psalmist we sing praise to our God while we have being.

In **2 Kings 4:42-44** we find a little-known episode about feeding a sizeable group of people with a handful of loaves, an account that anticipates the feeding of the huge crowds of four and five thousand by Jesus. Pay attention to the elements of this story: an anonymous donor, a compassionate inclination, a skeptical servant, a confident prophet and a surprising outcome! Watch for these elements in the Gospel accounts of the feeding miracle.

In **Mark's** telling of the feeding of the five thousand, he is probably alluding to God's provision of manna to the Israelites in the wilderness (Ex 16). He stresses the deserted setting and describes the people as shepherdless sheep (Num 27:15-17). Jesus intends to take his disciples away for some rest and review after their return from a preaching mission, but the crowds track them down. How does Jesus respond to this interruption? How do you suppose the disciples feel? What do you make of their concern in verses 35-36? Perhaps Jesus is calling their bluff here. Put yourself in the disciples' shoes for the rest of the episode. What new insight about Jesus do they gain? What do we learn? (For Jesus' later feeding of four thousand, see Mk 8:1-10.)

In **John's** Gospel, the feeding of the five thousand stands as the fourth "sign" of Jesus' glory. Compare John 6:1-15 with Mark's account. Here Jesus takes the initiative. He tests Philip. Does Philip pass the test? Knowing about Jesus' first miracle at Cana, how might Philip have answered differently? Here the people see the feeding as a sign and conclude that Jesus is the prophet of whom Moses spoke (Deut 18:15), but Jesus resists their impromptu acclamation. Yes, this sign does reveal Jesus as a prophet like Moses, as Jesus earlier had implied (Jn 5:46), and more than a prophet.

Continuing in **John 6:22-59** (and postponing verses 16-21 to week six), we encounter a "difficult" teaching discourse. Enthralled by the feeding miracle, the crowds look for Jesus. He challenges them to see what the sign pointed to, namely something beyond physical food. Thus this discourse focuses on true bread and eternal life. Read it carefully. Jesus presents himself enigmatically as the bread of life. Pay attention to the relationship between Jesus and the Father, the interplay of God's initiative and human belief, and the mysterious linkage between bread and wine and Jesus' body and blood. Perhaps the Eucharist is also in view here. Meditate on the connection between the provision of manna in the wilderness (Ex 16), the feeding of the five thousand and Jesus' giving of his flesh for the life of the world. Here is an epiphany: Jesus is the living bread that came down from heaven; if we take him into ourselves by believing, he takes us into himself and gives us eternal life.

RESPONDING TO GOD

This week, remembering that your Creator sustains you, be thankful for what you have to eat and your ability to secure it. Even more, especially if you are able to participate in the Eucharist or Communion, be thankful for the bread of life that sustains you eternally.

Closing Prayer. O Jesus, feed me with yourself today so that I may abide in you and you in me, for your flesh is true food and your blood is true drink. Amen.

WEEK SIX OF EPIPHANY
Beginning the Sunday between February 4 and 10
(If the last Sunday of Epiphany, use week nine.)

Peace! Be Still!

Last week we watched Jesus miraculously multiply the physical substance of food and discerned significant implications for our souls. This week we focus on two more of his nature miracles and their spiritual meaning: Jesus stills a storm and Jesus walks on water. These divine "interventions" in the created order recall the parting of the Red Sea in the exodus and anticipate our future delivery from the chaotic powers of evil in the eschaton. Indeed, the story of the demon-possessed tomb-dweller in Mark 5 amounts to a stunning real-life parable of our salvation by the redeeming power of Jesus. Psalm 107 provides a fitting antiphonal prayer in light of these gospel epiphanies in which Jesus commands the forces of destruction: Peace! Be still!

Approaching God. I give thanks to you, O Lord, for you are good and your steadfast love endures forever; you redeem us from trouble and gather us to yourself.

Presenting Myself. Sometimes I am lost and bewildered, sometimes I feel trapped and burdened, sometimes I lie sick and sorrowful, and sometimes I just feel overwhelmed; in all such times, O Lord, I cry to you in my trouble and trust you to save me from distress.

Inviting God's Presence. Come and be present with me today, O Lord; make the raging storm be still, hush the waves around me; bring me in peace to the haven I desire. Amen.

LISTENING TO GOD
Psalm 107; Exodus 14; **Mark 4:35-41;**
Mark 5:1-20; **John 6:16-21**

Read through **Psalm 107** once or twice in order to detect the structure. The opening verses set the theme: thankfulness for God's redemptive acts that show his unchanging love. From verse 4 we may surmise a reference to Israel's return from exile. Then come four stanzas with the same pattern: predicament, redemption, call to gratitude, closing thought. The predicaments—lostness, imprisonment, (moral) sickness and storm-tossed seas—may be ways of describing the exile or simply universal parables of the human condition. Can you identify with any of them? The last section (verses 33-42) reflects on the reversals in our human experience that God brings about by his judgment and grace.

In **Exodus 14,** we're presented with the dramatic event in which God through Moses parts the Red Sea so that the Israelites can escape the pursuing Egyptians. Then at God's command Moses releases the walls of water to crash down on the charioteers. Put yourself in the place of the people trapped between the uncrossable Red Sea and the unstoppable Egyptian army. What do they feel and think? Then what do they learn about Yahweh, their God and deliverer? After this epiphany the people, full of awe, believe in the Lord and trust in Moses as their leader.

In **Mark 4,** Jesus and his group are caught in a fierce storm at sea. How bad is the storm? Pretty bad, if experienced fishermen are scared. How curious that Jesus would be soundly asleep in the boat. Roused, Jesus rebukes the wind and waves—and also the disciples. How fair is it to expect them to have enough faith to stay calm during such a storm? Whatever they may have failed to grasp before this point, what do they now understand about Jesus as a result of this epiphany? Perhaps they begin to connect their experience to the Red Sea story or various psalms. Indeed, for an apt reflection on this episode, reread Psalm 107:23-31. Do these texts speak to your life in any way right now?

Mark 5:1-20 gives us the dramatic story of the Garasene demoniac. First, pay attention to all the details in Mark's portrayal of the tormented man. What do they say about his condition and, symbolically, about the human condition? Next, study the strange encounter between Jesus and the demon-possessed man. Ironically, it's the demons that reveal Jesus' identity and recognize his authority. Then picture the scene after the man is healed, using your emotions as well as your mind. Finally, consider the surprising reaction of the (probably Gentile) townsfolk. Jesus refuses the man's request to go with him and instead commissions him to become a witness to the very community that's so afraid of him. Here is the Epiphany pattern: transforming encounter, bold proclamation. Mark places the casting out of the demons right after the stilling of the storm; do you see a connection? Again, Psalm 107 can provide a fitting meditation on this redemptive action by Jesus.

We return to **John 6** and the fifth sign revealing Christ's glory, another nature miracle: Jesus walks on water. John mentions strong wind, but the parallel accounts (Mt 14:22-33; Mk 6:45-52) make clear that the disciples are struggling, and Jesus comes to help. How do they react? Jesus identifies himself to put them at ease—"Don't worry; it's me"—and also to imply his divine identity—"I am, but don't be afraid." Matthew and Mark report the calming of the wind once Jesus gets into the boat; Matthew alone tells about Peter walking on the water. John suggests a further miracle in the speed of reaching at their destination (see Ps 107:30). With echoes of the Red Sea crossing, Jesus demonstrates a creator-like authority over nature and a redeemer-like power to save.

RESPONDING TO GOD

The Scriptures this week speak of God's power and predisposition to rescue us when we're in trouble. Do any of the stories fit your situation just now: trapped with no way out, caught in a storm that could sink you, tormented by forces beyond your control or facing a headwind that makes progress seem impossible? Let the epiphanies of these passages renew your confidence in Jesus.

Closing Prayer. I thank you, O Lord, for your steadfast love and for all your wonderful works to humankind; I will extol you in the congregation of your people and proclaim you to all those around me. Amen.

WEEK SEVEN OF EPIPHANY
Beginning the Sunday between February 11 and 17
(If the last Sunday of Epiphany, use week nine.)

I Am the Light of the World

Light is a universal spiritual metaphor. Many teachers offer their wisdom as a source of enlightenment. But in the same way that Jesus' healing once ratified his authority to forgive sins (Mk 2), his restoring of physical sight validates his claim "I am the light of the world." This week we examine several episodes in which Jesus heals people who are blind. More importantly, we think about the issue of spiritual blindness. If we cannot admit the possibility of our own blindness, how can we gain—or regain—sight? Of course, this is what the season of Epiphany elucidates: our need for eye-opening encounters with Christ.

Approaching God. Lord Jesus, you are the light of the world; whoever follows you will never walk in darkness but have the light of life.

Presenting Myself. I confess that at times I am blind to your light and I walk in darkness, but today, Lord Jesus, I desire to walk in the light and have fellowship with you. Amen.

Inviting God's Presence. Jesus, Son of David, have mercy on me. Open my eyes that I may see your light. Jesus, Son of David, have mercy on me.

LISTENING TO GOD
Mark 10:46-52; John 8:12-20; John 9;
1 John 1:5-10; Psalm 146

The healing in **Mark** of Bartimaeus, a blind beggar, is the second restoring of sight miracle in the Gospel (the other occurs in 8:22-26). Put yourself in the shoes of Bartimaeus. You hear the excited wave of conversation as Jesus approaches on the road. What do you feel? What do you do? They tell you to shut up, but you shout even louder. You make a scene. Suddenly they are calling for you. It's him, his voice. He asks you a simple question. Dare you say what you want? Dare you hope in this Jesus?

In **John 8,** Jesus is participating in the Feast of Tabernacles (Succoth) in Jerusalem. He uses aspects of the festival to dramatize his identity and mission. For example, in John 7:37-39, in keeping with the daily water procession, he compares himself to a river of living water. Now, with implicit reference to the evening lamp-lighting ceremony in the temple court, he declares himself the "light of the world." To follow Jesus is to walk in light, to have life. An argument with the Pharisees ensues, which only shows that they cannot see the light.

What seems to precipitate the miracle in **John 9,** the sixth sign of John's gospel? Take some time to ponder Jesus' surprising answer to the disciples' question. In this case, in contrast to the two incidents in Mark above, Jesus takes the initiative. He sends the man to a pool called "Sent," where he regains his sight. After his life-changing encounter with Jesus, the man becomes a stalwart exhibit for Jesus' healing power. But the authorities refuse to see it. What's their problem? Everyone seems to be against him. And why is Jesus out of sight during all of this? Finally, Jesus comes looking for the man and in a poignant exchange, he reveals himself and invites belief; indeed, he accepts the man's worship. Reflect on the paradoxical judgment of Jesus; he is the light that both brings sight and causes blindness. And you? What do you see?

The epistle of **1 John** makes metaphorical use of light and darkness, the same themes we've been exploring during Epiphany. God is pure light. To walk with God is to walk in the light and to walk in the light,

John insists, is to love one another. But what about the darkness in our hearts and in our relationships? Jesus can bring light to these places if we will admit our wrongdoings and own our moral weaknesses. If we confess our sins, he will forgive and cleanse us. But if like the Pharisees in John 9 we deny our sinfulness, we will remain in darkness as if blind. What do you need to confess and who do you need to concretely love this week, so as to walk in Christ's light?

Psalm 146 is one of the five Hallel songs that conclude the Psalter, so named because each begins and ends with *Hallelu Yah,* or "Praise the Lord." And this is a fitting psalm to rehearse in prayer as the final week of Epiphany approaches. How easy to imagine healed Bartimaeus or the formerly blind man of John 9 voicing the opening of this psalm: an exuberant vow to praise God always. You may want to memorize verses 5-6 as a beatitude that reminds you where to look for help and in whom to put your hope. The catalogue of God's gracious actions in verses 7-9 recalls the various signs that have revealed to us the light and love of Christ during Epiphany.

RESPONDING TO GOD

The season of Epiphany is about seeing and saying. The Pharisees in John 9 claim that they are not blind, but of course they cannot see that they cannot see. This week, admit the likelihood that you too have blind spots, and humbly ask God to open your eyes to more of the light of Christ. And whatever he allows you to see this week, be willing to tell someone about it.

Closing Prayer. Praise the Lord! Praise the Lord, O my soul! You, Lord God, made heaven and earth, the sea and all that is in them; you keep faith forever; you set the prisoners free and open the eyes of the blind. I will praise you O Lord as long as I live; I will sing praises to you all my life long. Amen.

WEEK EIGHT OF EPIPHANY
Beginning the Sunday between February 18 and 24
(If the last Sunday of Epiphany, use week nine.)

Who Do You Say That I Am?

During Epiphany we have walked alongside Jesus' disciples as they listened to his kingdom teachings, pondered his subtle claims about himself, observed his exchanges with admirers and critics, and witnessed his amazing progression of miracles. To top it off, we now look at one of the three recorded occasions when Jesus raised someone from the dead (for the other two, see Lk 7 and Jn 11). What do all these words and works reveal about this itinerant rabbi from Nazareth? When Jesus asks, "Who do you say that I am?" Peter blurts it out: "You are God's Messiah!" But are they ready to take in the next epiphany, the revelation of what this will mean? As John makes clear, even believers struggled to grasp Jesus' true identity and destiny. Of course, Jesus' question echoes down through time to us.

Approaching God. Praise the Lord! Great are your works, O Lord, full of honor and majesty, faithful and just; and great are your words, O Lord, trustworthy and established, faithful and upright. Your praise endures forever. Amen.

Presenting Myself. I want to be your follower, Lord Jesus; I want to live for more than my own self-fulfillment, even if it requires sacrifice and suffering; I believe by adhering to your word I will increasingly know the truth and the truth will make me free.

Inviting God's Presence. Lord Jesus, I need the help of your Spirit if I am truly to deny myself, take up my cross and follow you. Amen.

LISTENING TO GOD
2 Kings 4:8-37; **Mark 5:21-43; Mark 8:27-38;**
John 8:21-38; Psalm 111

The prophets Elijah and Elisha both perform miracles that anticipate those of Jesus. The intriguing story of Elisha and the Shunammite woman in **2 Kings 4** actually contains two miracles. Read the passage attentively, taking in the details and absorbing the drama. How would you describe the relationship between the prophet and this prosperous woman? How does she demonstrate her faith in God? How does Elisha show his faith? How does this story speak to you? Glance at 2 Kings 8:1-6 for an interesting follow-up to this story.

Two miracles intertwine in **Mark 5,** increasing the dramatic tension of the story. Rehearse the narrative three times, imagining in turn that you are Jairus, then the anonymous woman and then one of the three disciples. How do you experience Jesus? Compare the two miracles for similarities and differences. For example, both involve marginalized females (the woman unclean from her bleeding, the girl merely a girl), both emphasize the role of faith and both show Jesus' compassion. In one an adult with an incurable condition takes the initiative; in the other a man intercedes for his dying daughter. The woman has suffered from hemorrhages for as long as the girl has been alive. What about Jesus impresses you? Consider his compassion—how he listens to the woman, how he speaks to the girl (*talitha cum* means "rise, lamb"). Consider his power—how it goes out from him, how it even can raise the dead.

Jesus' question to his disciples in **Mark 8** culminates the first half of this Gospel. His followers have seen enough to draw a conclusion. Peter speaks up for the group (the parallel passage in Mt 16 makes clear that Peter's insight comes by revelation from the Father). Now Jesus begins to reveal that he will undergo suffering and death—and resurrection. What do you make of Peter's reaction and the fierce rebuke it evokes? Jesus spells out the implication of his destiny for them. It's not what they expect: deliberate self-denial, risk of capital punishment and forfeiture of independence. How could this be the path for the one anointed with power over nature, sickness, evil and even death? Yet in the paradox of costly discipleship, Jesus promises life and alludes to a coming day of glory, judgment and sovereign power.

John also portrays Jesus telling his followers about his impending death. Just after declaring himself to be the light of the world, he speaks of "going away" to an inaccessible place. In the same breath he curiously asserts that his hearers will die in their sins apart from him. Try to understand Jesus' meaning in this somewhat awkward dialogue. He describes himself as "from above," he uses the "I am" expression in a way suggestive of divinity, he equates his words and actions with those of the Father, and he insists that adhering to his teachings brings enlightenment and freedom. Our response to these proclamations shows whether or not we are spiritually aligned with God.

Psalm 111 calls us to give wholehearted thanks to the Lord and to praise him publicly. It is an acrostic poem: each of its twenty-two lines begins with a different letter of the Hebrew alphabet. The first half of the psalm (verses 2-7a) highlights the works of God, and the second (verses 7b-10) his words. Perhaps these divisions correspond to the exodus and to the giving of the law, respectively. On this second to last week of Epiphany, this psalm invites us to study the power of Christ's works and the wisdom of his teachings. As John 8 brings out, if we embrace Jesus' words, we will know the truth and the truth will set us free.

RESPONDING TO GOD

Perhaps you could take some time this week to review the insights about Jesus that you've gained during these seven weeks of Epiphany. How have you observed his glory? What has he shown you through your devotions and your experiences? Joyfully reaffirm who you believe him to be and renew your willingness to follow him at all costs.

Closing Prayer. You sent redemption to your people in your Son Jesus; through him, you have commanded your covenant forever. Holy and awesome is your name. Amen.

Transfiguration Sunday
Beginning the Sunday before Ash Wednesday

Transforming Glory

On the first Sunday after the Feast of the Epiphany we focused on Jesus' baptism in the river; on this last Sunday we study Jesus' transfiguration on the mountain. Once again and even more dramatically we see his glory revealed and hear the confirming voice. For the disciples who experience this amazing and terrifying epiphany, it is transformative, as Peter's later testimony makes clear. Jesus' experience echoes that of Moses and Elijah in their day. This episode is a fitting culmination of the Epiphany season. As we have gazed each week at the face of Jesus in the Gospels of Mark and John, more and more of his glory has been unveiled. This final epiphany is dazzling, leaving us awed and speechless. Not only do we worship the majesty, we are changed by it; it is a transforming glory.

Approaching God. You are king, O Lord; let the peoples tremble! You sit enthroned upon the cherubim; let the earth quake! You are great, O Lord, and exalted over all. I praise your great and awesome name. You are holy, holy, holy!

Presenting Myself. You have placed a treasure—the knowledge of your glory in the face of Jesus—in the clay jar of my humanity so it will be clear that the extraordinary power belongs to you and does not come from me; I am humbly grateful, O Lord.

Inviting God's Presence. Shake me awake this day, O Lord, so that I may see your glory and hear your voice and be transformed. Amen.

LISTENING TO GOD

Psalm 99 (AC); Exodus 24:9-18; 34:29-35 (AC);
1 Kings 19:11-12; **Luke 9:28-36 (C);**
2 Peter 1:16-21 (A); **2 Corinthians 3:12-4:6 (BC)**

Psalm 99 prompts in us an echo of the threefold "Holy! Holy! Holy!" sung by the angelic beings before God's throne (see Is 6; Rev 4). It helps us to celebrate God's kingship, his love of justice and his merciful forgiveness. It reminds us that God answers those who pray, as he did the priests and prophets who called on him, especially Moses and Aaron, who encountered God at Mount Sinai (Ex 24), and Samuel, who first heard God's voice as a boy (1 Sam 3). Let this psalm shape your personal worship this week.

The passages in **Exodus** describe Moses' encounter with God's glory on Mount Sinai, and the text in **1 Kings** tells of Elijah's experience on Mount Horeb. These two towering figures will appear with Jesus in his transfiguring encounter with God on a mountain. Study each passage. What is Moses' experience when he goes up? After he comes down? Have you ever been around someone whose encounters with God gave them, at least for a time, a kind of holy aura? Has something like this ever happened to you? Now compare the experience of Elijah with that of Moses. What is similar, what is different? Sometimes, maybe most times, God's presence and glory are revealed to us in a "sheer silence" or "quiet whisper." Might you find space this week to be still and silent and attentive to the voice of God?

Luke and the other two Synoptic Gospels record the transfiguration episode (see Mk 9:2-9; Mt 17:1-9) just after Jesus' crucial exchange with his disciples about his messianic identity and destiny and his call to self-denial and potential martyrdom. What Peter, James and John experience a week later makes for a striking juxtaposition of suffering with glory. Reflect on the various details in Luke's account. What is Jesus doing on the mountain? How does his appearance change? Why Moses and Elijah? (Law and prophets? Exodus and eschaton?) They speak about Jesus' departure. Why does Peter blurt out a plan for organizing the experience? What do the cloud and voice remind you of? Why the command to listen? As always, put yourself in the story and see what you learn.

Later in life in **2 Peter 1,** the apostle Peter refers to his experience on the mountain. How does he describe it? What did it mean to him? For one thing, it bolstered his confidence in the prophetic messages of the Scripture: the writers were moved by the Holy Spirit and thus "spoke from God." Peter's eyewitness account of the glory likewise bolsters *our* confidence in the good news.

In **2 Corinthians** Paul weaves a tapestry of reflections on the theme of glory (chapters 3—5 form the larger context for our passage). He speaks of the relative glories of the old and new covenants. He refers to Moses and his shining face by way of analogy. He dramatizes the glory of the Lord as revealed in the face of Jesus. He declares that as we gaze at Jesus (as we've been doing during Epiphany) the Spirit is transforming us by degrees of glory into his image. And whatever suffering we endure, Paul reassures us, is slight and momentary when compared to the glory God has promised us, a glory that is weighty and eternal (2 Cor 4:16-18).

RESPONDING TO GOD

After reflecting on the transfiguration story and its related texts, step back at some point this week and allow yourself to meditate in this way: Could Jesus be inviting you to go with him to the mountain and enter into a posture of prayer and attentiveness so that he can reveal more of his glory to you, glory that will transform you over time?

Closing Prayer. O God, you spoke light out of darkness at creation and you have shone in my heart to give the light of the knowledge of your glory in the face of Jesus Christ; help me now to reflect this light in all that I say or do this day. Amen.

The Cycle of Life

Lent

The Paschal Triduum

Easter

5

Lent
Humbled in the Turning

Lent is a double journey—a journey together (and alone)
toward the mystery of God's redemptive embrace in the death
and resurrection of Christ. At the same time, it is
a journey into the depths of our humanity.

DON E. SALIERS

A journey, a pilgrimage! Yet, as we begin it, as we make the first step
into the "bright sadness" of Lent, we see—far, far away—the destination.
It is the joy of Easter, it is the entrance into the glory of the Kingdom.

ALEXANDER SCHMEMANN

Alone in the art gallery at Regent College, I stared at a piece by Erica Grimm-Vance, a Vancouver artist. The work both intrigued and troubled me. It was a narrow, vertical rectangle roughly one foot wide and five feet high. A haunting image, veiled by a layer of encaustic, filled the top third of the piece while a heavy black panel of steel formed the bottom two-thirds. A half-inch band of gold leaf created a shimmering boundary between the two parts. The image? A bird skeleton stretched out with a pair of extended white-feathered wings attached by thin bones. The lightly tinted encaustic over the gray graphite drawing generated a subtle luminosity, like liminal light at dawn. The piece was titled *Grace and Gravity*, an allusion to writings by the twentieth-century French mystic and philosopher Simone Weil.

It was the first week of my sabbatical in 1997. I wanted to encounter God in fresh ways during this time, especially through the arts and the contemplative disciplines. To start it off I had signed up for a new experience, a poetry writing workshop taught by Luci Shaw. So I stood before this work of art intending to write a poem in response. Unsure of what I was seeing or what it meant, I wrote a few groping lines. Later I chose to write about the puzzling Grimm-Vance piece for my final workshop assignment, which required us to choose and explore a metaphor that conveyed some aspect of our spiritual selves. With my sabbatical in mind I reengaged with the artwork and wrote this poem—presciently, as it turned out:

> These months must be for me
> an exploration of Simone Weil's
> two movements of soul, dark gravity
> pulling down and its bright exception, grace.
>
> Here is what I must learn: I am this bird,
> skeletal, stripped of flesh and feather—
> the ineluctable pull of cold black earth—
> my flightless white bones left to weather.
>
> Only then will wings descend to take up
> my frame, animated once again, to race
> into the sea's early mist, the abrupt
> light of the sun rising in golden grace.

Just words for an assignment, a class exercise in thinking metaphorically. But I underestimated the power of image and the strength of metaphor, especially in the hands of the Spirit.

My summer in Vancouver ended, and back in New York I settled into a routine, promptly forgetting all about the art. But my sabbatical did not unfold as I had imagined or planned or even prayed. The simplest way to describe it is this: somehow I expected to join Jesus on the mountain of transfiguring glory but instead found myself alone and bewildered in the desert. As the months passed I grew increasingly confused, disappointed and even embarrassed by what I was *not* experiencing. What would I say to the generous donors who were underwriting this opportunity to go deep with God?

I had scheduled the sabbatical to conclude on Easter Sunday in what I thought was a clever and fitting touch. But as Lent began that February, I just wanted those final six weeks to go by quickly and bring my "spiritual failure" to an end. Easter didn't hold the promise of joy so much as the prospect of relief, a return to "normal" existence, minus the heightened spiritual expectations.

Some weeks after Easter, I met with my spiritual mentor for help in understanding my experience. At one point, knowing I had been writing poems, he asked to see them. I showed him several, including the one about *Grace and Gravity*. Rereading it after seven months, I was stunned. It was as if God had told me at the start what my experience would be, but I had lacked the ears to hear. Doug gently helped me regain perspective. Yes, I had been in the desert, but I had not been alone. Yes, I had been tested, but I had not failed. And yes, I had been humbled, but in turning from my spiritual pride and sense of entitlement, I was now open to a new encounter with God's transforming presence.

Each year the season of Lent asks us to embrace a spiritual gravity, a downward movement of soul, a turning from our self-sufficiency and sinfulness. In such quiet turning, we are humbled and thus made ready to receive from God a fresh and joyous grace.

THE HEART OF LENT

"Remember that you are dust, and to dust you shall return." With these words the priest or pastor marks a cross on our foreheads with ashes as we stand or kneel in silence. This day, Ash Wednesday, marks the beginning of Lent, the six-week season that leads up to Pascha (Good Friday, Holy Saturday and Easter Sunday). Dust and ashes. These symbolize two themes at the heart of Lent: our creaturely mortality and our moral culpability. Finite beings and sinful persons, we are destined to die. And so we humble ourselves before the eternal God who created us and the holy God who must, if we are to live, redeem us. The dust speaks of our bodily dependence and the ashes signify our spiritual penitence. Ash Wednesday sets the tone for the season: humility, simplicity, sobriety and even sorrow.

But the great Orthodox theologian Alexander Schmemann speaks of a "bright sadness" that is the true message and gift of Lent. Yes, during these weeks we become especially mindful of the sinfulness that alienates us from God, indeed, of the human evil that nailed Jesus to those rough beams. And this we lament with sadness. At the same time, we understand that by his death Jesus secured for us forgiveness and eternal life. We are like prisoners whose release draws near or refugees on our way back home or patients for whom the cure is working. Lent is sobering, but it leads to Easter!

We can think of Lent as both a sojourn and a journey. We have two opportunities to identify with Jesus, one at the start of his public ministry and one near the end. The sojourn occurs in the desert as Jesus spends forty days alone in self-reflection and discernment of God's way. The journey takes place on the road to Jerusalem as Jesus moves toward his dark destiny. The sojourn causes us to look inward and acknowledge our human and spiritual vulnerabilities; the journey bids us look outward and weigh the costs of discipleship. Both involve turning.

In the solitary sojourn, we turn away from our sins and temptations and toward God and his great mercy. This is otherwise known as repentance. And while we usually don't put ourselves in a desolate environment for forty days, we can choose a posture of humility and undertake practices that sharpen our spiritual awareness. These include prayer and Scripture meditation, moral inventory and behavior change, fasting and other forms of abstinence, acts of generosity and service. As Jesus entered the desert keenly aware of his baptism, during Lent we too rehearse and reaffirm our own baptismal promises: to renounce Satan and all evil powers and sinful desires, to trust in the grace of Christ as our Savior, to follow him as our Lord. As we turn inward and turn Godward, we can trust him to turn toward us with spiritual grace (see Ps 138:6; Jas 4:6).

"When the days drew near for him to be taken up, he set his face to go to Jerusalem" (Lk 9:51). Resolutely Jesus turns toward death in fulfillment of his mission, and he asks his followers to go with him. This is the pivot from self-gratification to self-denial, from seeking acclaim to risking scorn, from the seduction of power to the prospect of suffering. In so turning we plunge into the paradox of the cross-and-empty-tomb gospel. These truths are simply too profound to take in over a mere Friday through Sunday, so we use the season of Lent to prepare. Lent allows us to enter into the power of Pascha more deeply.

The word *lent* comes from a Saxon word that originally meant "length" and was used to denote springtime (*lencton*, in Old English). So in the northern hemisphere, at least, we observe Lent during a time of year when the days are lengthening and signs of new life are appearing. Even as Lent progresses with its somber themes and ascetic disciplines, the natural world reminds us of the coming resurrection. Even as we prepare for the anguished hours of Good Friday and the unfathomable silence of Holy Saturday, we anticipate the glorious joy of Resurrection Sunday. These six weeks, suggests Schmemann, are like walking in a still-darkened valley even as the morning sun lights the tops of the mountains around us. Bright sadness, indeed.

LENT IN CHURCH AND CULTURAL TRADITION

Historically, Lent developed in relation to Easter, the fast in preparation for the feast. In the first two centuries, the church observed only a two-day fast: on Friday to commemorate Jesus' death and on Saturday to mark his entombment. This was a mourning fast, in keeping with sorrow and compassion for Jesus and also in remembrance of his words, "The days will come when the bridegroom is taken away from them, and then they will fast" (Mt 9:15). By the third century, the fast had been extended to the six days prior to Easter. Nothing but water, bread and salt were eaten for the first four days, and a complete fast was undertaken for the final two. By the time of the Council of Nicaea in 325, some churches were observing a forty-day period, with reference no doubt to the forty-day experiences of Moses (Ex 34), Elijah (1 Kings 19) and, above all, Jesus (Mt 4).

Three purposes characterized the pre-paschal practice of the early churches. First, with Easter as a signal day for baptisms (along with Epiphany and Pentecost), the baptismal candidates underwent an intensive catechetical process in the weeks before Easter. Similarly, Holy Week proved a propitious time for the church to reconcile and restore to fellowship those who had been separated from the church because of egregious sin; thus the public penitence prior to Pascha. Third, the church recognized the value of fasting and prayer for its own spiritual sake, as Adolf Adam outlines:

> Christians also saw in fasting a way of preparing for the reception of the Spirit, a powerful weapon in the fight against evil spirits, an appropriate preparation for such religious actions as the reception of baptism and the eucharist, and finally, a way of being able to help the poor with money that would otherwise have been spent on food.

The themes from these original purposes are woven into the fabric of our own Lenten experience.

While a consensus eventually developed around a forty-day Lent, the actual count of days has varied in different eras and parts of the church. Some have taken the forty days literally and some symbolically. Roman Catholics today measure Lent from Ash Wednesday through Maundy Thursday, which totals thirty-eight days, excluding Sundays. Some Protestants consider Lent to extend through Holy Saturday, thus totaling exactly forty days. The Orthodox churches have no Ash Wednesday but begin Lent the evening of the seventh Sunday before Easter and keep forty days of fasting, including Sundays, ending on the Friday before Holy Week.

The Orthodox actually set aside four weeks to get ready for Lent—preparation for the season of preparation. Each of five preceding Sundays is dedicated to a preparatory theme:

- Zacchaeus Sunday: desire to see Jesus
- Sunday of the Publican and Pharisee: humility
- Sunday of the Prodigal Son: return from exile
- Meat-fare Sunday (last day to eat meat): the last judgment
- Cheese-fare Sunday (last day to eat dairy): forgiveness

During vespers on the final Sunday, Orthodox congregants verbally request forgiveness from and extend it to one another. Then begins the Great Lent, the first day of which is called Clean Monday (Is 1:16-17). In contrast to Western churches, which omit all "alleluias" in worship during Lent, the Orthodox increase their use of the word to signify their joy in fasting. This note of joy is further amplified during the two-day interlude between the end of Lent and the start of Holy Week: Lazarus Saturday, which foreshadows Christ's resurrection, and Palm Sunday, which prefigures his royal triumph.

For many centuries the Western church—especially Catholics, Anglicans and Lutherans—also emphasized pre-Lent by marking the three Sundays before Ash Wednesday, but this practice has largely disappeared. These preliminary weeks, however, do correspond to the tradition of Carnival (Latin for "putting away meat") celebrated in many Latin countries with great feasting and celebration leading up to Ash Wednesday. In the United States, we have the revelry of Mardi Gras, or "Fat Tuesday" in French. This day is also called Shrove Tuesday (from Middle English *shrive*, "to confess") or Pancake Tuesday, given the old practice of using up rich foods—butter, eggs, milk and sugar—before fasting began on the next day. Some churches offer a family pancake supper on this Tuesday as an alternative to Mardi Gras carousing.

The season of Lent may be signaled at church in various ways: the presence of the liturgical color purple (representing penitence), the use of confessional litanies, a somber tone for musical worship and the omission of "alleluias" from the service. The worship space can also be stripped of bright colors and ornamentation, the cross draped with a purple cloth and the windows progressively darkened over the weeks. Some churches enlist parishioners in preparing a booklet of spiritual meditations or artistic expressions to be used by the whole congregation to "journey with Jesus" during Lent.

THE CHRIST STORY IN LENT

During Epiphany we emphasized the glory of Christ being made known through his teachings and miracles—Epiphany completed the Cycle of Light. During Lent we continue to walk with Jesus, but our attention shifts from light to shadows: his increasingly hostile opponents, his growing heaviness of spirit, and his ominous talk of betrayal and death. With the disciples, we grow uneasy, almost appalled. Human sin, corrupt powers, even raw evil comes into view.

This light and shadow approach is only a general scheme; after all, Jesus encountered testing from the start, as when he was tempted and worked miracles right until the end, as when he raised Lazarus. We start Lent by joining Jesus in the place of solitude, we continue by walking with him toward Jerusalem and we end by kneeling beside him in dark Gethsemane. All along the way—the desert, the road, the garden—Jesus is tempted to go a different way, one that avoids anything like the cross. Repeatedly he says no.

The desert. Driven by the Spirit, Jesus goes into the wilderness. For forty days he fasts, prays and meditates on the convictions that have grown in him over the years in Nazareth. He thinks about God as Father and King. He thinks about himself as a beloved son and about his people as a chosen nation. He thinks about his role in bringing about the kingdom of God. At some level he knows this will involve suffering and eventually death. He wrestles with this. The tempter seeks to undermine his confidence in God's Word, both the voice at the river and the Torah of the synagogue. He attempts to dissuade Jesus from a path of self-denial, humility and powerlessness. The temptations grow most acute near the end of the forty days when he is most vulnerable:

"Why suffer? Turn these stones to bread and satisfy yourself. In the same way, you could feed the hungry poor!"

"Why stay hidden? Leap from this temple and promote yourself, for surely the angels will save you. You could prove your divine favor and win the people!"

"Why renounce wealth and power? Bow to me in this moment and exalt yourself. As ruler of the world, you could bring liberty and justice for all!"

Physical comfort. Public acclaim. Political power. If he is indeed the Son of God, why not exempt himself from suffering or exercise his prerogatives or claim his rightful position? But these would have been the right things gained by the wrong means: bread apart from Bread, glory separate from Glory, power independent of Power or, to put it in Genesis 3 terms, godlikeness apart from God. But unlike Eve and Adam, Jesus says no to the tempter and yes to the Father. No to self, yes to sacrifice. No to doubt, yes to faith. No to empires, yes to God's kingdom. No to idolatry, yes to obedience.

The road. "When the devil had finished every test, he departed from him until an opportune time" (Lk 4:13). Indeed, Jesus' temptations continue. His disciples urge him to seize the moment when the people clamor for him in Capernaum, but Jesus chooses to go elsewhere. The religious leaders accuse him of law-breaking and blasphemy, but Jesus refuses to conform in order to gain their approval. His family thinks he's out of his mind, but Jesus ignores their concern and redefines "family." The Pharisees ask for a public sign, but Jesus declines. The disciples desire to sit on thrones, but Jesus speaks of greatness through service. After miraculously eating, the people want to make him king, but Jesus withdraws to a mountain. And his most promising disciple, after an enlightened declaration of faith, quickly becomes the voice of Satan; Jesus issues a stinging rebuke. Jesus says no to every voice that diverts him from the path that God has chosen for him.

And that path leads to Gethsemane and Golgotha.

The garden. Think of Jesus praying in Gethsemane as the final scene of Lent. Here the temptations that started in the desert culminate. Here the test becomes most intense. Everything in Jesus shrinks from what lies ahead, certainly the physical torment, but even more the spiritual abyss. He is distressed and agitated and deeply grieved. He pleads to be spared the dreaded hour come round at last, the bitter cup of suffering. Three times he asks! But in the end he says yes; he wills to do his Father's will, whatever the cost.

And this is what Jesus asks of us during Lent, to say no and yes: "If any want to become my followers, let them deny themselves and take up their cross and follow me" (Mk 8:34).

INHABITING LENT

One March morning, while running with a friend who was thirtysomething and single, I casually asked him what he was giving up for Lent that year. "Sex . . . again," he ruefully replied. A slight pause and we both broke out laughing. "And you?" he asked. "Oh, just Starbucks coffee," I replied, and we laughed again.

This light exchange actually touches on two core elements of Lenten practice, namely addressing our temptations and denying ourselves certain enjoyments. Add prayer and Scripture and you have the basic means for inhabiting the season. The Book of Common Prayer, for example, extends a threefold invitation to observe Lent "by self-examination and repentance; by prayer, fasting, and self-denial; and by reading and meditating on God's holy Word." All such Lenten disciplines represent a kind of turning from a self-centered stance to a grace-filled humility.

Fasting. "There is no Lent without fasting," asserts Schmemann. While he may be overstating it, he also makes a crucial point, certainly one in keeping with the practice of the church over the centuries. But why is this the case?

Even though we know fasting is found throughout the Bible, some of us have misgivings about the practice. We immediately picture ascetics going to great lengths to "mortify" their flesh in order to overcome temptation or to please God or to reach a mystical state. Fasting may strike us as a type of self-punishment that reflects a negative view of the body with its needs, appetites and capacities for pleasure. Or we may suspect in it an emphasis on works over against grace.

Yes, there can be distortions and abuses, but rightly understood and practiced, fasting can bring great dividends. Lynne Baab, in her book *Fasting: Spiritual Freedom Beyond Our Appetites,* provides this simple definition: "Christian fasting is the voluntary denial of something for a specific period of time for a spiritual purpose." In this respect fasting is much like sabbath-keeping: a restriction that creates space for God. In recent years many Christians have rediscovered fasting along with other long-neglected disciplines that can deepen and enrich us. After all, Jesus thought fasting important. In response to the devil's temptation to turn stones to bread, Jesus quotes Deuteronomy:

> [The Lord] humbled you by letting you hunger, then by feeding you with manna, with which neither you nor your ancestors were acquainted, in order to make you understand that one does not live by bread alone, but by every word that comes from the mouth of the LORD. (Deut 8:3)

Humbled by hunger, the Israelites in the wilderness and Jesus in the desert understood experientially their daily dependence on God for physical sustenance; more profoundly, they relied on God for the life that lies beyond biology, life for our souls, our selves. "In him we live and move and have our being," affirms Paul (Acts 17:28). Hearing God's Word and doing God's will becomes food for us, teaches Jesus. Even more, he feeds us with himself: his flesh is true food and his blood is true drink. Indeed, each time we partake of the Eucharistic bread and wine, we mysteriously "feed on him in our hearts by faith, with thanksgiving," according to the Book of Common Prayer.

Fasting, then, is to deny ourselves food for a time in order to more vividly know Jesus as the source of our sustenance and being. It is to turn from the bread of the pantry to the bread of life and in this humbler state to rediscover our deepest hunger and remember our truest food. In this way, fasting draws us closer to God.

There are three basic types of fasting. First, a *partial* or *ascetical fast* entails restricting the diet by either cutting out certain foods or cutting out certain meals. For example, we might go without meat, fish, dairy, eggs and oil like the Eastern Orthodox. Or we might forgo select substances like caffeine or sweets. The tradition of fasting on certain days, especially Fridays (the day of Christ's death), goes back to the beginning of the church. One option is to skip one or more of a day's meals, say breakfast and lunch, for a given time, as Muslims do during Ramadan. Second, a *normal fast* means eating no food but drinking liquids, either water or juice. After two or three days of normal fasting, a person enters a physiological state called ketosis, which often coincides with heightened spiritual awareness. Third, in an *absolute* or *complete fast,* one consumes nothing at all (which necessarily limits this type to no more than two days). Be aware that some people should not engage in any type of fasting, especially pregnant or nursing women, anyone who is sick or has a medical condition like diabetes, the very old, the very young and people with eating disorders.

My own pattern each year is to fast from everything but juice and water on Ash Wednesday and on each Friday during Lent. At the end I fast from the Maundy Thursday Eucharist until I take Communion again on Easter Sunday. Such fasting helps me stay aware of the season and increases my sense of belonging to God. My fasting in Lent always amplifies the joy of my feasting on Easter.

Strictly speaking, fasting refers to not eating food, but we can appropriately extend the concept to other activities and substances. In our consumption-driven society, the practice of abstinence from certain things for certain periods can loosen the hold of our unhealthy appetites and destructive addictions. Marjorie Holmes claims:

> In a more tangible, visceral way than any other spiritual discipline, fasting reveals our excessive attachments and the assumptions that lie behind them. . . . Fasting brings us face to face with how we put the material world ahead of its spiritual Source.

This is why many people choose to give up something for Lent. If we are purposeful in what we choose, this type of fasting can recalibrate our degree of "need" for the thing given up. I remember the year I suspended weekday delivery of the *New York Times*, which I compulsively read first thing every morning, often at the expense of my devotions. Over the weeks of Lent, I slowly became content without the paper, so afterward I decided not to renew. This Lenten abstinence weaned me from a small but unhelpful dependence. Here are other things that I have given up for Lent in different years or that I've learned about from others:

- Eating desserts and sweets
- Buying expensive cups of coffee
- Drinking alcoholic beverages
- Purchasing books
- Watching television
- Reading books and magazines
- Wearing colorful jewelry or using makeup
- Listening to music or watching movies
- Eating overpackaged, overprocessed foods
- Shopping
- Using Facebook

None of these are in themselves bad, but any of them can become overly important in our lives. We are not to live by such things alone. To abstain for a time is to resist these subtle idolatries and to refocus our attention on God, who is our life.

Fasting and prayer. Almost always fasting is linked to prayer in Scripture. Consider how fasting can enhance praying during Lent. First, it makes space for God, both in our hearts and in our schedules. It weans us from our preoccupations and attunes us to God and his concerns. Fasting helps us listen to God. Practically, we can convert the skipped meal times to prayer times. If we just put in an extra hour at our work desks, what have we gained?

Second, fasting in some mysterious way strengthens our prayers, both our faith in asking and our discernment in listening. It was during a time of fasting that the leaders at Antioch heard from God about setting apart Paul and Barnabas for missionary work. Fasting and prayer also preceded the day they were sent off (Acts 13:1-3). Throughout history Christians have attested to the power of fasting in connection with intercession, including prayers for healing. One Lent I abstained from alcohol and linked this discipline with my prayers for a close friend struggling with his drinking problem.

Fasting and repentance. Throughout the Bible we find fasting as an expression of repentance, whether individual or corporate. For example, the prophet Joel proclaims:

> Yet even now, says the LORD,
>   return to me with all your heart,
> with fasting, with weeping, and with mourning;
>   rend your hearts and not your clothing. (Joel 2:12)

Starting with Ash Wednesday, Lent calls for us to examine ourselves, to admit to God (and others) our places and patterns of sin and to work at changing these with God's help. With the psalmist, we dare to pray:

> Search me, O God, and know my heart;
>   test me and know my thoughts.
> See if there is any wicked way in me,
>   and lead me in the way everlasting. (Ps 139:23-24)

We set aside times to quiet ourselves in the presence of God in order to take an honest look at ourselves. We think about our inner dispositions and our external behaviors, our hearts as well as our habits. It takes courage and humility to stand before the "penetrating gaze of holy love," which "falls on what is unholy and unloving within us." But remember, we confess to a God who loves us and who wants to transform us, who describes himself as "gracious and merciful, slow to anger, and abounding in steadfast love, and relenting from punishment" (Joel 2:13), the same God who gave himself for us and for our salvation.

There are many resources for moral inventory and the practice of repentance, starting with Scripture itself. For example, we can meditate on the Ten Commandments of Moses or the Beatitudes of Jesus. We can listen to prophetic pronouncements such as Isaiah 58 or study an instructive character such as Joseph or read through an epistle such as James. We can also make use of the seven penitential psalms: 6, 32, 38, 51, 101, 130 and 143. Whatever God shows us, we must act on: write to our estranged friend or stop looking at sullying images or refrain from snapping at our irritating colleague or revise our spending and giving habits.

Fasting and meditation. When we fast during Lent, we identify with Jesus in a tangible way: we keep the sojourn and we join the journey. The weeks slowly build in intensity until he enters the city to the joyful praise of the people and the angry plot of the authorities. The more that we can enter into his sufferings and death in that final, holy week, the more we will know both our own great sin and need and God's great goodness and love. We read and meditate on Scripture in this season in order to know Christ and to share in his sufferings, becoming like him in his death so as to share in the power of his resurrection (Phil 3:10).

THE GRAVITY OF LENT

"You turn us back to dust," writes the psalmist. But then he cries out, "Turn, O Lord! . . . Have compassion on your servants!" (Ps 90). This is the wisdom of Lent: to acknowledge our finitude and failings and to turn to the God who turns to us in mercy. So we practice the creaturely humility of fasting, the spiritual humility of prayer, the moral humility of repentance and, vicariously, the sacrificial humility of Christ himself.

In the gravity of Lent we choose a downward movement of soul, and in this turning we are humbled. In the humbling, we find a growing freedom and grace.

*   *   *

Preview of devotions in Lent. The first set of devotions accompany Ash Wednesday and focus on confession and fasting. Those of the first full week (week one) derive from Jesus' testing in the desert. Weeks two through four address three common sources of temptation, and week five explores the power of forgiveness. In addition to psalms and Gospel texts, I offer two continuous studies for the middle four weeks: the narrative of Joseph in Genesis, a story of descent and ascent, and the epistle of James, a mirror for self-examination. The final Sunday of Lent, Palm Sunday, marks the start of Holy Week, and I have included extra material for those who wish to intensify their devotions during the first four days.

Ash Wednesday
From Ash Wednesday to the following Sunday

A Sign of Our Mortality

We begin Lent by observing Ash Wednesday as a day of fasting, reflection and repentance. It helps to participate in a service (at our own or another church). In the service, we are marked on our foreheads with ashes—a smudge of a cross—as a sign of our mortality and a symbol of our penitence. We become conscious of our sinful condition as humans and our specific failings as individuals. The Scriptures prescribed by the Revised Common Lectionary lead us into a posture of humility for these weeks of Lent. We identify with David's psalm of confession after his most grievous moral failing, we hear the prophets cry out for authentic national repentance, we learn from Jesus about secrecy in prayer and fasting, and we study Paul's willingness to deny himself in faithfulness to his calling.

Approaching God. I turn to you, O Lord, with all my heart, for you are gracious and merciful, slow to anger, abounding in steadfast love and relenting from punishment. Amen.

Presenting Myself. I know my transgressions, and my sin is ever before me; against you, you alone, have I sinned and done what is evil in your sight, so that you are justified in your sentence and blameless when you pass judgment.

Inviting God's Presence. Have mercy on me, O God, according to your steadfast love; according to your abundant mercy blot out my transgressions; wash me thoroughly from my iniquity and cleanse me from my sin. Amen.

LISTENING TO GOD
Psalm 51 (ABC); Joel 2:1-17 (ABC);
Isaiah 58 (ABC); Matthew 6:1-21 (ABC);
2 Corinthians 5:20b—6:10 (ABC)

Psalm 51 represents King David's response to God after the prophet Nathan exposes his rape of Bathsheba and his arrangement to have her husband killed (see 2 Sam 11—12). David is filled with remorse and rightly humbles himself before God. He confesses his specific transgression but also acknowledges his innate propensity for inner dishonesty and outward wrongdoing. He asks for forgiveness and spiritual restoration. He pledges to live differently. Throughout the psalm, he confidently but without presumption rehearses God's propensity for mercy, forgiveness and redemption. Let this psalm help you express to God your own humility and repentance and your own desire for a clean heart.

The prophet **Joel** responds to a devastating plague of locusts that has come upon the nation and attributes this event to the judgment of God (Joel 1). In Joel 2:1-11, he likens the onslaught of insects to an invading army and thus evokes the impending Day of the Lord with all its fierce judgment. Joel calls for the people to respond with a collective fast and a season of repentance. "Return to me with all your heart," God says. Do you see anything befalling our nation or global community that should impel us to collective humility and repentance?

Isaiah 58 pointedly insists that God is not much interested in our ritual expressions of piety and repentance. No, what he wants of us is integrity and action: right relationships with our neighbors, fair treatment of our workers, steps to address injustice, generosity that helps the poor and sabbath-keeping that honors God. Beware hypocrisy. This Scripture bears reflection and response throughout the weeks of Lent.

Matthew 6 records Jesus' comments on three spiritual disciplines. Maybe Isaiah 58 is in his mind as he warns us not to "practice our piety" in public. Indeed, are we not tempted to garner the admiration of others—and perhaps even God—when we let our practices of spiritual devotion be known? What God cares about is our heart. He wants to see who we are when no one is looking and what we do with our time and money. As you give and pray and fast in this season, do so privately, quietly. Matthew incorporates the Lord's Prayer into this section of the Sermon on the Mount. Give thought to these familiar words in the context of Lent. The first sweep of the prayer focuses on God, his love, holiness and sovereign will. The second highlights our human needs, physical, spiritual and circumstantial. Be reminded of the sobering truth that our experience of forgiveness is linked to our willingness to forgive.

In **2 Corinthians 5,** Paul calls himself and his coworkers (and, by implication, us) ambassadors for Christ engaged in a ministry of reconciliation. In verses 20-21, he urges all to accept the exchange offered in Christ. Then in chapter 6 he describes with passionate candor the lengths to which he is willing to go as a servant of God. Read this catalog and take a moment to think about each element, perhaps jotting down your thoughts. Notice the categories: experiences of physical abuse and deprivation, costly choices of character and behavior, painful implications for public reputation and standing. Yet Paul, while not denying the hardship, considers himself richly rewarded. Lent turns us from our self-protecting and self-advancing instincts to a willingness to die to ourselves in order to be alive in God and faithful as ambassadors.

RESPONDING TO GOD

Use these few days to ponder how you want to observe Lent. Perhaps you can choose one or two areas of your life for repentance, that is, for change that aligns you more with what God expects. Also, what appetites or activities could you restrain over these next weeks to help you practice repentance and deepen your attention to God?

Closing Prayer. Almighty God, you have created us out of the dust of the earth: Grant that these ashes may be to us a sign of our mortality and penitence, that we may remember that it is only by your gracious gift that we are given everlasting life; through Jesus Christ our Savior. Amen. (Book of Common Prayer)

Facing Temptation

As humans created in God's image we have the ability to make moral choices—indeed, the responsibility to do so. But sadly, we have inherited the legacy of our original parents: a flawed moral capacity. We are unable to live fully in the way that God rightly requires. We are vulnerable to temptation. Jesus, too, is subject to temptation. He is tested not just in the desert at the start of his public leadership but throughout his years. And he proves faithful. From him we can gain wisdom and strength for facing temptation.

Approaching God. You are the Lord our God, you alone. You placed the first humans in the Garden and endowed them with moral responsibility. You freed your people from slavery in Egypt and brought them through the sea. You made a covenant with them at the mountain and gave them your commandments. And you led your Son into the desert to be tempted and he proved faithful. You are the Lord our God, you alone.

Presenting Myself. O Lord, I am a child of Adam and Eve, vulnerable to the wiles of the tempter; I am like the people of Israel, prone to forget your commandments; I am a faltering disciple of your Son Jesus, inclined to avoid the cost. O Lord, have mercy on me.

Inviting God's Presence. Lord God, strengthen me this day through the example of your Son who was tempted in every way but did not succumb, who was severely tested but did not falter. Amen.

LISTENING TO GOD
Genesis 3—4 (A);
Deuteronomy 5:1-21; 6:1-9; Psalm 1;
Matthew 4:1-11 (A); Mark 8:31-38 (B); James 1:12-16

Genesis 3 describes the first sin of the first humans and the devastating consequences for all of humanity and all of history. How does the serpent tempt the woman and the man (who is also present)? See how it subtly discredits the trustworthiness of God, how it entices them to satisfy their appetite not just for food and pleasure but for godlike knowledge. It gets them to disregard God's presence and provision and to act with arrogant autonomy. Trace the sad consequences of their choice. But note the hint of redemption (Gen 3:15) and the gesture of mercy (Gen 3:21). Study in **Genesis 4** the account of Cain's heinous sin: the competition, the anger, the warning, the deliberation, the deed and then the aftermath. What does the metaphor of sin as a lurking attacker suggest to you about facing temptation?

We find the famous Ten Commandments in **Deuteronomy 5.** Despite the emphatic charge of **Deuteronomy 6:1-9,** however, we rarely rehearse and reflect on them. This would be a good exercise for self-examination this week. For each prohibition, consider what the positive prescription might be. For example, what is life-giving (versus murderous) or marriage-honoring (versus adulterous)? How does Deuteronomy 6:4-9, with its call to love God, augment and sum up the commandments? To amplify your understanding, read Jesus' teachings in Matthew 5.

Psalm 1 opens the Psalter with a classic portrayal of the two paths in life, which Paul might describe as conformity to the world versus transformation by God's Word and will (Rom 12:2). Meditate on the contrasting metaphors of the wind-blown chaff and the fruitful tree. Enjoy the poetry of the psalm but also consider its practical application to your life given your current circumstances and temptations.

Matthew 4 tells about Jesus' forty days in the desert. Apparently Jesus thinks hard about his identity (who is he in relation to God?), wrestles with his vocation (what is he called to do?), and struggles with his doubts and fears (how much suffering is he willing to undergo?). Weakened from hunger he faces temptation. The essence is captured in the three exchanges with the devil. Reflect on each temptation. What is the heart of it? Why is it powerful? How does Jesus counter it? Then think about your own experience. How are you tempted to put your physical comforts ahead of your spiritual commitments? How are you tempted to presume on God's power and grace in order to prove something or impress someone? How are you tempted, in the interest of acquiring or protecting wealth and influence, to let someone or something other than God dictate your values and actions? Compare with Luke 4:1-13.

Jesus faces temptation again in **Mark 8.** This time, the seductive proposal comes through the earnest words of his close friend and trusted disciple. After Jesus discloses the very convictions he must have formed in the desert regarding his messianic identity and path of suffering, Peter takes him aside to talk him out of these dead-end notions. He envisions for Jesus—and himself—power and acclaim, not suffering and sacrifice. Jesus discerns the voice of Satan and again rejects it. He calls his would-be followers, including us, to the way of self-denial. Does temptation come to you through the unwitting words of your friends?

Blessed is the one who endures temptation and passes the test, writes **James.** He offers his own slant on the temptation progression that starts with simple desire and ends in death. What do you learn here about facing temptation?

RESPONDING TO GOD

The challenge for this and each week in Lent is to discern the shape of temptation in our own lives. How are we drawn, either subtly or blatantly, to put ourselves first over against choosing God's way?

Closing Prayer. Almighty God, whose blessed Son was led by the Spirit to be tempted by Satan: Come quickly to help us who are assaulted by many temptations; and, as you know the weaknesses of each of us, let each one find you mighty to save; through Jesus Christ your Son our Lord, who lives and reigns with you and the Holy Spirit, one God, now and for ever. Amen. (Book of Common Prayer)

Blinded by Pride

We are so easily blinded by pride. We hold back from confessing our sins and resist the work of repentance. We subtly interpret our gifts and blessings as signs of superiority over others. We assume it is better to be rich than poor, to be satisfied than hungry, to be buoyant than tearful. We readily form judgments of others and then downplay our own weaknesses. If we've been Christians a long while, we grow overly confident in our understandings and less open to instruction. Finally, we tend to put more stock in correct words than concrete actions. Our texts for this week speak to these temptations.

Approaching God. Happy are those whose transgression is forgiven, whose sin is covered, those to whom the Lord imputes no iniquity and in whose spirit there is no deceit; many are the torments of the wicked, but steadfast love surrounds those who trust in you, O Lord.

Presenting Myself. If I keep silent, I will waste away through my groaning all day long; for day and night your hand is heavy on me and my strength dries up as in the heat of summer. So I will not hide my sin from you but acknowledge it: I confess my transgressions, O Lord, and ask you to forgive my guilt.

Inviting God's Presence. Do not treat me like a horse or mule, without understanding and curbed by bit and bridle; rather, teach me the way I should go and counsel me with your eye on me, so that I may live this day in a manner pleasing to you. Amen.

LISTENING TO GOD
Psalm 32 (AC); Genesis 37;
Luke 6:17-49; John 3:1-21 (AB); James 1

Psalm 32 reports the happy release of someone who stops avoiding God and finally acknowledges the sin and guilt that has been eating away within. But why do we keep silent before God? What makes it hard to come clean? Shame? Pride? The psalmist turns from hiding from God to being hidden in him, from holding out to being held. This psalm calls us to act like humans, able to grow in wisdom and follow from the heart, not like beasts, which constantly must be reined in and made to comply.

The Joseph story opens in **Genesis 37** with a seventeen-year-old boy who is favored by his father and resented by his brothers. How are the characters in the story tempted, and how do they go wrong? Can you identify with any of them: Jacob in his favoritism? Joseph in his youthful arrogance? The brothers in their anger, jealousy, treachery or conspiracy of silence? Consider what grief each must bear as a result of his sin.

The teaching of Jesus in **Luke 6** arrests and challenges us. Ponder the blessings and woes. Why, from a kingdom-of-God point of view, might it be disadvantageous to be wealthy, sated, mirthful and well-esteemed? Why would God expect us to love our enemies with goodness and generosity? Why is it spiritually dangerous to judge others? The final two sections require us to connect our inward selves with our outward lives: our words reveal our hearts and our actions reveal our faith. Trace out the role that pride plays in the patterns that Jesus addresses. (The themes from this sermon will reappear in the later weeks of Lent.)

Early in the Gospel of **John** we read of the encounter at night between Nicodemus, a leading Pharisee, and Jesus, the upstart rabbi. Three themes bear reflection. First, the declaration of God's great love for all humanity and his intent not to condemn but to save. Second, the allusion to the story in Numbers 21 in which the people are healed through a bronze serpent affixed to a pole, a prefiguring of Jesus on the cross. Third, the temptation toward pride, spiritual or otherwise. Why does Nicodemus come at night? Why do he and his fellow Pharisees resist Jesus' teaching? What posture should we take if our spiritual life depends on birth from above and the blowing/breathing of the wind/Spirit? (Nicodemus eventually becomes a believer—Jn 7:50-52; 19:38-42.)

James has been likened to a commentary on Jesus' teaching. Because of its practical instructions on the moral life, it makes for an effective "mirror" during Lent. Work your way through chapter 1. Temptations and trials can lead to maturity if we respond wisely. If we lack wisdom, we can freely ask and expect God to freely give. James echoes Jesus' wisdom when he points out the danger of being in a "high" position (rich and powerful) and the advantage of being "lowly." There is a pride that is foolish and a boasting that is fitting. But we can take heart; such temptations are not irresistible. The question is this: will we act on what we have heard from God, or will our faith be largely rhetorical? We are blessed when we do the Word: avoiding anger and arrogance, caring for those in need, and refusing to conform to the distortions of our culture.

RESPONDING TO GOD

This week, examine yourself for the dangerous and often subtle tendency toward pride. The suggested opening prayers will assist you in making confession and receiving forgiveness. Identify one area in which you are tempted to spiritual pride and then choose a means to practice greater humility in that aspect of your life this week.

Closing Prayer. Father God, you so loved the world that you gave your Son that we might have eternal life in him. O Jesus, you allowed yourself to be lifted up on a cross for us. O Spirit, you blow as you will and bring new birth to those who are open to you. And since you resist the proud and give grace to the humble, O Lord, help me this week to grow in humility and imitate your self-giving love. Amen.

Bent by Prejudice

Some people are easy to love, some are difficult and some almost impossible. But Jesus teaches that, after the call to love God wholly, the command to love our neighbors as ourselves (Lev 19:18) is the second greatest. He goes even further, telling us to love our enemies, those who sell us out, do us wrong or keep us down. But we have many ways of qualifying these stark requirements and justifying our hierarchies of merit and preference. We are bent by prejudice. This week's Scriptures teach that there is no room to elevate ourselves above others or exempt ourselves from showing mercy. Jesus shows us how to love and tells us to "go and do likewise."

Approaching God. You, O Lord, are a great God, a great King above all gods. In your hands are the depths of the earth; the heights of the mountains are yours also; the sea is yours, for you made it, and the dry land, which your hands have formed.

Presenting Myself. Today, O Lord, I bow down and worship you; I kneel before you as my maker. You are my God and I am one of your people; I am like a sheep of your pasture. Have mercy on me, O Lord, for my heart is prone to go astray and to disregard your ways.

Inviting God's Presence. O God, make your merciful presence known to me this day so that I may joyfully give thanks; let me hear your voice so that I may respond with an open heart. Amen.

LISTENING TO GOD
Psalm 95 (A); Genesis 39—40;
Luke 10:25-37; John 4:1-42 (A); James 2

Psalm 95 bids us approach God to joyfully worship and to carefully listen. We come gratefully aware of his grace as Creator, redeemer and king. We humble ourselves—bowing, kneeling—in reverence and awe. We pay close attention to his Word, ready to respond. As preparation for hearing God's voice today, and given the deceitfulness of sin, take some time for self-examination. Is there any hardness in your heart, like that of the Israelites at Massah ("testing") and Meribah ("quarrelsome"), who took God's grace for granted and provoked his disgust? (See Ex 17:1-7.) Read the sustained meditation on Psalm 95 in Hebrews 3:7—4:13 urging us as "partners of Christ" to obey God—today!—if we hear his voice. Reflect also on the scalpel-like power of God's Word to penetrate and uncover the intentions of our hearts.

Genesis 39 continues the Joseph story. Betrayed by his own kin and enslaved in a foreign land, Joseph is surely tempted to nurse hatred toward his brothers, hostility toward his masters and even resentment toward his God. But Joseph seemingly sets his hurts aside and invests himself in his new situation. By God's grace, he prospers. But only for a time. Study how he resists the seductions of Potiphar's wife. What are his reasons for saying no? She cruelly frames him, invoking racial prejudice. Joseph does the right thing yet ends up in prison. How would you feel toward God and toward Egyptians at this point? But again he makes the most of a grim predicament. **Genesis 40** recounts a spike of hope and then a crushing disappointment. Joseph has descended to the depths. If this is his desert, what might be his temptations? His situation is ripe for self-pity, anger and despair. Can you identify with him to any extent? Compare Joseph to Jesus, who was willing to descend into great humiliation (Phil 2:5-8).

Examine the exchange in **Luke 10.** Jesus' side of it consists of a question, an assurance, a story, a second question with a twist and finally a simple command. How much like the lawyer are you? Where are you tempted to justify yourself, to explain how your current way of living is reasonable, all things considered? But Jesus tells a story where a Jew (presumably) is loved by an "enemy" who does not consider the inconvenience, the physical risk, the monetary cost, the potential ingratitude or the ongoing obligation. He sees the need and simply responds. Neighbors show mercy to neighbors.

In **John 4,** Jesus chooses to travel through the territory of the mixed-race, religiously heterodox Samaritans, a people much despised by most Jews. Study his encounter with the woman, whose coming to the well alone at noon suggests her social ostracism. He confounds her expectation of prejudice and spiritually entices her. He reveals himself as the Messiah—and she is changed. Now study the encounter with the disciples returning from their own opportunity in town to speak of, say, "living bread." It seems they have missed a harvest because of their prejudice. Are there people you find hard to reach out to because they differ from you in ethnicity or religion or social standing?

James 2 warns us that our acts and, even worse, patterns of favoritism toward some and prejudice toward others belie our belief in Jesus. If we should favor anyone, it should be the poor and the socially outcast. Think about how the powerful tend to use their power. As Jesus warns the lawyer in Luke 10, it is not our place to judge the worthiness of others but simply to show them mercy. Genuine faith reveals itself in compassionate actions. What do you see in James' mirror today?

RESPONDING TO GOD

Psalm 95 warns of ingratitude that hardens our hearts, and James decries prejudice that contradicts our faith. Jesus calls us to show mercy to all of our neighbors and even our enemies. If God speaks to you this week, respond with a soft heart and concrete action.

Closing Prayer. Creator and Father of all, you love every person you have made; forgive any prejudice that leads me to love some neighbors more than others, and give me opportunity this week to show mercy to someone in need. Amen.

Possessed by Possessions

Last week focused on the call to love our neighbors as ourselves. This week highlights the call to love God with our whole being. There can be no other gods, no idols, no rival allegiances. But in our consumer culture we are easily lured by money and all that money can buy or bring. We can be possessed by our possessions. Jesus taught extensively and repeatedly about money. He warns against greed and the accumulation of material things. He invites us to trust the Father who knows our needs and provides for us, the God who alone can raise us from the depths and ransom us from death. Jesus calls us to follow him with all that we are and all that we have. In so doing we become rich toward God.

Approaching God. O God, you yearn jealously for the spirit that you have made to dwell in us; you oppose the proud and indulgent but give grace to the humble.

Presenting Myself. O Lord, I have not loved you with my whole heart: I acknowledge my attachment to possessions and my failure to be generous; I confess my difficulty in being content with what I have and my desire to acquire even more; O Lord, have mercy on me.

Inviting God's Presence. O Lord, draw near to me as I draw near to you this day. Amen.

LISTENING TO GOD
Psalm 49; Genesis 41; **Luke 12:13-34;**
Luke 18:18-30; James 3:13—4:12

Psalm 49 sets the stage for this week's reflection on the seduction and ultimate futility of wealth. The opening verses identify this as a wisdom psalm that speaks to all humankind. Then the psalm divides into two parts. The first stresses the inevitability of death regardless of wealth or status; no payment can forestall one's death. The refrain (verse 12) reiterates the point: money cannot buy an eternal abode. The second half introduces a redemptive note: yes, death will herd us all to Sheol, but God will ransom the souls of those who trust in him. How does this wisdom shape your perspective toward your wealth or that of others?

By **Genesis 41** Joseph has been in Egypt for thirteen years, mostly languishing in prison. Now a sudden ascent from the darkest depths to the very heights of power! Can you detect evidence of Joseph's growth in character over these years? Note the combination of remarkable humility and shrewd initiative. When Pharaoh asks if he can interpret dreams, Joseph does not claim the ability—he surely would have in his arrogant youth—but simply points to God. Yet at the opportune moment he boldly proposes a fourteen-year economic plan that impresses Pharaoh. Joseph's story invites our reflection about patient endurance and confident trust. God will rescue and exalt us in his own way and his own time. Again, meditate on Jesus' exaltation after suffering (Phil 2:6-11).

The section in **Luke 12** presents a sharp challenge to the majority of us in North America. Read carefully and examine your own tendencies. How do you guard against greed? Jesus says the antidote to greed is generosity. What do you find yourself worrying about or anxiously striving for? Meditate on what it means to be rich toward God. Or to strive for his kingdom. What does Jesus teach about the Father? Perhaps his assurances will help you renew your trust in the gracious provision of God.

The exchange in **Luke 18** with a wealthy leader dramatizes how serious Jesus is about the dangers of money. The inquirer is confident of his moral and social standing, so Jesus tests him. Jesus purposely leaves out the commandments that pertain to unalloyed loyalty to God and the one about covetousness. Then he presents the telling challenge. Why is it hard for someone wealthy—as most of us are—to enter the kingdom? We are prone to idolatry, to unwittingly giving our allegiance to people and things other than God. So idols gain power over us. Over and over, we must ask God to free us. In the case of the idol Money, we must repeatedly choose to forgo purchases, to adjust our lifestyle and to give funds away. Jesus assures us that everything given up comes back to us through sharing in the community of God's people and, ultimately, through the eternal possessions of the world to come.

James provides further wisdom on the problem of covetousness. He identifies envy, ambition and greed as underlying causes of disorder and conflict in our lives. Ask yourself: Whom do I envy? What motivates my ambitions? What things do I crave? But, alas, these instincts are encouraged in our consumer culture and woven into its very fabric. To renounce them puts us at odds, at enmity, with most people and what they consider normal. Startlingly, James asserts that we cannot be friends with the world and friends with God at the same time. Like Jesus with the rich ruler, James calls us to submit ourselves humbly and wholeheartedly to the God who tolerates no rivals for our allegiance.

RESPONDING TO GOD

As you inventory your heart this week, and perhaps your assets and possessions, is there some choice that you could make to resist the seduction of idolatry and to reaffirm your full allegiance to Jesus? Is there something to give up or give away? Is there some way to practice contentment with what you have? Is there some means of trusting God for your needs?

Closing Prayer. O Generous Father, who feeds the ravens and clothes the lilies, free me this day from all anxiety about the things I have and the things I do not have; rather, help me stay focused on your kingdom so that I might grow rich toward you and store up treasure in heaven; through Jesus Christ your Son, who gave up everything for us. Amen.

Out of the Depths

Lent began with intimations of our mortality as sinful persons. The texts for this fifth week return us to those themes. Will a powerful man choose to forgive brothers who have betrayed him? Will a father receive back a rebellious son at the cost of his own humiliation? Will another son release his resentment and be reconciled to his family? Our sins set us against God and divide us from each other, in both cases leading to a kind of death. Out of the depths we cry to God. To the penitent he offers forgiveness and to the estranged he brings reconciliation. He can even bring the dead back to life, as in the story of Lazarus.

Approaching God. If you, O Lord, should mark iniquities, who could stand? But there is forgiveness with you so that you may be revered. With you there is steadfast love and great power to redeem; it is you who will redeem us from all our iniquities.

Presenting Myself. Out of the depths I cry to you, O Lord. Lord, hear my voice! Let your ears be attentive to the sound of my supplications!

Inviting God's Presence. Come, O Lord, I am waiting for you today; my soul waits and in your Word I put my hope. Amen.

LISTENING TO GOD

Psalm 130 (A); Genesis 42—45; Luke 15 (C); John 11 (A); John 12:1-8 (ABC); James 4:13—5:20

Simply and elegantly, **Psalm 130** expresses the themes of Lent. No matter how deep our discouragement, like Joseph in his prison we can cry out and the Lord will hear. No matter how sordid or shameful our sins, like David after his adultery we can cry out and the Lord will forgive. No matter how beyond hope our situation, like Mary and Martha at the death of their brother we can cry out and the Lord will redeem. Like Jesus on the cross, we cry out and then wait for God to act. I suggest praying this psalm daily this week, perhaps even memorizing it.

These next chapters of the Joseph story in **Genesis** read like a movie script. Work through them unhurriedly. Notice the details. Enter the drama. Feel the emotions. This is a story of reconciliation. But at first Joseph struggles within himself. The forgiveness does not come easily. With actions that border on a cruel joke, he manipulates his brothers. But in the end he relents and embraces them. The brothers are stunned; they never imagined that their treacherous deed could be redeemed or their lost brother restored. Do you find yourself anywhere in this story?

In **Luke 15,** Jesus tells a poignant story about a father and his sons. What precipitates the three-part parable? Notice the progression: the good shepherd searches for the one lost sheep of ninety-nine, the good woman searches for the one lost coin of ten, and the good father seemingly seeks the one lost son of two, except there is a twist. Are not both sons lost in relation to their father? In hiking up his robes and racing through the village, the father humiliates himself in order to embrace the disgraced young man as a son again. What a picture of God's seeking and reconciling love! But what about the resentful older son? Will he also respond to his father's initiating grace and reenter the family circle? By not finishing the parable, Jesus leaves this question in the air. Where does this story speak to you? Are you like either the prodigal or the dutiful son in your relationship with God? With the Pharisees, are you being challenged to embrace unconditionally someone you find offensive?

John 11. In the story of Joseph, the brother presumed dead is found to be alive; in the parable of the prodigal, the brother who runs off returns as if from the dead; but in the story of Lazarus here the brother is truly dead—and buried. Jesus responds with the final and most amazing sign in the Gospel of John. Read the story for all its dramatic tension. Observe Jesus' enigmatic behavior and cryptic words. Put yourself in the place of Mary and Martha, his close friends. Do *you* believe his words? Here is Jesus, shortly before his own death, raising his friend from that deepest, darkest of places.

John 12. Mary, partly in gratitude for her brother's return and partly in intuitive anticipation of Jesus' death, enacts an extravagant outpouring of costly perfume. Jesus is deeply touched and defends her against Judas's callous indignation. Meditating on this tender moment will begin to prepare you for the sober days of Holy Week just ahead.

The final sections of **James** remind us of the fleeting nature of our lives and their contingence on the will of God. We can be gone as quickly as the morning mist. And wealth is no protection, especially when gained by the exploitation of workers. If we are among those who suffer exploitation or injustice, we are called to patient endurance and to faith-filled prayer until the day comes when God raises us up from our depths.

RESPONDING TO GOD

As this season of self-examination and repentance nears its end, have you opened your deepest and darkest places before God? Is there any way in which you are far from God and ashamed to go to him? Is there anyone who has hurt you and is hard to forgive? With God's help, let this be a week of forgiveness and reconciliation, as befits your situation.

Closing Prayer. O Jesus, you who welcomed sinners and embraced the lost, I turn to ask once again your mercy and to receive once more your grace; help me to forgive anyone who has harmed me and to reconcile with those from whom I am estranged. I ask this, O Lord, in light of your steadfast love and your great power to redeem. Amen.

Palm Sunday and the start of Holy Week

Beginning the sixth Sunday in Lent

Hosanna! Hosanna!

Although aware of the danger, Jesus at a certain point "set[s] his face to go to Jerusalem" (Lk 9:51). Later, after he raises Lazarus, the threats against him intensify into a death plot. Now he arrives in the city with its teeming pilgrims and hostile Pharisees. As we rehearse his messianic entrance on this last Sunday of Lent, we sing with exuberance and we wince with foreboding. "Hosanna! Hosanna!" actually expresses both impulses—our joyous praise to the King and our humble plea for a Savior—since the literal meaning of *hosanna* is "Save, I pray." It is a fitting start to a holy week.

Approaching God. This is the day that you have made, O Lord; I will rejoice and be glad in it. I will give thanks to you, for you are good; your steadfast love endures forever!

Presenting Myself. Hosanna! Save me, O Lord! I thank you that you *have* answered me and *have* become my salvation. You are my God and I give you thanks; you are my God and I extol you.

Inviting God's Presence. Hosanna! Blessed is the one who comes in the name of the Lord—the righteous king of Israel, the ruler of all the earth. Hosanna in the highest!

LISTENING TO GOD

**Psalm 118 (ABC); John 12:12-19 (B); Philippians 2:5-11 (ABC);
Isaiah 42:1-9; 49:1-7; 50:4-11 (ABC); John 12:20-50 (ABC);
Hebrews 9:11-14 (ABC); 1 Corinthians 1:18-31 (ABC)**

For Palm Sunday:

Psalm 118 was most likely a liturgical psalm sung by the Israelites at the annual pilgrim festival to celebrate Passover. As you read it, conjecture which lines might have been spoken or sung by the various participants: the cantor, the "representative," the approaching pilgrims and the welcoming congregation. The psalm opens (and closes) with affirmation of God's goodness and steadfast love. A kinglike figure gives testimony of God's rescue from the siege of hostile opponents, echoing the ancient victory song from the crossing of the Red Sea (Ex 15). With the procession, this "king" reaches the gates of the city or temple where there is a liturgical exchange. The pilgrims are welcomed in with blessing and all proceed to the altar for worship. As you meditate, let this psalm give expression to your own trust in God for salvation (verses 14, 17, 25, 28). Further, let the psalm resonate prophetically as you picture Jesus entering Jerusalem for the Passover festival and the week of his Passion.

John 12. Each Gospel writer narrates Jesus' orchestrated entry into Jerusalem at the time of the Passover festival. Like the throngs of other arriving pilgrims, he is greeted with the familiar blessing from Psalm 118, but, as John indicates, the shouts for Jesus carry an enlarged meaning. Many hail him as if a king or Messiah, especially those abuzz with the report of the raising of Lazarus. Others wonder who he is. John leaves out the details of securing the colt but quotes Zechariah 9:9 to make the messianic implications clear. The Pharisees certainly get the point. All is coming to a climax now: the rising hopes of the people, the hostile opposition of the leaders, the intense emotions of Jesus (Lk 19:41-48) and his sober clarity about what he must undergo. Today, at the outset of this momentous week, add your own "hosannas" to the festive shouts and implicit prayers of the people. (See also Mt 21:1-11; Mk 11:1-11; Lk 19:28-40.)

Paul urges the **Philippians** to cultivate a mindset or posture that conforms to the contours of the Jesus Story. This shape is succinctly presented in what might be an early hymn: self-emptying, self-sacrifice and then trusting God for exaltation. Reflection on such large christological themes—incarnation, atonement, vindication, enthronement—places the events of this coming week into profound theological perspective. And moves us to bend *our* knees and voice *our* praise.

For Monday-Wednesday:

These three "servant songs" from **Isaiah** progressively portray a unique figure who brings redemption to Israel and to all nations, ultimately through his suffering. **Isaiah 42:** Verses 1-4 describe the servant and his universal mission; in verses 5-9 God speaks in confirmation to the righteous servant. Called and empowered by God, gentle with the weak but strong within himself, he will faithfully bring justice to the world. Through him, the Creator will inaugurate a new covenant of light and liberation. **Isaiah 49:** When the servant speaks, he understands himself to be called, shaped and protected by God. Despite discouragement, he rehearses his mission to restore Israel. God, in fact, enlarges the mission: light to the Gentiles and universal salvation. But abhorrence and subjugation come before recognition, suffering before glory. **Isaiah 50:** Finally, God helps his humiliated servant; he vindicates his faithful one. We too must be attentive and obedient to the voice of the servant, trusting in God's light rather than walking in our own self-kindled light.

In **John 12** we gain greater insight into Jesus' thoughts as he approaches his death. Some Greeks (Gentile proselytes) ask to "see" Jesus. Presumably they both meet him, and through his words they better understand him. What do you see? What is the connection between death and glory? What does it mean to lose our lives? John doesn't describe Gethsemane, but he does portray Jesus' anguish at the hour now upon him and his overriding desire for God's glory. Ponder the series of cryptic statements by which Jesus reveals the meaning of his death: the judgment of this world, the defeat of Satan, the drawing of all people, the light of eternal life. Will we believe these meanings this week? Will we walk in this light?

The writer of **Hebrews** makes an extended presentation of Jesus as both priest and sacrifice. In chapters 9 and 10, the contrast is drawn between the earthly tent (tabernacle, temple) and the true sanctuary (heaven itself), between the annual offerings by the Levitical priests and the once-and-for-all sacrifice by the eternal high priest, and between the blood of animals and the blood of Christ. In this Holy Week, we meditate on Christ as our high priest who offered himself as our sacrifice to purify our consciences from futile works so as to enable living worship.

Paul offers the **Corinthians** a soaring discourse on "Christ crucified" as the power and wisdom of God. He contrasts this with human prowess and intellect. How can a man nailed to a cross, that instrument of torture and execution, represent anything other than weakness and foolishness? Likewise those who believe in such a one? But Paul expounds the paradox. Do we not sometimes face similar bafflement or derision when others know of our deep faith, not so much in God but in Jesus and his literal blood? This week we once again embrace the weakness and believe the foolishness.

RESPONDING TO GOD

Let Palm Sunday mark your entry into this most holy of weeks. Indeed, it is a week to follow him and to enter vicariously into his suffering. In your heart, lay your coat in the road before him, wave your palm branch over him and shout your hosannas to him. This joyous welcome will help us remember over the rest of holy week that the suffering servant becomes the triumphant King.

Closing Prayer. Hosanna! Blessed is the one who comes in the name of the Lord! Blessed are you, my leader! My high priest! My holy sacrifice! My Savior! Hosanna in the highest! Amen.

6

The Paschal Triduum
Healed in the Dying

He was wounded for our transgressions,
crushed for our iniquities;
upon him was the punishment that made us whole,
and by his bruises we are healed.

ISAIAH 53:5

The liturgical year did not come into existence on a draughtsman's table nor does
it owe its existence to shrewd thinking and careful planning, but rather . . . it
emanates, and derives its growth, from a heart, a center. This heart of the
liturgical year is the passion and resurrection of Christ.

ADOLF ADAM

When I came into the simple worship space of our church for the Maundy Thursday service, immediately I was struck by the large cross suspended horizontally about fifteen feet above the seats near the front of the altar. It was the same design as the small cross that had hung behind the altar during Lent, but this one, made of rough mahogany, loomed ten feet tall and heavy. Ropes from the ends of the crossbar attached it to the ceiling; another rope affixed to the foot passed through a pulley on the ceiling and ran down taut to a wooden cranking device bolted to the left edge of the altar platform. Albert Pedulla, an artist in our community, had created this arrangement, this artistic piece—part visual, part performance, part liturgical—to enhance our experience of worship at the beginning of the Paschal Triduum, the Great Three Days.

Each year I eagerly looked forward to this service at All Angels' Church; I loved its symbolism, its poignancy, how it felt both choreographed and casual. The Bible readings rehearsed the original Passover (Ex 12), the practice of the Lord's Supper in the earliest churches (1 Cor 11) and the Last Supper itself, when Jesus washed his disciples' feet (Jn 13).

The sermon meditation that evening was titled "Weight of the Cross, Weight of Glory." The speaker quoted two contrasting invitations from Jesus: "Come to me, all who are weary and carrying heavy burdens" and "If any want to become my followers, let them take up their cross." One promised rest and the other presaged death. "What weighs on you tonight?" the speaker asked. "Sickness? Grief? Marriage strain? Work troubles? Debt? Loneliness? Death?" Then he rehearsed the weight that Jesus had borne, from his desert temptation to his Gethsemane anguish to his Golgotha stumble under the beam that would bear his dying body. All of this borne for us, for our healing, our salvation. Finally, he urged us to entrust ourselves, burdens and all, to Jesus, who wanted to wash our dirty feet, to serve us bread and wine, and to turn our "slight momentary affliction" into an "eternal weight of glory" (2 Cor 4:17).

Next we enacted an ancient ritual that echoed that long-ago Thursday evening. Along one end of the chapel six chairs were set out, and before each a basin of warm water rested. When ready, any of us could go to an empty seat and have someone gently wash and dry our feet. In turn we would kneel before the chair and wait to wash another's feet. Friends washed friends' feet, husbands washed wives', children washed parents', strangers washed strangers'. There was something sweetly touching, literally, about these sometimes tearful, sometimes ticklish, but always tender gestures of service and love.

Then we enacted the other crucial aspect of that original evening, the sacrament of Christ's body and blood. True, we did this every Sunday, but on this night, the night that Jesus was "handed over to suffering and death," the night on which he first said, "Take, eat, this is my body. . . . Drink this, all of you, this is my blood," it always carried added meaning.

As the last ones received a wafer into their hands and sipped from the silver chalice, the soft singing of choruses ended and the lights dimmed. We watched in silence as solemnly, ceremoniously the elements and vessels of communion were put away, the candles extinguished and removed, the altar cleared of all objects and stripped of its cloth, until nothing remained but the cold slab of a table, which was then slowly pushed back until it hit the rear wall with an ominous, resounding thud. With a series of rhythmic ticks on the rim of a drum, the music started and grew into a haunting, disconcerting, improvised mix of didjeridoo, violin and percussion.

Next, Albert walked forward and acolytes brought a bowl of water in which he washed his hands. The music diminished into those same drum-rim ticks, which gave way to rhythmic clicks of the crank as Albert slowly lowered the cross, ratcheting it down until it hung at the front of the altar five feet off the floor. Now we could see it more clearly: a T-shaped carpenter's cross, workable enough for a real crucifixion, leather straps dangling at the end of each beam, a boxlike footrest attached near the bottom of the upright. The music resumed. A parishioner holding an eight-inch spike walked slowly forward; as the music reached a crescendo, she dropped the spike into the hollow footrest in synch with a single boom of the drum. Silence. This scene was repeated. After the third spike, the boom echoed in the dark stillness. A single light shone on the forbidding cross. One by one, when we were ready, we went out into the night.

The next day when we came for Good Friday observance, there hung the cross, stark in the daytime. And there it hung during the silence of Holy Saturday. But on Easter, with the chapel bathed in light and all things restored, it was gone and a new version of the cross hung behind the altar. It was the same shape but smaller, made of finished, light maple, without straps and pedestal but with a new feature where the beams intersected: a carved sunlike image in bright gold, its rays like tongues of fire radiating in a nimbus of Easter glory!

THE HEART OF THE PASCHAL TRIDUUM

In keeping with ancient tradition, we treat the period from the Maundy Thursday gathering through the first Easter celebration as one uninterrupted service of worship. Together, these "three days" represent Pascha (Hebrew *pesach*, or "Passover"), the great saving act of God. As in the Exodus story of old when the blood of unblemished lambs protected the people from death so they could pass through the sea to freedom, so it is for us: Christ our Pascha, our Passover lamb, has been sacrificed for us; therefore we join the joyful feast (1 Cor 5:7-8).

Taken together, the death and resurrection of Jesus form the heart of the Christian Story, thus the Triduum represents the center of the Christian year. Think of the messianic prophecies we rehearsed in Advent, the mystery of the incarnation we pondered at Christmas, the revelation of the kingdom we studied during Epiphany. Then in Lent we readied ourselves for a dramatic endpoint, the cross, and in Easter we will celebrate an explosive new beginning, the empty tomb. Pascha then is both culmination and inauguration. At All Angels', these continuities were conveyed by the three crosses, similar in design but differing in purpose: the Lenten cross to prepare us, the Paschal cross to overwhelm us and the Easter cross to uplift us.

What is the meaning of the cross? On one hand we can find shelves and shelves of books parsing its theological complexity. On the other, young children "get it" and respond in genuine faith. Why Jesus had to die in this way, what God accomplished by it and how this changes our lives and destinies: these are mysteries into which the "angels long to look" (1 Pet 1:12). This is why inhabiting the Paschal Triduum year after year will not grow tiresome; each cycle allows us to plumb more deeply and embrace more fully the terrible glory of the cross.

We start with our dire condition, as Lent impresses on us each year. Left to ourselves we human creatures would be in trouble, huge trouble: we've offended God's holiness, we've violated his moral law, we've racked up a massive spiritual debt, we've betrayed his loving covenant with us, and we've completely lost our way in his world. We cannot extricate ourselves: there is no way to make it up to God, no way to avoid the penalties, no way to buy ourselves out of hock, no way to reverse the relational estrangement or find our way back home.

In rehearsing these descriptions of our predicament, we must not make the mistake of underplaying the solution from God's side, as if he needed only to calm down like an angry parent, commute our sentence like a lenient president, cover our debt like a wealthy relative, invite us back like a forgiving spouse or swoop in to extract us like a search-and-rescue pilot.

No, the cross forces a different reckoning. God's action comes at an incalculable cost, as the major biblical metaphors convey. But the biblical terms can become sterile for us; we need to crack open their doctrinal casings each year and let the meaning of what Christ has done spill out anew:

> *Atonement*: his blood sacrifice on our behalf
> *Justification*: his acceptance of our legal sentence
> *Redemption*: his payment to buy us out of slavery
> *Reconciliation*: his absorption of pain to restore relationship
> *Salvation*: his expenditure of life to rescue us from death

Oh, the depth of our sin, the height of God's love and the breadth of his abundant grace!

The apostle Peter, quoting the messianic prophecy of Isaiah 53, employs another metaphor for our salvation, this one from the realm of medicine: "He himself bore our sins in his body on the cross, so that, free from sins, we might live for righteousness; by his wounds you have been healed" (1 Pet 2:24). On the literal level, as Matthew 8:17 asserts, Jesus "took our infirmities and bore our diseases" when he cast out demons and cured sicknesses. And we too, at different times and in various ways, receive healing for our psyches and bodies as signs of his kingdom. But Isaiah's and Peter's use of this image represents a larger idea: full salvation through Christ's suffering and death. Spiritually we are infirm, diseased, ill—terminally so. The remedy is the confounding spiritual transaction whereby Jesus assumes the conditions of our sickness with its inevitable outcome so that we in exchange can receive his perfect health.

This then is the heart of the paschal mystery that we absorb in this holy Triduum: by his dying, we are healed.

PASCHAL TRIDUUM
IN CHURCH AND CULTURE

Originally, the first Christians recalled and celebrated the death and res-
urrection of Jesus in a single day—and they did so once a week, on the
Lord's Day! But it was not long, probably by the end of the first century,
before a more elaborate annual Pascha was established. In that sense, as
Laurence Stookey has suggested in response to the maxim that every
Sunday is a little Easter, "Every Easter is a great Sunday." With the
Council of Nicaea in 325, the date for Easter was fixed—the first Sunday
after the first full moon on or after the spring equinox of March 21—and
the threefold character of Pascha established. St. Augustine was the first
to refer to "the most holy triduum of the crucified, buried, and risen
Lord."

The Great Three Days begins at sundown on Thursday and concludes
at sundown on Sunday. The church's public liturgies over these days—
or, more properly, the progressive aspects of the one integral paschal
observance—can richly inform our personal meditation and worship as
well.

Maundy Thursday. The designation "Maundy" is thought to be an
English corruption of the Latin *mandatum*, as in the "new commandment" *(novum mandatum)* that Jesus gave his disciples on this night:
"Just as I have loved you, you also should love one another" (Jn 13:34).
An expression of this mandate by actual footwashing may be offered for
the whole congregation; more typically, in keeping with historical tradition, the act may be performed symbolically by the priest or pastor who
washes the feet of a small representative group, often numbering twelve.
Then follows the Eucharist. This is both a commemoration of Jesus' Last
Supper with his disciples and a sacramental participation in his sacrificial death; hence this paschal meal feels both wistful (imagining that
portentous evening in the upper room) and wondrous (appropriating
once again the spiritual meaning of his body and blood).

Then the transition to Good Friday begins. The stripping of the altar,
as described earlier, symbolizes the stripping of Jesus, his clothes and his
dignity, before the crucifixion. Often a veil is draped over the sanctuary
cross. Some churches also suspend use of the organ. Thus we have what

has been called "the fast of the eyes" and "the fast of the ears" during the Triduum. In recent decades many churches have adopted a service of *Tenebrae* (Latin for "darkness" or "gloom"), which has its roots in a monastic liturgy of the Middle Ages. A series of Scriptures and prayers is read, and after each reading one of a set of candles (often twelve) is extinguished, and the church lights progressively dimmed, until one lone candle flickers on the altar. The darkness captures our sadness and anticipates the noontime eclipse of light during the crucifixion. There is no closing blessing because the service will not conclude until the end of the first Easter gathering.

Good Friday. The term "Good Friday" may in fact be a corruption of an earlier English phrase, "God's Friday," in the same way that our "goodbye" is a contraction of the sixteenth-century phrase "God be with ye." Of course "good" also carries the idea of holy, as well as the affirmation that the day is beneficial because on it Christ secured our salvation.

Good Friday services vary in format depending on a church's tradition, but the historic liturgy usually includes three parts: the Service of the Word, the Solemn intercessions and the Veneration (or Adoration) of the Cross. For the first of these, the lectionary readings include the fourth servant song of Isaiah (Is 52:13—53:12), Psalm 22 ("My God, my God, why have you forsaken me?") and Hebrews 10:15-25. The account of the Passion is read from John's Gospel, and at the mention of "Golgotha" (Jn 19:17) the people stand and remain standing until the end.

The Solemn Intercessions derive from very early liturgical material, a form of "bidding prayer" in which the leader "bids" the people pray along certain lines: in this case for Christ's church throughout the world, for all the nations of the world and all in civil authority, for all who suffer any kind of affliction in body or mind, and for the response of all people to the gospel and love of Christ.

The Veneration of the Cross provides an opportunity for worshipers to meditate on the powerful significance of this symbol of our faith. Usually a large cross or crucifix is brought to the front of the church for contemplation. In addition to prescribed prayers or chants, worshipers may come forward to genuflect (bend or touch one knee to the ground) or touch the cross out of profound respect for what Jesus endured on such an instrument of torture. (Roman Catholics at this point celebrate Communion with elements pre-sanctified on Maundy Thursday, but most other traditions do not offer Communion.) Again the gathering ends without a final blessing.

Holy Saturday and the Easter Vigil. This day is also called Silent Saturday or the Great Sabbath, representing the silence of the tomb and the "rest" of Jesus after finishing his great work of redemption. In the early church, the Christians continued to fast and use the day for quiet contemplation of Christ's death and repose. They would gather in the late evening for a liturgy in which solemnity gave way after midnight (and sometimes not until dawn) to the festive celebration of Christ's rising. Now, most liturgical churches hold a Saturday evening service called the Paschal Vigil or the Great Vigil of Easter that follows an ancient pattern, as summarized below.

The Service of Light. The congregation gathers in the darkness, usually outside the church, where a small fire has been kindled. From it the leader lights the large Easter or paschal candle, three times singing "The light of Christ"; the people responding each time "Thanks be to God." Each worshiper holds a small candle, which is then lit from the new Easter flame. Like the Israelites following the pillar of fire in the wilderness, we process behind the candle into the church. There some version of the Exsultet, an ancient Easter proclamation hymn, is sung or said as the call to worship, beginning:

> Rejoice now, heavenly hosts and choirs of angels,
> and let your trumpets shout Salvation
> for the victory of our mighty King
> Rejoice and sing now, all the round earth,
> bright with a glorious splendor,
> for darkness has been vanquished by our eternal King.
> (Book of Common Prayer)

The Liturgy of the Word. Through a series of Scripture readings, with a responsorial psalm and prayer after each, we rehearse the history of God's creation and salvation prior to Christ:

Genesis 1:1—2:4: The creation
Genesis 7:1-5, 11-18; 8:6-18; 9:8-13: The flood
Genesis 22:1-18: The sacrifice of Isaac
Exodus 14:10-31; 15:20-21: The exodus
Isaiah 55:1-11: The offer of abundant life
Proverbs 8:1-8, 19-21; 9:4-6: The call of wisdom
Ezekiel 36:24-28: The promise of a new heart
Ezekiel 37:1-14: The valley of dry bones
Zephaniah 3:14-20: The restoration after exile

An Epistle and Gospel reading are also prescribed in the lectionary, but the placement in the liturgy varies by tradition. Romans 6:3-11 anticipates and interprets the rite of baptism, in which we are united to Christ in his death and raised with him to walk in newness of life. With the Gospel proclamation of Jesus' rising (from one of the Synoptics), the church is once again filled with light and resounds with "alleluias" and triumphant music. Some churches use creative forms of music, drama or visual images in conjunction with these readings.

Baptism and Eucharist. What a marvelous moment for someone to be baptized and to formally enter into new life in Christ! Similarly, what an occasion for all of us to reaffirm our own baptismal vows to renounce evil and die to sin, to follow Christ and obey his teaching, to love our neighbors as ourselves, to represent the gospel with our lives, and to seek the righteousness and justice of God's kingdom. Lastly, what a holy opportunity to gather around the table to experience the living Lord in the breaking of the bread and in celebration of the paschal feast!

Prominent in the Eastern Orthodox celebration, reports Sue Lane Talley, are the "joyous disruptions" by the shout of the celebrants—"Christ is risen!"—to which the people roar in return, "Indeed, he is risen!" The confidence, the hope, the joy represented by these acclamations can never be taken away, she affirms, and illustrates this by recounting a dramatic scene:

> When an "official" atheist propagandist of the Soviet state, years ago, was berating a crowd of Russians, he was silenced simply by the cry of one old man, "Christ is risen!" and the unanimous, jubilant reply, "Indeed, He is risen!"

THE CHRIST STORY IN
THE PASCHAL TRIDUUM

Each Gospel writer devotes a disproportionate share of his narrative to the final week of Jesus' life. This allows us to meditate on his last hours: his celebration of Passover with his closest disciples, his betrayal by his friend Judas, his middle-of-the-night arrest in Gethsemane, his abandonment by his followers, his sham trial before the Jewish elders, his letdown when Peter denies him, his expedient condemnation by wavering Pilate, his torture and mockery by the Roman soldiers, his weakened trudge out of the city to Golgotha, his prolonged and excruciating death and, finally, his hasty burial in a donated tomb. In three of these scenes, the particular action of Jesus points beyond the moment to a greater aspect of his mission.

An enacted parable. John alone portrays the extraordinary scene of Jesus washing his disciples' feet. They are completely caught off-guard and embarrassed as their leader takes the lowly part of a servant. Peter tries to refuse the gesture. Once again Jesus makes the point that his followers must be willing to serve one another in humility. But he's also showing his tender love for these men who have followed him so loyally. He handles each man's rough feet, looks into each pair of eyes and speaks some word of affection to each, including tormented Judas. More profoundly, Jesus' action amounts to a parable of the fullest expression of his love to come. He discards his clothes, girds a towel about his waist, kneels to humbly serve, and eventually resumes his robe and place, thus picturing the great self-emptying and future return to glory described in Philippians 2.

A memorial meal. Later the same evening, Jesus provides another picture of his love. This time he infuses the most common elements of the meal—the bread, the wine—with new meaning. They represent him. They do not stand for some general spiritual quality such as the wisdom of his teaching; rather they signify his physical being, his flesh, his blood. He will give his body to be beaten, his blood to be spilled. And he will do this for them. He will be the lamb killed as an atoning sacrifice. More than crafting a parable to teach a truth, Jesus here creates a ritual for his disciples to perform repeatedly as a memorial: a vivid means of remembrance and a vital means of participation. By this meal Jesus intends to make his presence known and to give us his life. O sweet Communion!

A dreaded emblem. Required by Jewish law to spend the night of Passover in or near Jerusalem, Jesus and his disciples make their way to a garden on the western slope of the Mount of Olives. Jesus asks Peter, James and John to join him in prayer as he experiences the weight of what is coming. He becomes "distressed and agitated," according to Mark, "deeply grieved, even to death." Jesus pleads with God to spare him this ordeal: "Abba, Father, for you all things are possible; remove this cup from me; yet, not what I want, but what you want" (Mk 14:36). What is this cup? Old Testament writers speak of the "cup of God's wrath," which the wicked are made to drain to the dregs in judgment (Ps 75:8; Is 51:17). As John Stott explains: "It symbolized neither the physical pain of being flogged and crucified, nor the mental distress of being despised and rejected even by his own people, but rather the spiritual agony of bearing the sins of the world, in other words, of enduring the divine judgment which those sins deserved."

"My God, my God, why have you forsaken me?" Is not Jesus' wail from the cross after three hours of darkness the cry of one who has drunk from a terrible cup? Is it not a cry of real dereliction? As German theologian Jürgen Moltmann piercingly proclaims, "This suffering from God himself is the real torment in Christ's passion. This godforsakenness is the cup which he is not spared." We can only grasp at the full meaning of this moment as Jesus quotes the beginning of Psalm 22, a psalm of suffering and lament.

These three scenes from the story of Christ, each represented by a commonplace object—a towel, a loaf, a cup—point to three dimensions of Jesus' identity: the suffering servant, the sacrificial lamb and the God-forsaken Son.

INHABITING THE PASCHAL TRIDUUM

The forty days of Lent have prepared us for inhabiting the three days of Pascha. With a heightened awareness of our sinfulness and mortality, with a sharpened sense of Jesus' determined movement toward the cross, we now vicariously, spiritually enter into his Passion and death, by which we are healed. How can we meaningfully do this?

Sanctify the days! Safeguard this Friday, Saturday and Sunday, set them apart, make them sacred. If possible, take Friday off from work. As feasible, keep Saturday a quiet day. By all means make Sunday festive. This will take some forethought and planning (recall the prodigious preparations we make for Christmas; does not Pascha also merit intentionality?). We need to get our shopping done, clean and prepare our homes, plan for our meals and activities, and make provision for our spiritual engagement with God. Participate in the worship services that make up the Pascha experience. Spend some time alone each day reading, meditating and praying.

Consider incorporating visual or tangible symbols into your observance. One Ash Wednesday at All Angels' we each were given a two-inch flooring nail to carry in our pockets or purses during Lent. Over the weeks we fingered it when drawing out coins or saw it when emptying pockets. In Holy Week the simple object took on even greater symbolic weight. You might also wear a cross around your neck, perhaps hidden beneath your clothing as a reminder to yourself. We can also place a cross in a noticeable spot within our home as a visual cue during Holy Week. Or we can locate reproductions of art such as Rembrandt's *The Crucifixion* or Michelangelo's *Pieta* to display in our living space. We can learn from the Eastern Orthodox, who make extensive use of icons in their meditations and worship. Or we can fill our homes with music appropriate to the Triduum, whether classical like Bach's "St. Matthew's Passion" or contemporary selections.

On Good Friday, many Christians engage in a devotional exercise known as the Stations of the Cross, a practice first developed in the fifteenth century. It's also called the Way of the Cross *(Via Crucis)* or the Way of Sorrows *(Via Dolorosa).* Worshipers proceed through a series of fourteen "stations" that represent particular moments in the Passion of Christ, stopping at each for a Scripture reading, a meditation and a prayer. In liturgical churches the stations are typically identified by an image or sculptural rendering. In the traditional form, eight stations correspond to biblical scenes and six to elements from tradition. In 1991,

Pope John Paul II introduced a variation of the practice called the Scriptural Way of the Cross that focuses only on biblical scenes.

Traditional Way of the Cross	Scriptural Way of the Cross
1. Jesus is condemned to death	1. Jesus in Gethsemane
2. Jesus takes up the cross	2. Jesus betrayed and arrested
3. Jesus falls the first time	3. Jesus condemned by the Sanhedrin
4. Jesus meets his mother	4. Jesus denied by Peter
5. Simon of Cyrene carries the cross	5. Jesus judged by Pilate
6. Veronica wipes the face of Jesus	6. Jesus scourged and "crowned"
7. Jesus falls the second time	7. Jesus takes up his cross
8. Jesus meets the daughters of Jerusalem	8. Jesus is helped by Simon of Cyrene
9. Jesus falls the third time	9. Jesus meets the women of Jerusalem
10. Jesus is stripped of his garments	10. Jesus is crucified
11. Jesus is nailed to the cross	11. Jesus makes a promise to the good thief
12. Jesus dies on the cross	12. Jesus entrusts Mary and John to one another
13. Jesus' body is removed and held by Mary	13. Jesus dies on the cross
14. Jesus is laid in the tomb	14. Jesus is laid in the tomb

In some versions, the list is adjusted to conclude with the resurrection. (In the Roman Catholic Church over the last twenty years, a Stations of the Resurrection has been taking shape: The Way of Light [Via Lucis] focuses on fourteen biblical incidents beginning with the raising of Jesus.) Finding a church that offers the Stations of the Cross, either in a special service or for individual devotion, could enrich your Good Friday experience.

HEALING IN ITS WINGS

Eugene Peterson, in his meditation on the salvation wrought by Christ in history, discusses back-to-back episodes in the Gospel of Mark: the call to self-renunciation and cross-bearing after Peter's confession (Mk 8:27—9:1) and the astounding transfiguration on Mount Tabor (Mk 9:2-9). He identifies the first as the "ascetic" dimension of salvation and the second as the "aesthetic." The denial and the abundance, the barren and the beautiful, the suffering and the glory. Or, in terms of the Christian year, the Lenten and the Epiphanic. Noting Peter's reaction in each case, he observes: "On the road, Peter tried to avoid the cross; on the mountain he tried to grab the glory." Not so for us during these three holy days.

The Paschal Triduum draws us to the very foot of the cross. We choose to stand there—no, to kneel there—in all of our spiritual sickness. Our leader, whom we love, suffers—"godforsaken, God-cursed"—on our behalf. We watch him die. We weep. Then we wait. Why? Because evil cannot triumph. Because death cannot hold him. Because the gloom cannot forestall the glory.

For those of us who revere his name, "the sun of righteousness shall rise, with healing in its wings" (Mal 4:2)!

New Covenant, New Commandment

On Maundy Thursday, the eve of Christ's death, we focus our attention on the Passover meal he shared with his disciples. On this night he instituted what would come to be called the Lord's Supper, in which the eating of bread recalls his broken body and the drinking of wine remembers his spilled blood. By his atoning death he inaugurated a new covenant with all who put their faith in him. Also, Jesus washed his disciples' feet in an extraordinary gesture of humble service, after which he gave them a new commandment or mandate (Latin *mandatum*, from which we get "Maundy"). So we think today about self-giving love, Christ's for us and ours for one another.

Approaching God. O Jesus, on the night of your betrayal, knowing that the Father had given all things into your hands and that you had come from God and were returning to God, you showed your love for your disciples by washing their feet, even as you would soon give your very life for them.

Presenting Myself. O Jesus, here are my feet to receive your washing, here are my hands to receive your bread and wine.

Inviting God's Presence. O Jesus, Teacher and Lord, as you have set an example, help me this day and all my days to love and serve those around me, even as you have loved and served us all. Amen.

LISTENING TO GOD
Matthew 26:17-46; John 13 (ABC);
1 Corinthians 11:23-26 (ABC); Psalm 117

In **Matthew 26** Jesus eats his final meal with his inner circle of disciples. Imagine being present. Jesus' talk of a betrayer casts a shadow over the supper. His symbolic equation of the bread with his body and the wine with his blood adds to the ominous and momentous tone. Consider the significance of "blood" and "covenant" in the context of a Passover meal (see Ex 12). But the disciples do not really understand. Even as he foreshadows his death, Jesus looks ahead to the messianic banquet of the kingdom of God. Likewise for us, when we participate in the Eucharist or Lord's Supper, we not only look back in remembrance, we look forward in anticipation. After the customary hymn (probably from Ps 115—118), the men retire to a garden on the lower slopes of the Mount of Olives. Here Jesus agonizes in prayer. He is torn between his fear of what lies ahead—physical death, yes, but even more the spiritual ordeal—and his desire to obey his Father. He needs the support of his friends, but they let him down. And he knows they will soon desert him in their own fear; one will deny even knowing him. Are you facing any situation in your life in which your anxieties are at war with your allegiances? Let the honest, earnest example of Jesus shape the way you pray in your situation. (Parallels: Mk 14:12-42; Lk 22:7-46.)

John includes two distinctive elements in his account of the Passover meal: the foot washing and the new command. Jesus washes his disciples' feet, including those of Judas, as an act of love. Notice the strong self-awareness that precedes his self-effacing action. What does he want his followers to understand? What does he want us to understand? After Judas goes out into the night, Jesus gives them the mandate to love one another as he has loved them. Reflect on how Jesus' simple act of service with the basin prefigures his enormous act of sacrifice on the cross (see Phil 2:5-11). This is how he has loved us. This is how we are to love one another, by laying down our lives for each other. This is what Peter intends to do for Jesus but proves unable, at least at this point in his life.

Paul in his letter to the **Corinthians** gives us the first written account of how the Lord's Supper came to be practiced as a centerpiece of community life and worship in the early church. It is the same for us each time we partake: an act of remembrance, an act of thanksgiving, an act of proclamation.

Perhaps Jesus and the disciples sang **Psalm 117,** the shortest of the psalms, after their Passover meal. Succinct but significant, this psalm invites all people into the praise of the one true God. Like Jesus and the disciples at the table, we remember God's steadfast love in the past and express faith in his future faithfulness.

RESPONDING TO GOD

This is a day to renew our commitment to the new covenant by which we are made clean and promised a seat at the great banquet to come. This is a day to renew our commitment to love our fellow believers with the serving, sacrificing love of Jesus.

Closing Prayer. Almighty Father, whose dear Son on the night before he suffered instituted the Sacrament of his Body and Blood: Mercifully grant that we may receive it thankfully in remembrance of Jesus Christ our Lord, who in these holy mysteries gives us a pledge of eternal life; and who now lives and reigns with you and the Holy Spirit, one God, for ever and ever. Amen. (Book of Common Prayer)

Wounded for Our Transgressions

On this holiest of holy days, we are transfixed by Jesus' suffering and death on the cross. We experience a range of emotions: sadness, reverence, astonishment, gratitude. Why? Because we understand that what Jesus endured was for us and instead of us. He was wounded for our transgressions and he died for our sins—by the will of the Father and by his own will. His suffering exceeds our imagination and his motive goes beyond our comprehension. We are simultaneously dismayed and grateful: his torn flesh makes us whole, his bruises bring us healing, and his death gives us life.

Approaching God. O Jesus, you are the pioneer and perfecter of our faith; for the sake of the joy that was set before you, you endured the cross, disregarding its shame, and you have taken your seat at the right hand of the throne of God. All praise to you!

Presenting Myself. O Jesus, I am fixing my eyes on you this day: I see you betrayed and arrested in the garden, I see you falsely condemned by Caiaphas and Pilate; I see you flogged and mocked by the Romans; I see you dragging the cross to Golgotha; I see you crucified and crying out; I see you dead and lying cold in a borrowed tomb. O Jesus, I am fixing my eyes on you.

Inviting God's Presence. O Jesus, you endured so much for my sake;

on this holy day, give me strength to run with perseverance the race that is set before me, that I may not grow weary or lose heart. Amen.

LISTENING TO GOD

Psalm 22 (ABC); **Isaiah 52:13—53:12 (ABC);**
John 18:1—19:37 (ABC); Hebrews 12:1-3

Psalm 22 is read on Good Friday because of its astonishing correspondence to Jesus' experience of crucifixion, beginning with the anguished wail of abandonment that Jesus cries out from the cross. The psalmist composed his poem in two parts: an excruciating lament for his lonely endurance of hostility and abuse (verses 1-21) and a joyful celebration of his deliverance (verses 22-31). Notice in the first part how the psalmist alternates descriptions of his horrific predicament with affirmations of the God who seems so far away. The deliverance comes dramatically in verse 21. Then the psalmist fulfills his vow to testify before the assembly. See how the praise and celebration takes on universal proportions: the ends of the earth, all the nations, the generations not yet born. Use this psalm today in your meditation on Jesus' suffering, even as it reminds you of the great deliverance that follows.

In this fourth and final servant song, **Isaiah** completes the revelation of this unique figure and his unprecedented role. As we study this extraordinary passage, it yields deep and poignant insight. The first section presents a paradox: peoples and their rulers are astonished that someone once so marred and dehumanized has become so highly exalted. The next four sections explain. The servant grows up as an unremarkable man whose eventual afflictions lead people to despise and reject him. But his afflictions are not judgment from God; no, he suffers on account of our transgressions and endures punishment in our stead. He is the Lamb of God. He willingly and purposefully submits to his own execution. All of this is the will of the Lord so that many would be made righteous by the sacrifice of one, the righteous one. Therefore the servant will be exalted!

John, like each of the Gospel writers, gives prominent attention to the arrest, trial, execution and burial of Jesus. Each Gospel contains its own distinctive details. As you read and reread John's account or the others', seek to enter the story. Imagine yourself as one of the disciples, say, John or Mary Magdalene or Peter. Try even to imagine Jesus' experience. Such meditations will impress on you his complete humanity—his bodily pain, his emotional distress—but also his unique identity. We can ponder but not fully comprehend the enormity of what happens this day: the suffering of God for the salvation of humanity and all creation. (Parallels: Mt 26:47—27:61; Mk 14:43—15:47; Lk 22:47—23:56.)

The chapter preceding **Hebrews 12** recounts the exemplary faith of the many heroes in the history of God's people: Abel, Noah, Abraham, Sarah, Moses, Rahab, Samuel, David and those unnamed ones who did great deeds or endured great suffering. Our greatest model, however, is Jesus. When we consider how Jesus willingly endured crucifixion, that most shameful and cruel means of capital punishment, we gain strength and courage for our own struggles in the midst of a sin-distorted and unjust world. And we remember the joy that lies ahead!

RESPONDING TO GOD

This is a day, in the words of the famous hymn, to "survey the wondrous cross on which the prince of glory died" and to contemplate a "love so amazing, so divine" that it "demands my soul, my life, my all."

Closing Prayer. Almighty God, we pray you graciously to behold this your family, for whom our Lord Jesus Christ was willing to be betrayed, and given into the hands of sinners, and to suffer death upon the cross; who now lives and reigns with you and the Holy Spirit, one God, for ever and ever. Amen. (Book of Common Prayer)

Holy Saturday

Descended to the Dead

Today we think about Jesus lying dead in the tomb. His bruised and lacerated body, hastily wrapped, rests on a stone slab, cold and stiff in the darkness. Correspondingly, our hearts remain quiet. Yet in the spiritual realm, all is not quiet. A doctrinal tradition going back to the earliest era of the church declares that Christ, in the time between his death and his resurrection, descended to the dead, that is, to the precincts of hell itself, in order to liberate a throng of people. The "harrowing of hell," it is sometimes called. This doctrine is stated in the creeds—"He descended into hell"—and depicted in icons. Many Protestants dispute or downplay it because of the ambiguity of the scriptural texts. But whether Christ "recaptures" captives (see Eph 4:7-10) or simply proclaims the victory of the cross, some momentous event in the grand drama of God's redemption takes place on this holy sabbath. Christ's redemptive power plumbs the darkest depths before ascending to the brightest heights. Holy Saturday recognizes this wondrous mystery and invites us, quietly, to enter it.

Approaching God. Mysterious and merciful Father, you were the refuge for your Son even as his body lay dead in the silent tomb; I exult and rejoice in your steadfast love, for you deliver your beloved from the hands of the enemy and redeem all who commit their spirit into your hands.

Presenting Myself. My times are in your hand, O Lord; deliver me from the hand of my enemies, even death itself; let your face shine upon your servant and save me in your steadfast love. Amen.

Inviting God's Presence. Holy Father, as I remember today the silent tomb of your Son my Lord, let me know the presence of your steadfast love that never ceases and your mercies that remain ever new; great is your faithfulness, therefore I will hope in you. Amen.

LISTENING TO GOD
Psalm 31 (ABC); Lamentations 3:1-33 (ABC);
John 19:38-42 (ABC); 1 Peter 3:18—4:11 (ABC)

In **Psalm 31** David vividly expresses his predicament (besieged, afflicted, scorned, sorrowful) and desperately pleads for protection and deliverance. Repeatedly he affirms his trust in the steadfast love and goodness of God. He believes he will be rescued. Into God's hands he commits his spirit, his life. Compare David's posture of faith to that of Jesus, whose life rests in his Father's hands even as his body rests in the sealed tomb. In what ways do we need to heed David's closing exhortation: love the Lord, be strong, take courage, wait for the Lord who preserves the faithful?

Lamentations is attributed to Jeremiah and reflects the crushing reality of Judah's exile. God's judgment has fallen, the city and temple have been destroyed, and now the people languish in a foreign land. It is a kind of death. Jeremiah uses images of darkness, captivity and sickness. He laments their condition. Each chapter is an acrostic poem (each verse beginning with a successive letter of the Hebrew alphabet), and chapter 3 has 66 verses, three for each letter. Embedded at its heart (Lam 3:22-24) is a declaration of hope in God's steadfast love, his ever-new mercies and his great faithfulness. In just such hope, Jesus underwent death—a darkness, an exile—so that we could live by hope in the midst of our own afflictions and fears.

John gives a simple account of Jesus' burial. Joseph of Arimathea secures permission from Pilate to take the body. Nicodemus, the Pharisee who had sought out Jesus clandestinely (Jn 3), steps forward to help. Members probably of the Jewish ruling body, both had become secret disciples. Now they act openly. Joseph, a wealthy man, wraps and places the body in a new garden tomb—his own we learn from Matthew, who adds further details about the women who observed the burial and the Jews who arranged for a seal and guard. No more can be done as the sabbath begins, so Jesus lies unattended in the stone tomb. (See also Mt 27:57-66.)

Peter writes his epistle to Christians who face persecution and suffering. Earlier he has cited the example of Christ who, when suffering abuse, did not return abuse but entrusted himself to God (1 Pet 2:21-25). In chapter 3 he returns to Christ's suffering, "the righteous for the unrighteous," but now speaks of an activity of Christ beyond his "death in the flesh": his proclamation to the "spirits in prison" (1 Pet 3:19). This idea is echoed in 1 Peter 4:6, which says that the gospel was proclaimed "even to the dead" so that they might live in the spirit as God does. These texts are enigmatic, but from the beginning, they yielded an understanding that Jesus, alive in the Spirit, somehow descended to the realm of the dead, the abode of Satan, to accomplish something that was part of his great victory on the cross and vindication through the empty tomb. Theologians debate the interpretations: souls from Noah's time or souls from all of time? An offer of salvation or a dramatization of judgment? A plundering of Satan or a victory proclamation? Either way, we do well to pay attention to Peter's admonitions to live in light of all that Christ has done.

RESPONDING TO GOD

This is a day for quiet awareness of Christ's death and continued contemplation on its meaning for our lives.

Closing Prayer. O God, Creator of heaven and earth: Grant that as the crucified body of your dear Son was laid in the tomb and rested on this holy sabbath, so we might await with him the coming of the third day, and rise with him to newness of life; who now lives and reigns with you and the Holy Spirit, one God, for ever and ever. Amen. (Book of Common Prayer)

7

Easter
Heartened in the Rising

*The resurrection means rebirth out of impotence and indolence
to "the living hope," [which] means a passion for life
and a lived protest against death. . . . It lives from something different—
from the superabundance of God's future.*

JÜRGEN MOLTMANN

*The resurrection of Jesus is a sign of God's purpose and power
to restore his creation to its full stature and integrity. . . .
In the aftermath of Gethsemane, we catch a scent of Eden. . . .
The resurrection is like the first day of a new creation.*

ALISTER MCGRATH

The hero dies, and with him dies the dream. The people lose heart and
their hopes evaporate. Defeat looms. But then, by some miracle, the hero
returns to life. Amazed, overjoyed, the people take heart. With renewed
courage, they face their foes. Victory ensues.

So many stories and films tap into this archetypal plot. Take for example the heroes of three popular fantasies. In *The Lord of the Rings*, the
wizard Gandalf the Grey returns from the netherworld as Gandalf the
White, powerful wielder of light. In *The Matrix*, flatlined Neo is brought

back by Trinity's love and faith in him as the one who will free humanity from digital enslavement. In *Harry Potter and the Deathly Hallows*, when Harry sacrifices himself to save his friends, an avenue opens for him to resume his life and defeat his nemesis Lord Voldemort.

As readers or moviegoers, we get caught up in such stories. We feel dismay at the hero's death, and despair in the aftermath, but eventually we exult at the surprising return and enjoy satisfaction in the final triumph. The stories are mythic. Truly. They tap into the myth of the hero who journeys into deadly trials and returns transformed, or they draw on the ancient myth of a dying and rising god. Because they are archetypal, such stories work for us, over and over. They stir something deep in our consciousness.

But these are imaginative tales. What about the real world? Do we experience anything like these tumultuous reversals in our own lives?

I suppose we get inklings whenever we hear accounts in which someone is thought to be dead, or as good as dead, but subsequent events turn things about. Think of news stories where someone after a long period of diminishing hope is rescued from a mine collapse or found after going missing or freed from a kidnapper. Dramatic, moving. And how much more so if you or I were directly involved in such a story—the desperate spouse, the anguished roommate, the despairing parent—and the good news came to us? What joy, what relief, what waves of gratitude!

At the time of this writing, Ingrid Betancourt, a popular French-Colombian politician, was daringly rescued by Colombian commandos after six years of captivity in a remote jungle. With many others she had been held hostage by FARC, a leftist guerilla group. President Nicolas Sarkozy of France embraced Betancourt when she landed in Paris: "Dear Ingrid, we have been waiting for this so long. All of France is welcoming you back today." A happy nation, yes, but think of the immense joy of her family and friends. It was as if she had come back from the dead.

That same month, *Time* magazine featured Nelson Mandela on its cover in honor of his ninetieth birthday. This too put me in mind of the "return of the hero" motif. Half a life earlier, in 1962, when Mandela led the struggle against apartheid in South Africa and the hopes of the oppressed people rested on him, he was arrested and imprisoned for life.

He languished on Robben Island for twenty-seven years, cut off while the injustices of apartheid intensified. But then, against all odds, he was released from prison in 1990, an event broadcast around the world. The people were ecstatic, their hero had returned. He wielded his popularity and power to steer the nation toward peace rather than violence. For this Mandela received the 1993 Nobel Peace Prize. The next year he won the first-ever multiracial elections for president. During his five-year term he led South Africa down a path of truth, justice and reconciliation. Arguably, Nelson Mandela saved his nation.

But when we come to Jesus, it is a different story. It is not an account of deathlike disappearance by way of imprisonment or disease followed by a resurrection-like reappearance. No, the death is real and the corpse is buried. Real, too, is the man who returns, fully alive and demonstrably embodied. Nor is it a myth in the sense of a nonhistorical narrative that conveys a great human or spiritual truth. No, the Jesus story takes place in real time and space. As C. S. Lewis famously explained:

> Now as myth transcends thought, incarnation transcends myth. The heart of Christianity is a myth which is also a fact. The old myth of the Dying God, without ceasing to be myth, comes down from the heaven of legend and imagination to the earth of history. It happens—at a particular date, in a particular place, followed by definable historical consequences.

The followers of Jesus watched their leader die. They were disheartened—confused, afraid, grief-stricken and drained of hope. Despite Jesus' enigmatic statements about rising after three days, they had no expectation of his immediate resurrection. So when the women reported the tomb empty and word of his appearances reached them and, finally, they touched their risen friend themselves, joy eclipsed disbelief. They experienced what Tolkien calls *eucatastrophe*, the sudden turn of events that brings a disastrous story to an unexpectedly good conclusion, which "pierces you with a joy that brings tears."

"The Birth of Christ is the eucatastrophe of [human] history. The Resurrection is the eucatastrophe of the story of the Incarnation," asserts Tolkien, adding that "this story begins and ends in joy." As we inhabit

Easter, the eucatastrophe of the Jesus story, we too are filled with joy and deeply heartened.

THE HEART OF EASTER

A myriad of themes could fittingly occupy our spiritual attention over the seven weeks of this season, starting with the sheer fact of the resurrection and what it says about Jesus. But for the sake of simplicity, we will focus here on three ideas at the heart of our Easter experience.

Faith in the triumph of God. Jesus, by his crucifixion and resurrection—the one paschal event—overcame sin, death and evil. The resurrection of Jesus validated his teachings and vindicated his messianic claims. As the stunning implications sank in over time, his followers proclaimed him both Lord and Messiah. Here is how Peter put it when he first preached to the Jerusalem public some fifty days after Jesus rose:

> Jesus of Nazareth, a man attested to you by God with deeds of power, wonders, and signs that God did through him among you . . . this man, handed over to you according to the definite plan and foreknowledge of God, you crucified and killed. . . . But God raised him up, having freed him from death, because it was impossible for him to be held in its power. (Acts 2:22-24)

In Christ God triumphed. We could pile verse upon verse to make the point: "When he had made purification for sins, he sat down at the right hand of the Majesty on high" (Heb 1:3) or "Death has been swallowed up in victory" (1 Cor 15:54) or "He disarmed the rulers and authorities and made a public example of them" (Col 2:15).

The first disciples knew a deep connection with Jesus. He had called them, taught them, empowered them, indeed had loved them; in response they had joined his company, embraced his message, undertaken his mission and shared in his final meal. They were united with him in a spiritually mysterious way, they "in him" and he "in them." Through this union, they realized in retrospect, they had participated, somehow, in his dying and rising. By faith they shared in his triumph. And so do we! Our champion won a great battle for us. We've been freed from captivity to join an exuberant new exodus. Easter becomes for us each year an extended victory dance, a jubilee celebration.

Hope for the resurrection of the body. Yet we remain painfully aware of the suffering and sorrow in our lives. We all die. Even apart from headlines about insurgencies and famines, we can think of friends or family members who are facing their own frailty or mortality. Bright-spirited Ruth comes to my mind, a friend ravaged in her battle with endocrine cancer, or my elderly relative Alvah, his mind sharp but his body debilitated by stroke, or aging Phillipa, whose mind is mostly gone. We also remember the dear ones we've lost already to that pernicious thief death. What does Easter mean for them? Or, for that matter, for us who cannot escape the same end? Just this, as Paul put it: "He will transform the body of our humiliation that it may be conformed to the body of his glory, by the power that also enables him to make all things subject to himself" (Phil 3:21).

We believe in the resurrection of the body. Not the immortality of the soul as the Greeks did, not the dissolution of self in nirvana as Buddhists do, not the repeated cycle of reincarnation as Hindus do, not the progression of spirits to tiers of heaven as Mormons do and certainly not the abrupt end of conscious being as materialists do. No, our expectation is for new bodies fit to live in a new cosmos. Paul declares this mystery to the Corinthians: "We will not all die, but we will all be changed, . . . in the twinkling of an eye, at the last trumpet. . . . The dead will be raised imperishable, and we will be changed" (1 Cor 15:51-52).

This is our confident hope, not only for ourselves—our persons, our bodies—but also for our world. As Paul reveals elsewhere, "The creation itself will be set free from its bondage to decay and will obtain the freedom of the glory of the children of God" (Rom 8:21). At the end of time, God will renew all things, which includes primates and planets, human beings and human culture, and even spiritual entities about which we know so little. The resurrection of Jesus is the first fruits of this glorious new creation.

Love as the mark of the transformed heart. The victory already gained and the renewal sure to come have bearing on our lives now. Resurrection means the presence of Christ within us and the power of Christ to change us. Paul makes another sweeping announcement: "If anyone is in

Christ, there is a new creation: everything old has passed away; see, everything has become new!" (2 Cor 5:17). Paul grasped the practical implications of this spiritual reality: there are aspects of our character and behavior that need to be killed off, in keeping with Christ's death, and aspects that need to be brought to life, in keeping with his resurrection. We bear responsibility in this, but it is not simply a matter of our own willpower; paradoxically, another power is also at work, a transformative power: "You have stripped off the old self with its practices and have clothed yourselves with the new self, *which is being renewed* in knowledge according to the image of its creator" (Col 3:9-10). By his Spirit God gradually transforms us to be like his Son, an image marked supremely by self-giving love.

New spiritual freedom by virtue of God's triumph, the promise of new bodies in the world to come and the grace to grow into new and more loving selves—these gifts flow from the "super-abundance" of the resurrection and absorb us during the Great Fifty Days of Easter.

EASTER IN CHURCH AND
CULTURAL TRADITION

Within a century of Jesus' rising, the church had established the extended Easter season. But why fifty days? First, because the enormity of the resurrection invited a lengthy celebration. Second, Easter lasted until Pentecost (Greek for "fiftieth"), the day when the Holy Spirit was poured out. Third, the period corresponded to the Jewish spring harvest festival, which began with the Feast of Unleavened Bread (the barley harvest) and ended with the Festival of Weeks, or Shavuot (the wheat harvest). Note that over time, the focus of Shavuot shifted to commemorate the giving of the law on Mount Sinai. Finally, the numbers carried symbolic significance: seven (seven weeks of seven days) signifies fullness, as in the days of creation, and fifty suggests liberation and joy, as in the Year of Jubilee called for every fifty years in Leviticus 25.

In these earliest centuries, the church observed Easter by increasing the use of "alleluias" in worship and correspondingly suspending all fasting and the practice of kneeling in prayer. These gestures emphasized the standing of believers as those raised with Christ. Thus, the second-century church father Tertullian described Easter as "a most joyous space." Similarly, in the third century, Athanasius, bishop of Alexandria, wrote that Easter "extends its beams, with unobscured grace, to all the seven weeks of holy Pentecost."

Since the fourth century, the church has given formal significance to the first eight days, or octave, after Easter. The paschal celebration continues through special liturgies. During this week in ancient practice, the newly baptized gathered daily in white robes to be introduced to the mysteries of the faith, sometimes called the *mystagogical catecheses*. Easter Week still carries added significance in liturgical churches today. Easter Monday is a national holiday in many countries of Roman Catholic heritage. Eastern Orthodox believers, conceiving of the seven days after Easter as one continuous day, refer to the time as Bright Week (or sometimes Renewal Week). The liturgy is joyfully *sung* each day. Also, the doors of the iconostasis, the central icon wall or stand, are left open all week signifying the stone rolled back from the tomb.

The origin of the word *Easter* (in German, *ostern*) is disputed. Some postulate a derivation from the name of the Anglo-Saxon spring goddess Eostre; others propose a derivation from "east," the direction from which the sun rises. These tenuous associations with the fertility of springtime or the rising sun are possible, but not especially compelling. Stookey laments the English term as unfortunate over against the more widespread equivalents that derive from the theologically potent *pascha*: "In other tongues we find: *pasques*, Italian; *pâques*, French; *paaske*, Danish; *paasch*, Dutch; *pasg*, Welsh; and *pascua*, Spanish."

Of course, in the northern hemisphere Eastertide does coincide with spring, which means the rejuvenation of the landscape contributes to our reflection on new life. Likewise the tradition of Easter eggs. The egg symbolizes new life ready to break forth from a tomblike shell. Eggs may well have gained their Easter prominence in conjunction with the ending of the Lenten fast from dairy observed in parts of the church. Indeed, in the Orthodox tradition, worshipers bring baskets of eggs to the Easter service and the priest blesses them. Another Eastern custom is to give red-colored eggs to one another with this exchange of greetings: "Christ is risen!" and "He is risen, indeed!"

By tradition, each Sunday of Easter has a theme that is reflected in the lectionary readings. For example, the second is known as Thomas Sunday because it features the account of Jesus graciously accommodating his skeptical disciple. The third, Meal Sunday, focuses on the Emmaus story where Christ was known in the breaking of the bread. The fourth, Good Shepherd Sunday, draws its emphasis from the imagery of Psalm 23 and Jesus' description of himself in John 10. The fifth, I Am Sunday, derives from Jesus' declaration of himself as the source of life: "I am the vine." The sixth and seventh Sundays thematically relate to the ascension, which falls on the Thursday between them, and draw from Jesus' preparatory discourse and prayer on the eve of his death (Jn 14—17). The eighth Sunday, Pentecost, brings to closing crescendo the Great Fifty Days.

THE CHRIST STORY IN EASTER

This final chapter in Jesus' earthly life begins on the first day of the week after his execution. We don't know exactly what happened during the early morning hours, but Matthew conveys the enormity of it by speaking of a great earthquake and a dazzling angel; the stone is rolled back and the guards are scared stiff. The narrative picks up with the women arriving at the burial ground before first light. The tomb stands open and empty. Confusion ensues, as one might imagine and as the variations in the four Gospels imply: statements from strangers (men? angels?), messages hastily conveyed, disciples racing to see for themselves, conjectures about the body (moved? stolen?), tears, excitement, disbelief, hope. Certainty would not come until Jesus began to make his appearances.

Appearances. The Gospels tell us little about Mary Magdalene. She was one of a group of women, healed by Jesus, who followed him and supplied financial support. Jesus had expelled seven demons from her (Lk 8:2-3); otherwise Mary Magdalene is not mentioned until Christ's crucifixion. With a few other women she watches near the cross as he dies and observes as he is buried. Then she is the first to see him alive and to touch him. The encounter is tender (Jn 20:11-18), and the fact that Jesus chooses to reveal himself to her is theologically meaningful. Culturally inferior as a woman, spiritually suspect as a former demoniac and legally barred from being a witness, Mary nonetheless becomes the first herald of the resurrection, even if the men will have a hard time accepting her word.

There would be a string of such encounters, each poignant and powerful in its own way. He appears suddenly to the fearful disciples locked inside a house, patiently to one of his skeptical followers, incognito to two dispirited travelers going to Emmaus, appetizingly to seven tired fisherman on the lakeshore and belatedly to a fiery Pharisee dead-set against him. Jesus meets each one at his or her point of need. He allays the disciples' fears, he satisfies Thomas's doubts, he stirs up a fire in disheartened Cleopas, he forgives Simon Peter's threefold denial, and he changes Saul of Tarsus from persecutor to apostle. He meets and changes us as well.

Commission. On these occasions, whether in Galilee or Jerusalem, Jesus continues to instruct his followers about the kingdom of God and to impress on them their mission as its messengers. Starting in Jerusalem, then going to the rest of Israel and eventually expanding to all nations, they are to bear witness to him—his life, his teachings, his death, his resurrection—so that people everywhere become his followers and enter his kingdom. They will be acting on his God-given, resurrection-vindicated authority. Not only that, they will be acting in his God-given, resurrection-demonstrated power, which will be given to them in a baptism of Spirit. They are to remain in Jerusalem and wait for this gift.

Ascension. Having commissioned his followers, Jesus is ready to ascend into heaven. As his disciples watch, he is lifted up and lost to sight in a cloud. They stand there agape, staring up into the sky even as two men in white robes appear out of the blue to declare that one day Jesus will return in the same manner. Of course, Jesus did not spatially rise to some location in space; rather, he reentered the spiritual realm where God dwells. All of our language for this event is analogical since the ascension entails as much mystery as the incarnation, the atonement and the resurrection.

In truth, these mysteries belong together as one grand movement of God for the salvation of humanity and creation: Christ Jesus emptied himself of divine prerogative in order to take on our flesh, he further humbled himself by submitting to execution on a cross and he descended to the lowest place, the realm of the dead; but God raised him up from death and exalted him to the highest place, the realm of glory (Phil 2:5-11). C. S. Lewis suggests this analogy:

> One has the picture of a diver, stripping off garment after garment, making himself naked, then flashing for a moment in the air, and then down through the green, and warm, and sunlit water into the pitch black, cold, freezing water, down into the mud and slime, then up again, his lungs almost bursting, back again to the green and warm and sunlit water, and then at last out into sunshine, holding in his hand the dripping thing he went down to get. The thing is human nature; but associated with it, all nature, the new universe.

"When it says, 'He ascended,' what does it mean but that he had also descended to the lower parts of the earth?" teaches Paul, then concludes, "He who descended is the same one who ascended far above all the heavens, so that he might fill all things" (Eph 4:9-10).

The ascension represents the completion of God's work in Christ incarnate and, proleptically, the completion of Christ's work in us as we are "raised up . . . with him and seated . . . with him in the heavenly places" (Eph 2:6). Too often we treat this event and its meaning as little more than a coda to the main score—very few churches celebrate Ascension Day—but we neglect this rich doctrine to our own impoverishment.

INHABITING EASTER

As with Christmas, Easter is both a day and a season. If celebrating the twelve days of Christmas is a challenge, keeping the fifty days of Easter is ten times harder. There's no catchy song ("On the first day of Easter . . ."), no decorations to keep up a while longer and, from most of our churches, no encouragement or support. Easter Sunday? No problem. We know how to make this day special: nice outfits, arrangements of lilies and other bright flowers, a heightened liturgy full of alleluias, triumphal music with added brass, cheerful exclamations of "He is risen!" all around. But by the next Sunday we have usually moved on to our next topic or returned to our old routine. This is unfortunate because the implications of the resurrection—its explosive force—call for an extended period of exploration and appropriation. Easter cannot be done in a day.

But by all means make the most of the inaugural Sunday! First, if you belong to a nonliturgical church, you might consider participating in the Easter Vigil at a nearby Episcopal or Lutheran or Catholic church. As described in chapter six, the Great Vigil is an extended liturgy observed on Saturday night to rejoice in Christ's rising as the culmination of the Paschal Triduum. Or, you might choose to attend one of the Easter sunrise services sure to be offered in your community.

If you gather for worship at your usual hour, find appropriate ways to heighten your expectation beforehand and continue your celebration afterward. I like to rise early on Easter morning, shower and dress, then sit quietly in the room where we've placed fresh flowers and set out the family Easter basket with its goodies and gifts (for example, for many years it included a new semiprecious stone egg for our son). I read one of the Gospel accounts of the resurrection and maybe 1 Corinthians 15 or Romans 8; I pray; and then I put on some joyous music, usually the Easter portion of Handel's *Messiah*. After church, we like to share a meal with family and friends, either in one of our homes or at a restaurant. Following my period of fasting, this dinner always provides particular delight.

In line with tradition of the Easter octave, the days immediately after the Feast of the Resurrection most readily lend themselves to purposeful reflection. The drama of Holy Week remains vivid in our minds and the exuberance of Easter Day carries over. Let the exhilarating shock of the resurrection itself continue—the great reversal, the death of death, the shattered door, the harrowing of hell, the beautiful metamorphosis, the explosion of life! No metaphor measures up, no superlative suffices. As Madeleine L'Engle once exclaimed about Easter, "It is almost too brilliant for me to contemplate; it is like looking directly into the sun; I am burned and blinded by life." Speaking practically, we will want to shape our schedule and commitments for this week so as to safeguard time for contemplation and personal worship.

However, the spirit of this week and all of Eastertide is not obligatory but rather celebratory, joyful and, as the Orthodox remind us, bright. Easter is one long feast! It is fitting that Easter should last longer than Lent, that the feasting should exceed the fasting. A great way to maintain this perspective is by, well, eating. Why not host a different group of friends for dinner each week during the season? Or go to lunch with a group of fellow worshipers after church each Sunday? Or maybe just allow yourself some culinary treats that you normally limit in your diet, as a delightful reminder of God's life-giving grace?

In recent years Charlene and I have set up some visual reminders to help sustain our awareness of the season. For example, I place a simple, painted wooden egg on the top of my dresser so that I see it each morning as I get dressed. Also, we have chosen a spot at the bottom of our stairway for hanging small prints or photographs that represent the current liturgical season. For Easter, we put up an intaglio print titled "Lazarus," an abstract image of a series of receding rectangular openings. It daily reminds us of the empty tomb. Here is one more small gesture we've chosen: fresh flowers on the table throughout this season of new life. Along with such visual symbols, we can also inhabit Easter through music.

Some of us may want to get outdoors into the resurgence of the spring landscape. Even when we lived in upper Manhattan, many a Sunday afternoon Charlene and I would walk to nearby Fort Tryon Park to stroll in the heather garden or look out over the Hudson River at the soaring Palisades on the New Jersey side. For many years the novelist and poet Wendell Berry has spent Sunday mornings taking a meditative walk in the woods near his farm in northern Kentucky. He has captured his observations and musings in a series of "sabbath poems" published as *A Timbered Choir*, as in these lines, which dramatize the resurrection:

The earth shakes, grinding its deep stone;
All night the cold wind heaves and pries;
Creation strains sinew and bone
Against the dark door where he lies.

The stem bent, pent in seed, grows straight
And stands. Pain breaks in song. Surprising
The merely dead, graves fill with light
Like opened eyes. He rests in rising.

The Feast of the Ascension of Our Lord falls on the fortieth day of Easter, always the Thursday of the sixth week. As noted earlier, this is a much-neglected day in the church calendar, although some parishes commemorate the feast on the following Sunday. Even if there is no service to attend, we can "sanctify" the day in our personal lives. Perhaps we could take a day or half a day off from work to spend some hours in retreat. Or we could invite a small group of friends for an ascension dinner and creatively rehearse and celebrate the completion of Christ's work on our behalf. Or we could simply find a spot outdoors—a park, a hillside, a body of water—some place where we can see the open sky and clouds, to sit for an hour of meditation on the exaltation of Christ to glory.

Finally, as for the transforming of our hearts, a simple gardening analogy may help. Our plants don't grow to full flower or fruition overnight. We tend the soil, we prune, we water and feed, and then we wait patiently. God causes the growth. Jesus taught exactly this: "I am the vine, you are the branches. Those who abide in me and I in them bear much fruit" (Jn 15:5). We abide by prayer and worship and reflection and obedient action. Indeed, the devotional resources of this book are intended for this very purpose. As we remain in vital connection with Jesus over these weeks, we could choose an aspect of ourselves, just one, in which we desire change, in which we want to love God more fully or love others more selflessly. It could be less doubt and more faith. Or less procrastination and more discipline. Or less irritability and more patience. Or less lying and more honesty. Or less indulgence and more generosity. Whatever. Ask Jesus to renew this one part of your "self" over these weeks; ask that the fruit would benefit others and honor the Father.

LORD OF THE DANCE

During Lent we humbly confront our own mortality as sin-prone humans. For three days in Holy Week we plumb the depth of love that would suffer death in our stead. On Easter Sunday we sing amazed "alleluias" in light of Christ's triumph. In the weeks of the Easter season we allow the power of the resurrection to charge us with hope for our new bodies and to change us within our new selves. In this spiritual choreography—turning, dying, rising—we are humbled, we are healed and we are heartened.

As we rehearse these movements, especially if we are young, healthy, thriving and optimistic, sometimes the meaning of the resurrection seems more a beautiful idea than an urgent necessity. But the days will come when we no longer rehearse but utterly depend on these truths. This was the case for Malcolm Muggeridge, the famous twentieth-century English journalist and media personality. In his seventies, with growing awareness of his failing body and waning years, he described waking in the night with a sensation of being suspended between life and death:

> [I] see my ancient carcass, prone between the sheets, stained and worn like a scrap of paper dropped in the gutter, muddy and marred with being trodden underfoot, and, hovering over it, myself, like a butterfly released from its chrysalis stage and ready to fly away. . . . Yet in the limbo between living and dying, as the night clocks tick remorselessly on, and the black sky implacably shows not one single streak or scratch of gray, I hear those words: I am the resurrection and the life, and feel myself to be carried along on a great tide of joy and peace.

These are the words of our risen hero. This is the hope we hold against the darkness. This is the vast tide that carries us for the Great Fifty Days and beyond. This is the rising by which we are heartened and our feet set in jubilant motion. As Wendy Wright exults, picturing Jesus dancing on his grave: "All in our lives that is limiting, sorrowful, or dead becomes the dance floor on which we celebrate our Easter joy."

*   *   *

Preview of devotions in Easter. These devotions celebrate the rising of Jesus from the grave and explore the various ways this good news enlivens our hearts and heartens our lives. Even though Easter Sunday is the third day of the Paschal Triduum, its devotional material is included here. Then each week we look at a different appearance of the risen Jesus. On the Thursday of week six we mark the ascension of Jesus. In the final week we find ourselves waiting with the company of disciples for the promised Holy Spirit.

The lectionary calls for readings from Acts during Easter, but I have deferred these accounts of the early church to the first two months of Ordinary Time to better preserve the order of the story. (Paul's encounter with Christ, which we read in week five, is the one exception.) The devotions include two extended sections of Scripture. First, in the upperroom discourse of John 14—17, Jesus says many things to prepare his disciples; we will follow what must have been their postresurrection learning curve. Second, in Ephesians Paul explores the theological and practical implications of God's redemptive plan in Christ, giving us a fitting guide to the transformed life.

The Feast of the Resurrection of the Lord
Beginning Easter Sunday

He Is Risen Indeed!

Alleluia, Christ is risen!" "He is risen indeed!" This bold announcement and jubilant response should reverberate each day of the Easter octave. We exult as in a great victory. We shout as at hearing good news. We sing as if brimming with joy and hope. The narrative from John's Gospel tells the Easter story, along with the anticipations found in the Old Testament and the glorious implications spelled out in the New Testament. Live inside the resurrection story this week and let its power and joy inhabit you.

Approaching God. Alleluia! Lord Jesus Christ, you are the first and the last, you are the living one; you were dead and now you are alive forever and ever, and you have the keys to death and Hades. Joyful praise to you, risen Lord! Alleluia!

Presenting Myself. Alleluia! With glad confidence I enter your presence. I rejoice in your salvation and give thanks for your steadfast love; I celebrate your triumph over death and sing of your mercies forever. Alleluia!

Inviting God's Presence. Alleluia! Living Lord, show yourself to me this day; may I hear you speak my name so that my heart will be full of joy and my lips quick to announce the news: He is risen indeed! Alleluia!

LISTENING TO GOD

Psalm 118:1-2, 14-24 (ABC); **Isaiah 25:6-9 (ABC)**;
John 20:1-18 (ABC); Acts 10:34-43 (ABC); Revelation 1:1-18

We turn again to **Psalm 118,** as we did on Palm Sunday a week ago. Now we read a portion of the psalm in light of the resurrection. It could very well express the thoughts of the risen Lord, a song of victory and vindication, a jubilant thanksgiving after being rescued from death. It may also give expression to our thoughts as we recall resurrection-type experiences in our own lives. It certainly invites us to marvel that the rejected stone has become the cornerstone and our mourning has been turned to gladness. We rejoice in the greatest of all the days the Lord has made.

Isaiah 25:6-9 expresses themes that resonate with the potent implications of Christ's resurrection. Isaiah describes a messianic banquet on the mountain of God: the richest foods and the choicest wines provided by God for all people. God not only supplies; he also removes: he destroys the shroud of death and he wipes away the tears of each person. This scene anticipates the resurrection of the dead inaugurated by Christ. It is a picture of shalom in the kingdom of God. It is an Easter vision of life in the presence of the living God.

We read **John's** account of the empty tomb and the first appearance of the risen Lord. Mary Magdalene (and other women, according to the Synoptic Gospels) arrives at the grave before dawn only to find the tomb vacant. She assumes the body has been moved and runs to tell Peter and John. They race to the tomb and in the growing light discover only grave clothes. In what sense do you think John begins to believe? Later Mary returns, overwhelmed by consternation and grief. Follow this remarkable scene. Meditate on the moment of Mary's recognition. How arresting, how tender, when Jesus simply says her name. Why does Jesus tell her, "Do not hold on to me"? Immediately Jesus sends her as a witness— an apostle to the apostles! What would his words mean to them? What about Jesus from this passage impresses you and leads you to love and worship him?

Always on Easter the church reads **Acts 10,** the concise proclamation of the gospel by Peter to those gathered in the home of Cornelius. In effect, we fast-forward to the understanding of Jesus' life, death and resurrection that the apostles developed over the following weeks and months. Read it several times, carefully. Here is the story of Christ we have been following since Epiphany, which reaches its climax with the rising of Jesus from the grave.

In the opening chapter of the **Revelation to John,** we flash forward even further. The aged apostle John experiences a vision, an epiphany. He is given to see again the risen Christ. But this is different from those initial bodily appearances in Jerusalem; this is an encounter with the Lord in his glorified state, more like the transfiguration years before. First, in verses 1-8, examine the ways that John speaks of the triune God, especially how he neatly capsules the story of Christ: his life (the faithful witness), his death and resurrection (the firstborn from the dead), and his ascended glory (the ruler of the kings of the earth). From verses 9-18, meditate on the seer's vision. Let the images and metaphors ignite your imagination. Put yourself in John's shoes—which you might want to immediately remove! In this vision, this "one like a Son of Man" describes himself in terms of resurrection and victory over Death and Hades.

RESPONDING TO GOD

This is a week for wonder and worship: the one who was dead is now alive forever and ever! Find ways to focus your attention on the resurrection each day this week. It is like a display of spiritual fireworks dazzling us with each burst: Life! Power! Love! Triumph! Transformation! Hope! Joy!

Closing Prayer. Almighty God, who through your only-begotten Son Jesus Christ overcame death and opened to us the gate of everlasting life: Grant that we, who celebrate with joy the day of the Lord's resurrection, may be raised from the death of sin by your life-giving Spirit; through Jesus Christ our Lord, who lives and reigns with you and the Holy Spirit, one God, now and for ever. Amen. (Book of Common Prayer)

Not Seeing, Yet Believing

As we enter the second week of the Great Fifty Days, we remain full of joy and gratitude, which Psalm 150 helps us to express. John tells about the disciples' first postresurrection encounters with Jesus, who speaks peace to their fearful hearts and reassurance to their doubtful minds. Centuries later, Jesus' words also pronounce a blessing on all who, while not seeing firsthand, yet believe. Likewise, Paul wants the Corinthians (and us) to have full confidence in the resurrection of our bodies after death and wants the Ephesians (and us) to fully know the immeasurable greatness of God's power for those who believe.

Approaching God. Blessed be you, O God, who raised to life our Lord Jesus Christ, for you have blessed us in Christ with every spiritual blessing in the heavenly places, just as you chose us in Christ before the foundation of the world to be holy and blameless before you in love. Amen.

Presenting Myself. Lord Jesus Christ, in you alone do I believe and on you alone have I set my hope, so that I might live always for the praise of your glory. Alleluia! Amen.

Inviting God's Presence. God of our Lord Jesus Christ and Father of glory, give me a spirit of wisdom and revelation this day as I come to know you and the greatness of your resurrection power. Amen.

LISTENING TO GOD

Psalm 150 (C); **John 20:19-31 (ABC);**
1 Corinthians 15:1-34; Ephesians 1

Short but emphatic, **Psalm 150** concludes the Psalter with a rousing exhortation to praise the Lord. It calls on humans to praise God on the earth; it calls on angels to praise him in the heavens. We praise God for all that he has done by his power—especially his raising of Jesus—and we praise him for all that he is—his surpassing greatness. We praise him with music and movement, with lilting harps and crashing cymbals, with exuberant dance and quiet devotion. In celebration of the resurrection, we call on all creation to praise the Lord!

John reports that Jesus appeared to his disciples on the night of his resurrection. They have locked themselves in a room. Suddenly, startlingly, Jesus stands among them. Imagine the moment. What does he say and what does he do? At a certain point, Jesus commissions them— and, by implication, us. Meditate on the profound implications of his simple words (verse 22). What might they mean for our lives? Then Jesus breathes on them ("in-spires," the same word used in Gen 2 when God breathes into the dust-formed human the breath of life). He imparts the Holy Spirit, at least in some measure, since the full baptism awaits Pentecost. As they are sent to proclaim and embody the gospel, those hearers that embrace it will know forgiveness while those who reject it will remain under judgment. Compare the first scene to the second, in which Jesus gently confronts Thomas in his doubts. Consider Thomas's chastened declaration—he is the first to acknowledge Jesus as God. Finally, take heart from the beatitude in verse 29!

Paul presents a lengthy argument to the **Corinthians** in response to the disbelief of some regarding the resurrection of the dead. They accept that Christ was raised but not that his followers will be raised. Perhaps they object to the idea of long-dead corpses rising, or perhaps they hold a highly spiritualized view of the afterlife in which bodies are unnecessary. It's not clear. At any rate, Paul argues the logical inseparability of the two resurrections, Christ's and ours. In verses 1-11, he reiterates the core of the gospel, which includes the resurrection and appearances of

Jesus. Then in verses 12-34, he makes his case. Can you follow the three parts of his argument? No resurrection of the dead would mean no resurrection of Christ (verses 12-19). But since Christ has been raised, others must surely follow (verses 20-28). Finally, if there is no resurrection of the dead, why do we behave as we do (verses 29-34)? (Scholars don't know for sure what is meant by the practice of receiving "baptism on behalf of the dead.") No, we put our lives on the line because we believe that Christ's rising is the first fruits of a great harvest in which not only we, in our transformed bodies, but all aspects of reality will come fully under the rule of God.

We begin this week a survey of **Ephesians** that will continue throughout Easter. Chapter 1 sets the stage with a powerful exposition of all that God has done for us in Christ and an expansive prayer for all who put their faith in Christ. Paul blesses the God who has blessed us. The blessings belong to us because we belong to Christ. Note all that Paul declares to be true of us. Since Christ is now in the "heavenly places," the spiritual realm, so too is our inheritance. Again, note how Paul describes what is promised. Pause even now to give thanks for what God has destined. Next, absorb the meaning of Paul's prayer in verses 15-23. Not only does he want us to see and understand the riches of our spiritual blessings, he wants us to gain confidence in God's power to bring them fully about; the power that raised Jesus and exalted him to his right hand is the same power that is at work in us.

RESPONDING TO GOD

Rehearse with gratitude this week all of the blessings—the spiritual inheritance—secured for you through Jesus' death and resurrection. As you dwell on these, also dwell *in* them; let them shape your self-awareness and influence your actions this week.

Closing Prayer. With your disciple Thomas, I declare to you, Christ Jesus, with awe and allegiance: you are my Lord and my God! Amen.

Our Eyes Opened

In these weeks of Easter we celebrate that Jesus is alive and present in the world by his Spirit. But sometimes he seems absent from our own lives. At times we do not experience his presence, we lose sight of his promises or we doubt the depth of his love. The experience of Cleopas and his companion on the way to Emmaus reassures us this week that even when beset by disappointment and grief, Christ comes to walk with us. We are never orphaned, never abandoned, never alone. In time and often in unexpected ways, our eyes are opened to God's presence and we are given to comprehend once again his immeasurable love for us in Christ. So we ask God to open our eyes this week to see him anew.

Approaching God. I extol you, O Lord, for you raised your Son from death and through him defeated the powers of evil; he cried to you for help and you restored him to life; I sing praise to you, O Lord, and give thanks to your holy name.

Presenting Myself. You have turned my mourning into dancing; you have taken off my sackcloth and clothed me with joy, so that my soul may praise you and not be silent. O Lord, I will give thanks to you forever. Amen.

Inviting God's Presence. O Jesus, my risen Lord, as you did for your disciples in Emmaus, open my mind to your Scriptures and my eyes to your presence this day, that I may act on your Word and take joy in your grace. Amen.

LISTENING TO GOD
Psalm 30 (C); **Luke 24:13-43 (AB);**
1 Corinthians 15:35-58; Ephesians 2

In **Psalm 30** David rejoices at his recovery from a grave illness; it's as if he has come back from the dead. In verses 6-10, he admits to a previous posture of overconfidence but now acknowledges that when God "hides his face," he is undone. So he renews his dependence on God's gracious help. Consider how this psalm resonates with Jesus' experience of forsakenness, death and deliverance. In the same way that David sings praises to God, whose anger lasts a moment but whose mercy endures a lifetime, we cannot remain silent at the resurrection of our crucified Lord: mourning turns to dancing, weeping to joy and dismay to thanksgiving.

Luke 24 describes how, on the day of his resurrection, Jesus joins two despondent disciples walking to the village of Emmaus. However, "their eyes are kept from recognizing him." Jesus is present but they are unaware. Still, Jesus listens to their implicit prayers (their hurts, their questions, their needs) and teaches them about himself from the Scriptures. At the table he breaks bread to feed them, and then their eyes are finally opened. How does this story speak to you? Do you sometimes question Jesus' presence in your life? Do your prayers sometimes seem futile or your Bible reading sterile? Don't let Jesus walk off down the road. Invite him to stay with you. Look for him in the Word and in the Sacrament. Ask him to make his presence known.

We turn again to **1 Corinthians 15** and the second half of Paul's great discussion of resurrection. Now he addresses not if but how the dead are raised and in what form. Paul begins with two analogies: seeds and bodies. How do these analogies convey both continuity and transformation? Paul then applies these ideas to resurrection. The "seeds" of our physical bodies become transformed into spiritual bodies, which have a new glory because they are imperishable. Just as Christ was raised with a body "fit for heaven," so too will we receive new bodies—in the image of his! Paul concludes his teaching in soaring fashion. Meditate on the transformation that is promised so that we can inherit the kingdom of God. We are caught up in the great victory of Christ that ultimately swallows death itself. Alleluia!

Through Paul's letter to the **Ephesians** we continue to explore our new life in Christ. In 2:1-10, Paul speaks of our spiritual state before our union with Christ in the starkest of terms: death. What does this mean? Do we believe this is true for our friends who reject Jesus? "But God . . ." rings the glorious counter to our helpless condition. We regain life, we are raised up and we are seated in glory: in Christ. What moves God to do this for us? His rich mercy, his great love, his immeasurable grace. What are the implications of such grace for your life this week? In the second half of chapter 2, study how Christ's death and resurrection bring peace and reconciliation to estranged and hostile groups who now share in the "one new humanity" created in Christ.

RESPONDING TO GOD

In this season, we want to be especially alert to the presence of the risen Christ. If these are days of need for you, trust that he walks alongside you and invites you to pour out your heart to him. Read his Word with your heart open to his burning revelation. Then look for him in the breaking of the bread at the table of empowering grace.

Closing Prayer. O God, whose blessed Son made himself known to his disciples in the breaking of bread: Open the eyes of our faith, that we may behold him in all his redeeming work; who lives and reigns with you, in the unity of the Holy Spirit, one God, now and for ever. Amen. (Book of Common Prayer)

Come Have Breakfast

The Lord as shepherd is the traditional theme for the fourth Sunday of Easter. The lectionary readings include the familiar Psalm 23 ("The Lord is my shepherd"), John 10 ("I am the good shepherd") and John 21 ("Feed my sheep"). In the latter, Jesus literally feeds his followers by the Sea of Galilee. There's a bit of mystery about this account. First, Jesus gets his disciples' attention with a miracle, but afterward he simply invites them to come have breakfast. The men are pretty sure it's Jesus, but they don't want to ask him directly. Imagine the camaraderie around the charcoal fire: the hungry men, the welcome food, the questions asked, the stories recalled, the shared laughter and later the exchange that restores Peter. This is our risen Lord, wholly other yet still human, mysterious yet down-to-earth, forever one of us even as he is forever over us.

Approaching God. Lord God, Creator of all things, it is your plan to make known your great wisdom to the rulers and authorities in the heavenly places through your church, in accordance with your eternal purpose carried out in Christ Jesus our Lord, whom you raised from the dead for your eternal glory. Amen.

Presenting Myself. To that end, Lord God, I approach you boldly this day, confident by faith in the boundless riches of your glory; at the same time I come humbly, like a sheep to its shepherd, in need of provision and protection from your hand.

Inviting God's Presence. Risen Lord, good and gentle shepherd, renew my soul this day and lead me in right paths for your name's sake. Amen.

LISTENING TO GOD

Psalm 23 (ABC); John 10:1-30 (ABC);
John 21:1-19 (C); John 14 (A); Ephesians 3

Meditate on **Psalm 23** long enough to get past its familiarity. Try reading it in light of the resurrection. God provides what we need bodily and spiritually. He walks with us in places of darkness and danger and reassures us in our fears of death. How have you experienced such care of late? Where do you need it? Think of the last section as a portrayal of the ultimate triumph over all enemies of goodness and grace, including death itself. We will feast at the sumptuous table of God and enjoy his presence forever. The Eucharist is our repeated foretaste of this resurrection feast.

In **John 10,** Jesus likens people to sheep and calls himself a good shepherd. What makes Jesus a good shepherd? What is it like to be one of his "sheep"? What do you make of his words about laying down his life and taking it up again? Jesus knows us intimately and he wants us to know him, to recognize his voice. If we follow him, he will watch over us and lead us into life abundant and eternal.

In **John 21,** we have the third appearance of Jesus to his disciples in John's narrative. At Simon Peter's restless behest, seven of them go fishing, but they catch nothing. At dawn Jesus calls to them from the shore with some fishing advice. At first they don't know that it is him, but the huge haul of fish triggers recognition (compare Lk 5:1-11). Why do you think Peter plunges in and swims to shore? Just imagine the scene: Peter sheepishly standing before Jesus, dripping wet, still ashamed of his earlier threefold denial yet anxious to be reconciled. I suspect he doesn't know what to do with himself—perhaps this is why he single-handedly pulls in the net and, apparently, counts the fish. But Jesus puts them all at ease with his invitation to breakfast (loaves and fishes!). Soon, he pulls Peter aside for a painful but reconciling exchange (note how he calls him "Simon," not "Peter" the rock). Jesus extends grace after Peter's failure and recommissions him to shepherdlike leadership. In what ways can you identify with Peter? What about Jesus moves you today?

John 14 begins our focus on the discourse between Jesus and his followers on the eve of his death, which we will read in light of the resurrection. Here Jesus speaks of his leaving and returning, of a coming absence and a new kind of presence, of a home he will prepare for them and a home he will make within them, of love for his Father and love for his followers, of troubled hearts and transcending peace. Trace the promises and mark the commands. Let this passage both encourage and challenge you. Jesus is our way to the love, truth and life of the Father; because he lives, we also will live.

Paul, in **Ephesians 3,** describes his God-given mission to make known a mystery, the good news of God's grace offered to all humanity. Through the multiethnic, international, transhistorical church, God intends to display his universal wisdom as revealed in his resurrected Son. Take time to reflect on this overwhelming mandate to us as members of the church. Then consider Paul's prayer for us: for spiritual empowerment, for the indwelling presence of Christ, for comprehension of the dimensions of God's love, indeed, for the fullness of God filling our lives. Don't be reticent to pray these things for yourself.

RESPONDING TO GOD

Do you need the Lord to shepherd you in some way? Do you need to have a conversation with Jesus, as it were, about some failure for which you feel guilty or ashamed? Is your heart troubled over something? Do you need to be strengthened in your inner being? Let this be a week for turning to God and finding grace.

Closing Prayer. Now may the God of peace, who brought back from the dead our Lord Jesus, the great shepherd of the sheep, by the blood of the eternal covenant, make us complete in everything good so that we may do his will, working among us that which is pleasing in his sight, through Jesus Christ, to whom be the glory forever and ever. Amen.

Clothed with the New Self

In this fifth week of Easter, we focus on the transformation of our lives. First, we read of Jesus' appearance to Saul "as to one untimely born." Saul is heading in one direction, full of hostility toward Jesus, but when confronted by the risen Christ, he is radically changed and sent in the opposite direction. Later he explains to the Ephesian church that all of us must take off the "old self," like stripping off dirty garments, and be clothed with the "new self," which is being created in the image of Christ. How does this work? There is mystery here, but according to Jesus the answer lies in staying vitally connected to him, the true vine.

Approaching God. Praise the Lord! Let all in the heavens—angel hosts, shining stars, towering clouds—praise your name, O Lord; for you commanded and they were created. Let all on the earth—sea and mountain, wind and snow, wild lands and wildlife, men and women—praise your name, O Lord; for your name alone is exalted. Your glory surpasses heaven and earth. Praise the Lord!

Presenting Myself. Lord Jesus, true source of all life, sustain me like a vine sustains its branches; for only by staying close to you can I lead a life worthy of you, only by abiding in you can I bear fruit pleasing to you.

Inviting God's Presence. Spirit of God, nourish my soul and renew my mind this day, so that my true self would grow more like Christ, full of truthfulness, goodness and love. Amen.

LISTENING TO GOD
Psalm 148 (C); **Acts 9:1-22 (C)**; John 15; **Ephesians 4**

We turn to **Psalm 148,** another of the praise psalms at the end of the Psalter. First it calls on the inhabitants of the heavens in descending order—from angelic to cosmic to atmospheric—to praise their Creator. Then the psalm calls on the denizens of the earth in rough ascending order—from ominous depths to surface weather to forests and fauna to humans great and small—to praise the God of glory, who rescues his faithful and draws us close to himself. Let this litany help you to praise the living king of creation.

In **Acts 9,** Luke records the dramatic conversion of Saul from persecutor to preacher. The risen Jesus appears to Saul not in a body that could be touched but with blinding light and audible voice. Then through a matching pair of visions, God orchestrates Saul's encounter with Ananias, by whom he is healed and baptized. Note the three days of darkness and fasting reminiscent of Jesus' time in the tomb. Your own conversion may not be as dramatic as Saul's, but let this story prompt reflection on the ways God has intersected your life, turning you around and sending you in new directions. Give thanks to him who by resurrection power can transform lives, even those dead set against him. (For Paul's own testimony about his conversion, see Acts 22:1-16 and 26:1-23.)

In **John 15,** as Jesus makes his way with his friends toward the garden where he will be betrayed, he uses the grapevines at hand to teach them how they must live in a world of hostile opposition. Jesus is our source of spiritual life and vitality. We can be fruitful in our lives only if we stay vitally connected to him. How do we do this? By absorbing his teaching as nourishment. By doing what he commands, most especially loving one another sacrificially. By prayer, Scripture, worship and sacrament. By community, service and witness. And ultimately by his sheer grace. May Jesus' joy be yours as you abide in him this week.

With **Ephesians 4,** Paul (his new name signifies his transformation) makes the turn from the theological to the practical, from doxology to doing. Study it in sections. The overall point is to lead a life worthy of the great calling already unfolded in the letter, a calling that entails unity among believers. The risen and ascended Lord gives gifts to each of us and gifted leaders to all of us. These help us to grow to our full spiritual stature and equip us for service in the church and world. We are to imitate Christ by giving ourselves in love. Such life requires the ongoing transformation of our selves. Note the Spirit's part in this and note our part. We must choose to put off the behaviors and attitudes of our old selves and put on the marks of our new ones.

RESPONDING TO GOD

Are you wearing some part of your old self like a piece of shabby clothing? Choose one tendency of yours to discard this week and a corresponding quality to wear instead. In choosing to keep Christ's Word in this respect, you can ask him for the spiritual help you need, confident that he will grant it since it is his will that you bear fruit that befits someone he has chosen as friend.

Closing Prayer. Lord Jesus, thank you for choosing me and changing me, even as you chose and changed your servant Paul; continue your transforming work in me this day and this week as I seek to stay close to you, my source of love and joy. Amen.

The Ascension of the Lord

He Is Exalted!

On Thursday of this week, the fortieth day after Easter Sunday, we mark the ascension of Jesus, the mysterious departure of his physical presence from the earth. Jesus had spoken of this before he died (see Jn 16). At least three themes are in play here: the return of Jesus to his Father and to sovereign glory, the impending arrival of the promised Holy Spirit, and the commissioning of Jesus' followers to proclaim the gospel throughout the world. These final two weeks of Easter invite us to worship the ascended and enthroned king, to rejoice in his presence by the Spirit and to remember our calling to be witnesses. He is exalted!

Approaching God. Lord Jesus Christ, you are the most high, you have ascended into heaven, you sit enthroned at the right hand of the Father and you are sovereign over all the earth: praise to you, Lord Christ, joyful praise to you!

Presenting Myself. Lord Jesus Christ: you are exalted, I am abased; you shine with glory, I shy away; you are holy, I am not holy: Lord, have mercy on me as I kneel before you this day, have mercy on me as I behold you, risen and enthroned. Amen.

Inviting God's Presence. Father of Glory, by your Spirit enlighten the eyes of my heart that I may know you this day. Amen.

LISTENING TO GOD

Psalm 47 (ABC); Luke 24:36-53 (ABC); John 16:4b-33; Ephesians 5:1—6:9; Ephesians 1:15-23 (ABC)

Psalm 47 can be read as a kind of coronation song, but the king in view is not the mere ruler of a small nation; no, this king is God himself. His hand may be evident in Israel's history (verses 1-4) but the psalm quickly takes on universal scope. In the end, the peoples and leaders of all nations come to him and the might of all militaries belong to him. He is king of all the earth; by all means—applause, music, poetry—let us praise him!

In this **Luke** passage we return to that first night after Jesus' resurrection. The bewildered disciples are startled when Jesus appears. But fright turns to incredulous joy as Jesus proves his physicality. He opens their minds to understand the Scriptures (oh, that he would do that over and over for us) and rehearses his messiahship (suffering, death, resurrection, proclamation). This message offers forgiveness and transformation for all who are willing to turn to Jesus. Though he has withdrawn from us bodily, he is present with us spiritually, so we worship him with joy and bear him witness in the world.

In **John 16** we continue to eavesdrop on the intimate conversation between Jesus and his friends on the night of his arrest. Some of Jesus' words allude to his death and resurrection, some to his coming (incarnation) and going (ascension). There will be both sorrow and joy. Trace all that Jesus promises: sending of the Advocate, guidance into truth, unquenchable joy, direct access to the Father, peace in the face of persecution, and courage. Ask Jesus to take you deeper into the experience of one of these spiritual provisions this week.

We continue in **Ephesians 5** to absorb Paul's instruction on living in light of the risen and exalted Christ. We have choices to make about how we will live and with whom we will identify. Paul especially warns against sexual promiscuity, moral compromise and idolatrous greed. He calls us to wake up, to rise from our own deathlike condition and be bathed in the light of the resurrection. Our lives can be full of what is good and right and true, full of the very Spirit of God. Where are you prone to the wrong kind of inebriation: Sexual desire? Ambition? Greed? Unwholesome entertainment? Social attention? Alcohol? Power? (Note in 5:21—6:9 how Paul calls for mutual submission in the basic household relationships of his day, over against the abusive patterns of power that commonly prevailed.) Paul invites us, even urges us, to be intoxicated with the Spirit of light and life. Open yourself anew to that Spirit.

For Ascension Day, the church reads Paul's prayer in **Ephesians 1,** so we return to it this week. Let Paul's elevated orison become your own request of God. Pray with a keen awareness that the Jesus who promised the Spirit of truth and opened the minds of his disciples to the Scriptures is now enthroned at the right hand of the Father. His power for us is immeasurably great and his intention is to enlighten our hearts and fill us with the fullness of his presence. Ask for this.

RESPONDING TO GOD

As you vicariously identify with the disciples, who saw Jesus taken into heaven, let yourself stand this week at the thematic intersection of Christ's departure from us into glory, Christ's presence in us by the Spirit and Christ's witness through us to the world. In your choices this week, how can you "make the most of the time" in light of these three realities?

Closing Prayer. Lord God, by your immeasurably great power, you raised Christ Jesus from the dead and seated him at your right hand in the heavenly places, far above all rule and authority and power and dominion, with a name greater than any other name, not only in this age but also in the age to come; glory and honor to you, risen and ascended King! Amen.

Waiting for the Spirit

This final week of Easter, we continue with the themes of Christ's exaltation, the promise of the Spirit and the call to mission. We are in the ten-day period between Jesus' departure in the body and his coming in the Spirit. As in Advent, we are waiting, praying and letting our desire intensify. We want to experience the fullness of God in our lives. We are waiting for the Spirit. We need his revelation of truth, his protection against spiritual darkness and his power for witness and service.

Approaching God. You, O Lord, are King! Let the planet itself rejoice, let the cosmos proclaim your righteousness, let all the people behold your glory, for you, O Lord, are most high over all creation, you are exalted above all powers; praise and allegiance belong to you, Almighty King! Amen.

Presenting Myself. Lord Jesus Christ, in this fallen world I am vulnerable to the pull of temptation and the powers of darkness; I need your protection and guidance, I need your Spirit; strengthen me this week, O Lord, as I absorb your transforming Word and await your empowering Spirit. Amen.

Inviting God's Presence. Come, Holy Spirit.

LISTENING TO GOD
Psalm 97 (C); **Acts 1:1-26 (ABC);**
John 17 (ABC); Ephesians 6; **Revelation 22 (C)**

The Lord reigns as king, proclaims **Psalm 97.** Recalling Mount Sinai (Ex 19), the psalmist describes creation's response to God's royal presence. All beings become aware of his glory: idolaters turn in shame, angels bow in awe (verse 7; see also Heb 1:6), God's people rejoice in gratitude. And we who love the Lord, righteous and just, must, like him, hate evil. We stand against it, confident in God's protection and full of hope for our ultimate rescue. Thus Psalm 97 is an apt resurrection and ascension song. It can help you this week to rejoice in the dawning of the light.

Luke opens **Acts 1** by recapping the forty days from resurrection to ascension. Imagine yourself as one of the 120 or so women and men; Jesus has presented himself alive over the course of several weeks now. On these occasions he has pointedly talked about the kingdom of God and the coming Holy Spirit. You still have questions. Now he is gone, apparently for good. Two mysterious people (men? angels?) announce he will return one day in like manner. Your community reconvenes in Jerusalem to wait and pray. You are trying to digest what you've seen and heard. What is this baptism of Spirit that will bring new power? Why must you wait? For how long? Then what? Let these vicarious imaginings awaken a fresh desire for the fullness of God's Spirit in your own life.

In **John 17,** the soaring conclusion of Jesus' extended discourse before he died, Jesus prays intimately to his Father and openly before his friends. He rehearses his identity and mission; he intercedes for his followers and their mission; he even prays for those of us who will believe generations later. Trace the now familiar themes: glory, life, God's name, God's words, sanctification, truth, joy, oneness, love, the world. Meditate on how Jesus prays for us: our protection from evil in the world into which we are sent (as he was sent); our spiritual union with him (as he and the Father indwelt one another); our transformation by his truth (as he was sanctified by obedience); our profound unity as believers (as he was full of divine love). Jesus, through his suffering and death, glorified his Father; the Father, through the resurrection and ascension, glorified his

Son. Jesus desires and thus prays that ultimately we would see and share in this very same glory.

Paul ends his letter to the **Ephesians** on two of the same themes found in John 17: protection from evil and prayer for believers. Paul emphatically teaches that we contend against spiritual enemies, whether powers that inhabit and inhibit our human institutions or forces of evil that work against us in the spiritual realms. God provides strength and protection, but it's incumbent on us to avail ourselves. So think about the spiritual armor available to us: truthfulness, justice, readiness to act, faith, confidence in God's grace and knowledge of God's Word. All of these are mediated by the Spirit, who also infuses and empowers our prayers. And by making prayer integral to our lives, we stay spiritually alert, mutually strengthened and courageous in witness.

We began the Easter season with John's vision of the risen Christ in Revelation 1; we read now the conclusion in **Revelation 22.** The images point to resurrection life: the sparkling river, the fecund tree, the medicinal leaves, the perpetual light, the transformed community. The ascended Jesus assures us of his return. He will be like a bright morning star. Even now he invites each of us to "Come!" and offers the water of life as a gift. And we say, "Yes, let it be so! Come, Lord Jesus!"

RESPONDING TO GOD

The disciples already had received much from Jesus. But he had promised them more: the presence of his Spirit, holy within them. They were eager for it, waiting and praying and encouraging one another. This week, follow their example by asking God for a renewed awareness and fresh filling of his Spirit.

Closing Prayer. Father in heaven, you give good gifts to all who ask; risen and exalted Jesus, you promise always to be with us: be gracious to me this week and give your Holy Spirit in fresh measure that I may be guarded from evil, changed by truth and filled with power. Come, Holy Spirit, come. Amen.

The Cycles of Love

ORDINARY TIME

8

Ordinary Time
Empowered in the Pouring Out

We do not need to carry out grand things in order to show
a great love for God and for our neighbor.
It is the intensity of love we put into our gestures that
makes them something beautiful for God.

MOTHER TERESA

Because of what has been made known in Christ, no time can again be
regarded as ordinary in the sense of dull or commonplace.
The liturgical calendar as a whole exists in large part to remind us
that Christ has sanctified all of time, bringing us and the whole
of our experience into the orbit of resurrection. What we deem ordinary,
God has transformed into the extraordinary by his divine grace.

LAURENCE HULL STOOKEY

For those first hundred-plus followers of Jesus waiting together in Jerusalem as instructed, Pentecost breaks on them in stunning fashion. A roar like a windstorm. Bright flames dancing in the air. Ecstatic outbursts in unlearned languages. An inundation of presence and power. Extraordinary! Likewise the ensuing scene on the street and the later events in the city. This is the birth of the movement that will change the world. No wonder the ancient church chose to culminate Easter on Pentecost with the celebration of the Spirit poured out by the risen and ascended Lord.

Yet Pentecost also marks a beginning, the start of the long season we call Ordinary Time. Long as in six months. Ordinary in that the Sundays are simply numbered and there are no major feasts comparable to Christmas or Pascha. A time, in the words of Wendy Wright, "to become attentive to the call of discipleship both outer and inner. What are we called to do? . . . What are we called to be?" If the extraordinary event of Pentecost points the way—immersion in Spirit, empowerment for mission— then shouldn't our call to discipleship likewise be extraordinary?

If asked to name a Christian you consider "extraordinary," someone from your lifetime, who would you choose? For me it could be Billy Graham, the great evangelist, or Martin Luther King Jr., the great prophet for justice, or John Paul II, the great pope, or John Stott, the great Bible teacher, or Oscar Romero, the great opponent of oppression; but in the end I would choose Mother Teresa, the great—what shall we call her?— the great lover of the poor.

She was born Agnes Gonxha Bojaxhiu in 1910 in Albania. Her parents were devout Catholics, especially her mother, who modeled generosity toward the poor. At age eighteen, Agnes discerned a call to join a missionary order, the Sisters of Our Lady of Loretto. She journeyed to India for her two-year novitiate. Upon professing her vows, she took the name Teresa, after the recently sainted Thérèse of Lisieux, the patron saint of missionaries (1873-1897). For six years Teresa taught geography and history at a convent school in Calcutta, and for nine more served as the director of studies. In 1946, while traveling on a train, she reports, "I was quietly praying when I clearly felt a call within my calling. The message was very clear. I had to leave the convent and consecrate myself to helping the poor by living among them. It was a command." In 1948, with permission from Rome, she moved out and began her work among the poor. Soon other women joined her, many of them her former students, and in 1950 they were authorized as the Order of the Missionaries of Charity. Mother Teresa led the order for almost fifty years.

What did Teresa and her fellow sisters do? Simply put, they served the dying, the diseased, the orphaned, the poor and the outcast with the compassion of Christ—and also with compassion for Christ, as they saw in each needy person Christ himself:

> When we handle the sick and the needy we touch the suffering body of Christ and this touch will make us heroic; it will make us forget the repugnance and the natural tendencies in us. We need the eyes of deep faith to see Christ in the broken body and dirty clothes under which the most beautiful one among the sons of men hides. We shall need the hands of Christ to touch these bodies wounded by pain and suffering.

The Missionaries of Charity did this first in Calcutta, then throughout India and then around the world. After the airing in 1969 of *Something Beautiful for God,* a documentary by the British journalist Malcolm Muggeridge, Mother Teresa gained wider recognition in the West. In 1979, she was awarded the Nobel Peace Prize and accepted it in the name of the poor that she and her sisters served. Mother Teresa died in September 1997. At that time, the Missionaries of Charity were operating over six hundred centers in some 120 countries. In 2003, Pope John Paul II beatified Teresa, the second step on the path to sainthood, naming her Blessed Teresa of Calcutta.

Now that's extraordinary discipleship. Spirit-filled, self-sacrificing, mission-dedicated! But is such discipleship the expectation of God for all of us? My answer: yes and no.

Yes, because Jesus gives each of us his Holy Spirit and calls each of us to "lose our life for his sake" and enlists each of us as his ambassadors in the world. Yes, because every one of us is called to love God with our whole being and to love our neighbors as ourselves. Yes, because any one of us could be flying on an airplane or sitting in our backyard and, like Mother Teresa, receive a "call within our calling," that is, a leading from God to undertake a particular work in a given place for a certain period of time. And like her, we must be prepared to obey such a "command," whatever the risks or costs.

But no, because not all of us receive direction to engage in direct "ministry" as the main occupation of our lives. No, because there is no hierarchy of discipleship such that nuns, pastors and missionaries rank higher than, say, nannies, professors and merchants, and no dichotomy between sacred and secular such that preaching is more important than, say, parenting, or fasting more spiritual than farming. No, because God remains as eager to bless us as human beings made in his image as he is to use us as human agents deployed in his service. In fact, it is as we live our ordinary lives with extraordinary allegiance to his leadership that his mission moves forward in the world.

Mother Teresa taught as much herself:

> Do not think that love, in order to be genuine, has to be extraordinary. . . . We must love those who are nearest to us, in our own family. . . . Above all, your love has to start there. I want you to be the good news to those around you. I want you to be concerned about your next-door neighbor. . . . Do not pursue spectacular deeds. . . . In the work we have to do it does not matter how small and humble it may be, make it Christ's love in action. . . . What matters is the gift of yourself, the degree of love that you put into each one of your actions.

When Mother Teresa opened her first home for the dying poor, she entertained no ambitions for worldwide fame, no thoughts of meeting with presidents or accepting awards. Serving Christ would be its own reward: "You must not be afraid to say 'Yes' to Jesus, because there is no greater love than His love and no greater joy than His joy."

In the pouring out of ourselves for Christ, we find ourselves empowered with his love and joy. This happens in our everyday lives—among our family and friends, in the familiar settings of our neighborhoods, schools and places of work, in our domestic routines and leisure activities, indeed, during the commonplace days of our year. This is discipleship in Ordinary Time.

THE HEART OF ORDINARY TIME

In the Cycle of Light we celebrated the incarnation (God with us); in the Cycle of Life we contemplated salvation (God for us); now in Ordinary Time we concentrate on the outworking of that redemption (God through us). The incarnate and risen Christ is present in the world now in a different way: the Spirit indwells the believer to enable a fruitful life and empowers the church to engage in redemptive mission. We reveal his light, we exhibit his life and we embody his love.

"Tension is a creative force," Kathleen Norris observes in a musing about the doctrine of the Trinity, "but polarization, which seems an abiding sin of our age, is worse than useless." Too often we succumb to this latter tendency and set aspects of the Christian life into unhelpful opposition. We want to elevate one over the other as more spiritual or more important. Instead we should hold these elements in creative tension or complimentary pose or, better yet, see them as fruitful rhythms.

The two major cycles of the liturgical calendar draw us into rhythms of longing and fulfillment, fasting and feasting, preparation and proclamation. Over the months of Ordinary Time we can enter into additional rhythms of healthy discipleship: gathering for worship and dispersing for witness, tending to ourselves and caring for others, enjoying our rest and fulfilling our duties. As our anatomical hearts beat in systolic and diastolic rhythm, contracting and relaxing, taking in blood and pumping it out, so too should our spiritual hearts have cycles of engagement and withdrawal, giving and receiving, working and resting. Each of these expressions pulses with Spirit, each of these flows from love: our love for God, God's love for us, our love for neighbor, our love for ourselves.

I have structured the devotional material for Ordinary Time around three rhythms for faithful, Spirit-filled living in the midst of the world that God loves. Each rhythm entails a pair of complimentary themes.

World and church. The rhythm here is between our mission in the world and our worship in the community of fellow believers.

We participate in the mission of God. God purposes to rescue every person from their spiritual entrapment in sin, to put right all aspects of human society and culture, and to renew even creation itself. Consequently, our purposes in this flawed world mirror God's. How do we fulfill this great vision? A wide range of actions apply: proclaiming the message, helping the hurting, working for justice, serving the poor, confronting evil, fostering reconciliation, acting as cultural salt and light, and more. We engage in these actions both collectively and individually, by our support and by our direct involvement. In this sense, all of us are missionaries.

We belong to the people of God. All who have humbled themselves in faith before God and given their allegiance to Jesus and received the Holy Spirit, these make up the vast and diverse church around the globe. We can describe it many ways—the family of God, the body of Christ, the community of faith—but the idea is the same: Jesus Christ unites us in a way that is fundamentally greater than any other bond, whether familial, fraternal, political, cultural or national. "There is one body and one Spirit, just as you were called to the one hope of your calling, one Lord, one faith, one baptism, one God and Father of all, who is above all and through all and in all" (Eph 4:4-6). In local communities of this universal church, we praise God in worship, seek God in prayer, pay attention to God's word, receive grace at the Communion table, grow together in the faith, provoke one another to love and good deeds, and simply share our lives.

Consider how these two themes connect: worship fills us with joyful gratitude, gratitude moves us to earnest witness, witness often generates opposition, suffering draws us together and drives us to God, God heals and reinvigorates us, we move out again to serve, many people respond to God's grace, we regather to give thanks—you get the idea. There is a dynamic interplay between church and mission. Mark Labberton compellingly makes this point in *The Dangerous Act of Worship:*

> When worship is our response to the One who alone is worthy of it—Jesus Christ—then our lives are on their way to being turned inside out. Every dimension of self-centered living becomes endangered as we come to share God's self-giving heart. . . . Through the grace of worship, God applies the necessary antidote to what we assume is merely human—our selfishness. Worship sets us free from ourselves to be free for God and God's purposes in the world. The dangerous act of worshiping God in Jesus Christ necessarily draws us into the heart of God and sends us out to embody it, especially toward the poor, the forgotten and the oppressed.

God insists on both incorporating us into a nourishing, worshiping community and mobilizing us as his compassionate, transforming presence in the world. He supplies his Spirit to empower both endeavors. It will not do to give ourselves to the one and neglect the other; we need the full rhythm of worship and witness in our week-in, week-out lives.

Neighbor and self. Either of two extremes can undermine a healthy rhythm between giving of ourselves and caring for ourselves: we can grow so self-absorbed that we do little for others, or we can become so others-oriented that we allow ourselves little pleasure. How do we reconcile the apparent tension between Jesus' call to deny ourselves and lose our lives and his promise that through him we have life abundantly (Mk 8:34-35; Jn 10:10)?

We can love ourselves too much. When a wealthy leader consults Jesus about inheriting eternal life, Jesus puts the man's moral confidence to the test by telling him to cash out his assets, distribute everything and become a disciple with "treasure in heaven." The man cannot do it— cannot let go of that much money or muster that much compassion for the poor or put that much trust in God. What is his problem? Idolatry? Addiction? Pride? Greed? Maybe all of these to some extent, but it certainly includes self-centeredness. If virtually all of our time, energy and resources go into providing and enjoying a "good life" for ourselves, then there will be little left for those who (seemingly) have nothing to give in return. If we serve money, we cannot serve God. If we always put ourselves first, we cannot love our neighbors. It's just that simple.

We can love ourselves too little. Then again, maybe it's not that simple. Jesus told us to love our neighbors as ourselves, a measure that assumes we naturally take care of ourselves and our own. This is true and right. After all, God created humankind in his likeness, placed us in a lovely and resource-laden environment, and gave us meaningful responsibilities. We've been designed for spiritual intimacy, for social community, for fruitful stewardship, for intelligent discovery, for aesthetic pleasure, for personal achievement—for abundant life under the providence of God. He loves us and wants us to flourish. He cares about every aspect of our being. He cares so much that he became one of us—the incarnation affirms the goodness of our humanity. To denigrate ourselves, to devalue our bodies, to eschew pleasure, to exhaust ourselves in service, to think of God as austere and demanding, these impulses violate the gracious intentions of our Creator. It pleases God to bless us.

So how do we bring these two ideas together? Simply put, we are blessed to be a blessing (Gen 12:2). We don't resist the blessing and we don't refuse to bless. Instead, we develop a spiritual rhythm of enjoying the grace of God and showing the same generosity to others. As God blesses us, body and mind, heart and soul, we "bless" him with our whole being in return. And whatever we desire and delightedly receive from our Father, we turn around and eagerly seek for our fellow humans. We want to flourish but not to the exclusion of others, not at their unjust expense. We need to cultivate an underlying contentment in Christ, so that we can say with Paul, "In any and all circumstances I have learned the secret of being well-fed and of going hungry, of having plenty and of being in need. I can do all things through him who strengthens me" (Phil 4:12-13).

There is no rule book to tell us when to deny and when to enjoy ourselves, what to give and what to keep, how much to serve and how much to be served. Surely, however, our calendars, checkbooks and journals should record a rhythm of caring for neighbor and tending to self.

Work and rest. We instinctively understand the day-night cycle of wakefulness and sleep, and the weekly cycle of workdays and weekends. We know our bodies and minds need food and rest in order to be productive. But do we understand the spirituality of work and rest?

Our work is spiritual. Far too many of us think of our work as secular. For the most part, we take jobs or pursue careers to support ourselves and our families. What we do seems to have little direct bearing on the mission of God in the world. We are not in ministry like pastors and missionaries, although the helping professions come close. We don't see the connection between our jobs in law, business, government or construction and the kingdom of God, other than the opportunity to demonstrate ethical integrity or witness to colleagues or support missions from our earnings. Besides, some of us hate our jobs because of the inherent drudgery or the unfair boss or the depressing atmosphere or the grueling labor for low wages.

So, what's so spiritual about work? Only this: God created us with the capacity to work—farming, making, building, trading, inventing, organizing, creating, studying, teaching, governing, caretaking, imagining—

and God gave us the responsibility to work, that is, to cultivate and develop the unlimited potential of his good creation. Working is part of what it means to bear the image of God. After all, God worked in creating the universe. Yes, because of the Fall work has become difficult and distorted by sin—often rife with greed, exploitation, corruption—but it has not ceased to be good. God is honored by every human endeavor that comports with his good purposes for humanity and creation. Whether by parenting or studying or volunteering or making art or holding a job, we participate in the capacious work of God to redeem all things—persons, cultures, environments. As theologian Miroslav Volf asserts, "The noble products of human ingenuity, 'whatever is beautiful, true and good in human cultures', will be cleansed from impurity, perfected and transfigured to become a part of God's new creation."

So our work is indeed spiritual. In fact, recalling the first two rhythms, our work is part of our worship (love for God) and is one of the ways we serve others (love for neighbor).

Our rest is spiritual. Sleep is a gift from God. Sabbath is a provision from God. Seasons of celebration are a blessing from God. To enter into these rhythms is to receive God's grace. By these means God desires to renew us physically and spiritually. God himself actually set the pattern, so to speak, because after six days of creating, he rested. He commanded us to do the same. Furthermore, our times of rest become spaces for meeting God. As we rest, implicitly we acknowledge that he is at work when we are not and that he will provide for us and others. We are not meant to carry the weight of the world. Jesus says, "Come to me, all you that are weary and are carrying heavy burdens, and I will give you rest" (Mt 11:28). In effect, God says, "Give it a rest," because this too is spiritual.

Witness in the world and worship in community, care for neighbor and care for self, fruitful labor and refreshing rest, these are spiritual rhythms of Ordinary Time. As we pour ourselves out for God and others, God graciously pours himself into us.

ORDINARY TIME IN CHURCH AND CULTURE

Three colors—red, white and green—historically have been associated with Pentecost. On the feast day, the priests wear red vestments, recalling the flames of fire representing the Holy Spirit. In Great Britain the day is called Whitsun (derived from Middle English *whitsonday*, or "white Sunday"), perhaps stemming from the white robes worn for baptism or confirmation. Associated with the day in earlier times were May festivities called Whitsun Games or Whitsun Ales (the time of the new brews!). The color green highlights the seasonal turn to summer in the northern hemisphere. In Poland, for example, Pentecost is called "Green Holyday," in Germany, "Flowerfeast" and in Slovakia, "Summerfeast," hence the custom in such places of decorating homes with greenery. Thus green is the liturgical color for Ordinary Time, which is also known as the Green Season.

The first Sunday after Pentecost is Trinity Sunday. For over a thousand years, the church has given special attention to the doctrine of the triune God on this day, in part because of the christological and trinitarian controversies of the fourth and fifth centuries. Hence, on this Sunday, many churches recite the longer and seldom-used Athanasian Creed with its fuller exposition of the Trinity rather than the customary Apostles' or Nicene creeds. Trinity Sunday is an atypical feast since it celebrates not a biblical event but a theological doctrine. This feast day offers an occasion to worship the one God, the Father-Son-Spirit God, who is active in his trinitarian fullness from start (creation) to finish (new creation) and at every point between (blessing and salvation).

The designation "Ordinary Time" came into usage as a result of the liturgical reforms of the Second Vatican Council (the prior designation being simply "the Sundays after Epiphany" or "after Pentecost"). Protestants have largely followed suit.

Here are the notable feast days that punctuate the months of Ordinary Time, as observed mostly by the liturgical churches, especially Catholic, Orthodox, Anglican and Lutheran:

- The Transfiguration (August 6): Nowadays, the transfiguration is also commemorated on the last Sunday before Lent by many churches.

- The Assumption of Mary (or, in the East, the Dormition of the Theotokos) (August 15): This ancient feast honors Mary by commemorating the tradition of her passing into heaven.

- Holy Cross Day (September 14): This day focuses on the physical cross itself and commemorates the discovery of the "true cross" in 325 by St. Helena, the mother of the emperor Constantine.

- St. Michael and All Angels' (September 29): This day directs our attention to the mysterious order of beings who serve as messengers of God.

- All Saints Day (November 1): This feast honors those whose godly lives have been deemed exemplary, whether formally by the church or informally, and calls us to greater holiness; Halloween, then, is actually All Hallows Eve.

- Reign of Christ (last Sunday before Advent): This day calls us to worship the one who has all authority and to anticipate the glory of his coming eschatological reign.

Other commemorations include World Communion Sunday (first in October), Reformation Sunday (last in October) and Thanksgiving Day (fourth Thursday in November in the United States).

THE CHRIST STORY IN ORDINARY TIME

Luke succinctly closes his Gospel account on these notes: Jesus opens the minds of his disciples to understand the Scriptures as they pertain to him, he commissions them to proclaim to all nations repentance and forgiveness of sins in his name, he promises to clothe them with power from on high and then he blesses them even as he is carried into heaven. The end.

But then Luke writes volume two: Acts of the Apostles. The story continues, only now it focuses on those who are at once Christ's followers (disciples) and his sent ones (apostles). He reiterates at the start of Acts, like hook and eye, the same themes with which he ends his Gospel: Jesus' teaching about the kingdom, Spirit-baptism and worldwide witness, his cloudborne ascension and the angelic assurance of his return.

We can take our thematic cues for Ordinary Time right from Luke 24 and Acts 1: Christ at work in us and through us by his Spirit to announce his gracious salvation and extend his righteous rule to the people of the world, all in expectation of his glorious return.

Ordinary Time starts with Pentecost and ends with Reign of Christ Sunday. We begin by remembering the outpouring of Spirit and the immediacy of God's presence. This harkens back to the original creation when our access to God was unencumbered by sin, when the Creator "walked" with us "at the time of the evening breeze" (Gen 3:8). Now, as foretold by the prophets, God has put his Spirit within us and thereby restored a means of spiritual intimacy (Ezek 36:26). We end the season by celebrating Christ the King. This day looks forward to the new creation in which the home of God will be among us and we will dwell with him, once again unimpeded (Rev 21:1-3). Ordinary Time thus places us in the story between the Garden of Eden and the city of the eschaton, or, more properly, between Pentecost and the parousia (return) of Christ.

One additional point about Pentecost: the miracle of languages being miraculously uttered and understood represents a reversal of the confusion of tongues in the Tower of Babel story (Gen 11). The people of old, united linguistically, set out to build for themselves a great city with a tower reaching the heavens so as to make a great name for themselves. In response to their proud, independent, self-aggrandizing project, God scrambled their speech and scattered them. In contrast, the baptism of the Spirit empowers the church for a new and profound unity. In humble dependence on the Spirit, we now can pursue our human endeavors in ways intended to make *God's* name great, ways that acknowledge his authority and rule.

INHABITING ORDINARY TIME

In this season, we settle into the spiritual rhythms of living as disciples of Jesus. We gather in our churches and disperse into our neighborhoods. We worship and we witness. We seek to grow as individuals and we serve the needs of others. We rest our bodies and refresh our souls and we set out to do our God-given work. We engage in these rhythms day in and day out, week in and week out.

Two simple disciplines help us live well in the day-night cycle: receiving the day and releasing the day. The first is our disposition each morning: we gratefully accept the new day as a gift; we acknowledge God's goodness and invite his empowering presence; we commit to him our whole self and all our coming endeavors; then we set about our day in joyful dependence. The second is our disposition at the end of each day: we go over our day, recalling those points when we sensed most clearly God's closeness and care and those when we felt most disconnected or disconcerted; then we give thanks for God's presence in those experiences and confess our sins and failings; finally, we let go of the day, leaving in God's hands any things that we left undone and any that threaten to undo us. Then we enter peacefully into the gift of sleep. Both habits, the receiving and the releasing, immerse us in grace, as Dorothy Bass reminds us: "Those who can let go of the day, including its slights and sins, enter the next day forgiven and free. Those who fear the grave as little as their bed become available for bold and creative living. . . . We sleep well, as we live and die well, knowing that we are in God's embrace."

The key to our weekly rhythm is keeping the sabbath. We can think of this practice as a command (number four on the famous list of ten) or as a gift (in Jesus' words, "The sabbath was made for humankind"). Setting aside one day in seven—for rest, for reflection, for worship, for friendship, for nature, for quietness, for beauty—aligns us with the wisdom and grace of our Creator Father. It is a day to stop our working and rehearse the work of God in our lives; it is a day to cease our worrying and renew our dependence on his providence.

As a final resource for living in Ordinary Time, I commend the familiar prayer that Jesus taught his disciples and that many of us recite, often mindlessly, each week in church. What if we thought of the Lord's Prayer less as a recitation and more as a pattern, not just for praying but also for living as Christians? The prayer, as recorded in Luke 11, divides into two rhythmic parts: the first half centers on God, with implications for us, and the second half focuses on us, with assumptions about God.

Whenever we begin the music of prayer, we first hear from God an opening note of grace that elicits from us a response of trust and gratitude: *Dear Father—Abba, Papa—in heaven* . . . But the next note quickly draws our attention to God's holiness so that we step back from the initial embrace, as it were, and bow or kneel in reverence: *You are holy, holy, holy*. . . . We acknowledge God's rightful rule over the cosmos and recommit ourselves to seek first his kingdom: *Sovereign Lord, not my will but yours be done on earth and in my life, just as it is in heaven. . . .*

Then the prayer turns. Now we're free to simply ask for all that we need in order to live, remembering that we don't live by bread alone: *Father, feed me, feed all of us. . . .* Shifting from body to soul, we admit our wrongs, our failings, and ask for mercy, secure in our confidence that Christ paid our great debt and humble in our willingness to release anyone who owes us: *Father, forgive me and help me to forgive. . . .* Finally, we ask God to steer us clear of trouble and, should we encounter it, to either pull us out or enable us to endure: *Don't let me get in over my head, O God, and guard me against the evil one.*

This prayer of Jesus can serve as a pattern for our lives. Grateful for God's love, we love him in return. In awe of his holiness, we worship him. In response to his authority, we give our allegiance. As we live in the world in light of his rule, we look to him for provision and forgiveness and protection. We depend on God in body, soul and circumstance. All of this for the sake of his kingdom, by the power he has poured out and for the glory he deserves. Imagine the spiritual benefit if we would pray in this pattern each day during Ordinary Time, perhaps as part of receiving or releasing the day or giving sabbath attention to our Lord and our lives.

FOR HIM AND FOR HIS MISSION

In Ordinary Time we live out the extraordinary mysteries of the earlier cycles of the year, the light of God incarnate and the life of Christ resurrected. These shape what we are to do and who we are to be. This is the season of love. Jesus poured himself out in love and we seek to do the same. Not only that, he pours his love into our hearts through the Holy Spirit—the roaring wind, the living flame, the power of God (Rom 5:5). "For us and for our salvation he came down from heaven," we recite in the creed; during Ordinary Time especially, we echo in response, "For him and for his mission we go into the world."

*   *   *

Preview of devotions in Ordinary Time. The first week of Ordinary Time focuses on Pentecost and the power of the Holy Spirit. The second treats themes arising from Trinity Sunday. The material thereafter is organized into three eight-week sections corresponding to the three pairs of themes discussed above and outlined again below. The final unit centers on Reign of Christ Sunday and should be used in the week leading up to Advent.

World and church. We follow Acts 2—13 as the witness of the embryonic church spreads outward from Jerusalem in a dramatic series of surges and setbacks. The theme for each week comes from the Acts text. The Gospel readings all come from Luke (featured in Year C of the lectionary). The mission of the "church dispersed" entails preaching good news, facing persecution, setting people free and confronting powers. The life of the "church gathered" includes praying and giving, serving and suffering, embracing and reconciling, and giving and sending. The devotions alternate between these themes.

Neighbor and self. This cycle of love alternates between permission to love ourselves and the imperative to love our neighbor. Deuteronomy 6:4-5 commands us to love God with all our heart, soul and might, and Jesus, in quoting it, adds a fourth: all our mind (Mk 12:29-31). We are whole people, but comprised of these four overlapping dimensions. The devotions reflect on how God wants us to value and attend to each. These interweave with the neighbor-oriented themes of hospitality, generosity, justice and forgiveness. I have chosen a range of scriptural texts in keeping with the focus for each week, but the Gospel readings come primarily from Matthew (featured in lectionary Year A).

Work and rest. Four devotional themes focus on the broad idea of work: vocation, stewardship, society and culture, and four unfold dimensions of rest: daily bread, sabbath, beauty and thanksgiving. This too is a cycle of love. Out of love God created the world, and once it became damaged he acted at great cost to redeem it. Out of love he makes us stewards and sets us to work. Out of love he blesses us with bounty and gives us rest. Over the last few weeks the devotions also explore Revelation 21—22 and build toward a climactic celebration of Christ's kingly rule.

The Feast of Pentecost
Beginning the eighth Sunday after Easter

Wind and Fire

With the outpouring of the Spirit, the themes of resurrection and new life are amplified and the focus on the church and its mission introduced. This week we celebrate the gift of the Holy Spirit. The readings are full of images and metaphors that describe the mystery of the Spirit and his working. Wind and fire! We are rightly awed. We're also drawn by the invitation: receive the gift, be filled. Our experiences may range from quiet to dramatic—the Wind blows as it pleases—but in every case, we encounter the Being of God within our own being, his transforming, empowering and loving presence.

Approaching God. Lord God, you are always before me, always at my side to strengthen me; therefore my heart is joyful and I live in hope; for you will not abandon my soul to death even as you did not let your holy one experience decay. You have made known to me the ways of life and you will make me full of gladness with your presence. Amen.

Presenting Myself. Abba! Papa! Father! By the Spirit of adoption you have given me, I pray to you as your daughter/son: I need your Spirit to overcome my propensity to sin; I need your Spirit to give me hope in my sufferings; I need your Spirit to help me in prayer when I am weak. I need you, Holy Spirit.

Inviting God's Presence. Come, Holy Spirit, come and fill me anew. Amen.

LISTENING TO GOD

Psalm 104:24-34 (ABC); Ezekiel 37:1-14 (B);
John 7:37-39 (A); Acts 2:1-42 (ABC);
Romans 8:9-27 (BC); 1 Corinthians 12:1-13 (A)

This portion of **Psalm 104** is read on Pentecost in recognition that God not only feeds his creatures physically but renews us by his Spirit.

God gives **Ezekiel** this dramatic, even cinematic, vision during the time of Israel's exile in Babylon. The people see themselves as cut off, without hope, as good as dead. But Ezekiel's vision says otherwise. Further, it foreshadows the resurrection that Jesus will inaugurate. In your imagination, stand beside Ezekiel. Picture the aftermath of a war, the bleached bones of the thousands left unburied. How would you answer God's question (verse 3)? Whatever his doubts, Ezekiel twice prophesies and twice sees the unimaginable. Notice the interplay of breath, wind and spirit, all variations on the same Hebrew word. The Spirit who breathed life into humans at creation, who restored Israel after exile, who raised Jesus from the grave and who fell on the believers at Pentecost, this same Spirit fills us with life and guarantees the resurrection of our bodies after death.

In **John 7,** Jesus uses water as a metaphor for the Spirit, an image rich with Old Testament connotations: the river out of Eden (Gen 20), the water from the rock (Ex 17), the fountain of living water (Jer 17), and the river flowing from the temple (Ezek 47; also Rev 22). Jesus cries out on the seventh day of the Festival of Booths, perhaps at the joyful moment when the procession of priests is bringing the water from Siloam to pour as an offering on the altar. Echoing the psalmists (Ps 42; 63) whose thirsty souls are satisfied only in the presence of God, Jesus invites us to come to him not just for a quenching drink but for an ever-flowing spring.

Acts 2 describes the seminal outpouring or baptism or filling of the Holy Spirit. The Feast of Pentecost has drawn pilgrims from the nations to Jerusalem. Read the text carefully for what happens, using your senses. Noise. Wind. Fire. Languages. Crowds. Praise. Astonishment. Ridicule. Peter seizes the moment. Analyze his forthright proclamation. What does he assert about Jesus? What does he imply about the crowd? He offers God's gifts of baptism, forgiveness and Spirit to all who will repent and respond. And thousands do! As have millions since. The Spirit comes with power, the disciples preach with boldness, the people respond with repentance and the story of the church begins.

Paul reassures the **Romans** that living in line with the Spirit brings life and peace. All who belong to Jesus have the Spirit. Observe the benefits: guarantee of bodily resurrection, strength to resist sinful desires, assurance of God's fatherly love, hope of sharing in Christ's glory, help in times of weakness and even intercession for us when we have no words to pray. Grace upon grace!

To the **Corinthians** Paul explains spiritual gifts, those extraordinary abilities imparted to individuals for the purpose of serving the community of believers. God activates these gifts in us through the Spirit on various occasions for specific purposes. Whatever abilities the Spirit gives to you, whatever ways the Spirit works through you, these are always for the building up of the body of Christ and for the sake of our mission in the world. Paul goes on to discuss the body metaphor, emphasizing service and humility. But he places his strongest emphasis not on the spectacular gifts but on the greatest one: self-giving love.

RESPONDING TO GOD

This is a fitting time to open ourselves anew to the indwelling presence of God. Ask the Father to fill you. Ask Jesus to breathe on you. Ask the Spirit to intoxicate you. This week be still and receptive. Freely seek the benefits and gifts that Jesus promises and Paul describes. Above all, ask for love to increase in you.

Closing Prayer. Father in Heaven, together with your Son who sits at your right hand and your Spirit who dwells in all who belong to you, fill me this day and every day with your holy and loving presence, that I might live in a manner pleasing to you and readily act as your witness in this world. Amen.

Mystery of the Three-in-One

O n the first Sunday after Pentecost, the church considers and celebrates the trinitarian nature of God. While associated with a doctrine rather than an event in salvation history, this principle feast recognizes and honors the one triune God who has acted through all of time. Pentecost highlights the coming of the Spirit, but we must remember that the Spirit has always been at work: creating and sustaining the cosmos, forming and preserving Israel, choosing kings and speaking through prophets, overshadowing Mary and anointing Jesus, and, yes, baptizing and empowering the church. The simultaneous oneness and threeness of God is a mystery. The Father, Son and Spirit are coeternal and coequal, existing in a trinity of persons and a unity of being. Recall the sweep of the story from Advent to Pentecost this week as you contemplate the mystery of the Three-in-One.

Approaching God. Lord God, Three-in-One, you sit enthroned, high and lofty; your presence fills the place of your dwelling; seraphim attend to you with reverence; with them I call out: Holy, holy, holy is the Lord of hosts; the whole earth is full of your glory.

Presenting Myself. Lord God, before the fire of your consuming holiness, in the light of your shining glory, at the mystery of your threefold being, I fall to the floor and cry out: Woe am I! I am small before you, O Lord, I am unworthy in your presence, my lips are unclean and my heart impure; have mercy on me, O Lord, have mercy.

Inviting God's Presence. Lord God, touch my mouth with holy flame and wash my heart with pure water so that, renewed in your grace and filled with your Spirit, I can do your work in the world for the sake of your glory, Father, Son and Holy Spirit. Amen.

LISTENING TO GOD

Psalm 8 (AC); Isaiah 6:1-9 (B);
Matthew 28:16-20 (A); Romans 5:1-5 (C)

Psalm 8 exalts God and puts us in our place. When we look at God's creation, the vast cosmos—and this is even more true today given all our astronomical knowledge—we human beings stand utterly humbled. Who are we that God should even pay us attention? His being is majestic, his power unfathomable and his glory infinite. And yet we are made in God's image and entrusted with responsibility over the created order. So let this psalm both humble you and honor you, both move you to worship and inspire you to work.

In **Isaiah 6,** the prophet writes about the encounter with God that propelled him into mission. Isaiah is given a vision of God in his heavenly temple, an overwhelming vision. Look closely at the description of what he sees and what he experiences. With the account of Pentecost also in mind, contemplate the pattern in Isaiah 6: vision of God, conviction of sin, forgiveness, transformation and dispatch into mission. Recall other instances of this pattern, for example, Moses and the burning bush or Paul on the road to Damascus. In what ways does this match your experience?

We have in **Matthew 28** the famous Great Commission of Jesus. It fits well in this week of the year because of the trinitarian formula used in baptism and also the idea of Jesus continuing his mission through his followers. Although it may be familiar to you, study Christ's charge afresh this week. Take to heart what Jesus says about the scope of his authority, the extent of his love, the essential task of his ambassadors and the promise of his presence. As Jesus the Son heard the voice of the Father and saw the descent of the Spirit at his own baptism, so do all baptisms invoke the name of the one triune God: Father, Son and Holy Spirit.

Use these five verses from **Romans 5** as a meditation on the interrelatedness of the work of the Father, Son and Holy Spirit in our salvation and in our lives. What profound blessings are ours from God: peace, access, grace, hope and love! Let these move you to gratitude. Further, ponder how these blessings play out in situations where we find ourselves suffering. These spiritual graces become the foundation for our service to God in the world.

RESPONDING TO GOD

The proper response to the trinitarian mystery of God's being and working is wonder and worship, whether quiet contemplation of the cosmos (his majesty) or intense prostration before his throne (his holiness) or joyful remembrance of our baptism (his grace).

Closing Prayer. Father in Heaven, may your love be with me; Lord Jesus Christ, may your grace be with me; Holy Spirit, may your presence be with me—and with all your people in every place, this day and forevermore. Amen.

Proclaiming Good News

Jesus fills us with the Holy Spirit and sends us into the world. He wants us to proclaim the good news: the truth and grace of his life, the meaning of his death, the power of his resurrection, the glory of his exaltation, the presence of his Spirit and the promise to put all things right when he returns. We convey this message by all means: our words, of course, but also our willingness to pray for healing and other signs in the lives of others. The Scriptures this week portray various examples of gospel proclamation: a psalmist, a prophet, the twelve as sent by Jesus, Peter and John in Jerusalem just after Pentecost, and Paul years later in Athens. In each case, these witnesses declare God's glory and call for a response.

Approaching God. Lord of Glory, you are great and greatly to be praised; you are to be revered above all the powers that people foolishly admire and pursue, for you made and rule the universe; you deserve honor and majesty, O Lord; you are strong and beautiful.

Presenting Myself. O God my Creator, in you I live and move and have my being; O God my king, to you I give my allegiance; O God my Judge, before you I humble myself and trust in your mercy. Amen.

Inviting God's Presence. Refresh me with your presence, O Lord, and fill me with your Spirit, that I may be joyful in worship and bold in witness, for the sake of your name. Amen.

LISTENING TO GOD

Psalm 96; Isaiah 52:7-10;
Luke 9:1-6; Acts 3:1—4:22; Acts 17:16-33

Psalm 96 calls on us to sing in worship and shout in witness. Notice the energy and enthusiasm of this psalm. In fact, David uses it in the celebration after bringing the Ark of the Covenant into the city of Jerusalem (1 Chron 16). Trace out the attributes of God he emphasizes. Who does the psalmist call on to worship? What are appropriate ways of worship? Finally, meditate on the three roles of God that the psalmist proclaims: Creator, king and judge. Indeed, see how he governs and judges. To declare to all people the glory of this present and coming Lord is to announce good news of great joy.

Here's the scene in **Isaiah 52**: a lone runner makes his way up the heights toward the ruined city of Jerusalem and once in range shouts the good news of victory in battle ("Peace!" "Salvation!") and the triumph of their king ("He reigns!" "He returns!"). The sentinels on the walls spread the news and the people in the streets resound in relief and joy. God has comforted and redeemed his people; God has made his salvation known—and available—to all the nations. Meditate on this passage in light of our opportunities to announce good news in our spheres of influence. As Paul puts it in his own reflection on Isaiah, how can people respond to Jesus if they've never really heard about him, and how will they hear if no one speaks up? That's why we are sent and why our feet are "beautiful" (Rom 10:14-15).

In **Luke 9,** Jesus gathers his twelve disciples, invests them with spiritual authority and power, and sends them out to proclaim the kingdom of God. The news is good and the evidence is immediate. They offer hope and healing. They take nothing with them as they go, which means they must depend on God for protection and others for provision. There is no guarantee that people will welcome them or embrace their message. By this short-term assignment, Jesus begins to train them for the mission they will take up after Pentecost.

In **Acts 3 and 4,** we see the disciples in action shortly after Pentecost. As with Jesus, their preaching is both through word and action. In this case, the sign precipitates the sermon. Use your imagination to picture the sequence of scenes: the encounter with the beggar, his unrestrained excitement after being healed, the message to the astounded crowd, the intrusive arrest, the night in jail and the proclamation to the council. Look at how Peter describes Jesus and portrays salvation. Notice his use of irony: swapping the righteous one for a murderer, killing the author of life (3:14-15). Notice Peter's winsome promise of blessing for those who turn around and embrace God: wiping out of sins, times of refreshing, hope for universal restoration (3:19-21, 26). Peter and John, filled with the Holy Spirit, find the boldness to speak as witnesses and defend the name of Jesus. How does their example challenge and encourage you?

In **Acts 17** we find a fascinating account of Paul preaching the gospel in Athens, first in the synagogue, then in the marketplace and finally before an ancient council called the Areopagus, which may have met on the Areopagus, or "Mars Hill." What does Luke tell us about the city and its culture? Epicureans discounted deities and practiced serenity and detachment, while Stoics were more pantheistic and valued reason and duty. Study Paul's address. How does he connect to his audience? What are his major points—about God, about the human condition, about our proper response to God? How do people respond? Think about the principles from this story that you can apply in your own efforts to convey the good message to your friends.

RESPONDING TO GOD

Who can you pray for this week, that God would bring them healing or open their heart to the gospel? With whom can you begin a spiritual conversation this week, where you might have a chance to explain what you've learned and experienced in following Jesus?

Closing Prayer. Fill me, Holy Spirit, so that I may have power to bring healing in the name of Jesus and boldness to speak of his resurrection to those you may place in my path. Amen.

The Praying and Sharing Community

This week we have the first of four snapshots of the early church. Acts 2 outlines what the first believers devote themselves to: learning from the apostles about Jesus and his kingdom, sharing their lives and resources, remembering Christ's death at the table, and praying together. They gather in public places and share meals in private homes. They express love for God in their concerted praying and show love for each other in their concrete sharing.

Approaching God. Sovereign Lord, you made all things, earth and sky and sea and everything in them. Why do so many people rage against you? Why do so many leaders oppose you and your Messiah? Rightly, you laugh at them, sternly you warn them, and graciously you call them to turn to you for refuge and blessing. All praise to you, sovereign Lord.

Presenting Myself. Generous Father, too often I am preoccupied with the things I have or worried about the things I lack, but you know what I truly need, so today I am putting my trust in your goodness and focusing my attention on your gracious rule. Hallowed be your name. Amen.

Inviting God's Presence. Heavenly Father, fill me today with your Holy Spirit and cause me to know the reality of your kingdom, so that I would be quick to share my goods and bold to speak your Word. Amen.

LISTENING TO GOD

Psalm 2; Luke 11:1-13; **Luke 12:13-34;**
Acts 2:42-47; 4:23—5:11; Philippians 4:4-20

Psalm 2 figures in the prayer of the believers at the end of Acts 4, where it is ascribed to David. On first reading the psalm presents some harsh edges, but in the light of Christ its meaning becomes enlarged and deeply encouraging. In its original context, this "royal psalm" focused on the God-anointed king of his people. Read it in this light: rivals conspiring against the king, God's derision at their pretensions, the king's conviction about the divine favor toward him, a warning against actions that would provoke God's wrath. Next read it in a messianic light: earthly powers of all types foolishly disregarding God and his Christ ("anointed one"), God's affirmation of Christ as both King and Son and the one destined to inherit nations, and God's call for all to serve him and thus find refuge and blessing. (For other New Testament uses of the psalm see Acts 13:33; Heb 1:5; 5:5; Rev 2:27; 12:5; 19:15.)

In **Luke 11,** Jesus teaches about prayer in response to a request. Examine the Lord's prayer afresh—note that Luke's version is more spare than the more familiar form in Matthew 6. What might Jesus mean by "save us from the time of trial"? What is the point of the ensuing parable? Jesus encourages boldness and persistence, not because we can pester a reluctant God into a grudging response, but because we have a Father who wants to give good gifts, especially the Spirit, to us his children. So in any and every situation, feel free to ask, keep up the search and don't stop knocking.

In **Luke 12** Jesus teaches about sharing as opposed to hoarding. A request from the crowd precipitates a warning about greed and a parable about accumulation. Then Jesus addresses our normal concern about life's necessities: he discourages worry and striving and urges us instead to trust in the Father and to pursue his kingdom. God is pleased to bring us under the blessing of his rule. If our hearts are possessed by God rather than possessions, we will be free to gladly give. At the same time, it is the giving itself that loosens the idolatrous hold of money and frees our hearts to treasure God. Reflect on your own patterns of possessing and sharing in light of this teaching.

At the end of both **Acts 2 and 4,** Luke gives a summary description of life in the new church. But we must take care not to import our modern notions of "church"—this is a dynamic community and a burgeoning movement. Read 2:42-47 and imagine what it was like to be part of this exciting group in those very first months. Then read in 4:23-31 about one particularly dramatic occasion of community prayer. Trace how they draw on Psalm 2 to interpret their situation and inform their praying. How do they see themselves? What do they ask of God? What is God's response? Now study the second summary description (4:32-37) with its reference to great power and great grace. Finally, delve into the dramatic and sobering story of Ananias and Sapphira. How do they go wrong? What does the community learn? What should we learn?

Paul concludes his epistle to the **Philippians** with encouragement about prayer and affirmation of sharing. Always, he urges, we are to rejoice in the Lord. Rather than worry, we are to make our situations known to God with an underlying sense of gratitude and we will know an inexplicable peace. Paul expresses his gratitude to the Philippians for their financial help. Notice the fine line between thankfulness for having his needs met and reluctance to obligate them. He also posits a close relationship between financial sacrifice and spiritual reward. The bottom line: as we take care of others, God takes care of us.

RESPONDING TO GOD

Are you part of a small group of fellow Christians that meets regularly to share in each other's lives, to learn together, to seek God in prayer and to support one another in tangible ways? If not, could this be the time to find or form such a praying and sharing community?

Closing Prayer. Heavenly Father, give me today all that I need and help me to share with others; forgive my sins and help me to forgive others; keep me out of trouble and help me to stand by others; I ask these things according to your riches in glory in Chrst Jesus. Amen.

Facing Persecution

In our reading from Acts this week, God continues to pour out his Spirit on the early church for their mission in the world. Through the leaders, God displays remarkable signs of his presence and rule. The public watches in fascination and many become believers. But all of this does not prevent backlash and harassment. The authorities are threatened and they react. The disciples face persecution. It has always been so for the servants and messengers of God, including Jesus, as our other texts attest. But see how God exerts his power and provides for us when we undergo such hardships. He does not abandon us.

Approaching God. Lord Jesus, the Spirit of the Lord was upon you, anointing you to preach good news to the poor, to proclaim release to the captives and recovery of sight to the blind, to let the oppressed go free and to announce the time of the Lord's favor; yet people rose up against you and your apostles, as they do against your church today. Lord Jesus, have mercy.

Presenting Myself. O God, I know that you are for me, so in you, O Lord whose Word I praise, I put my trust; I am not afraid—what can a mere mortal do to me? I believe and so I will speak! Amen.

Inviting God's Presence. O Father, give me today the light of your glory in the face of your Son Jesus Christ—a treasure in this clay jar of my being—so that all would see that the extraordinary power comes from you and not from me. Amen.

LISTENING TO GOD
Psalm 56; 1 Kings 16:29—17:7; 19:1-18;
Luke 4:14-30; Acts 5:12-42; 2 Corinthians 4:5-15

David wrote **Psalm 56** based on his virtual captivity to the Philistines in Gath when he fled there to avoid the murderous pursuit of King Saul. David actually feigned madness as a self-protecting ploy (1 Sam 21:10-15). David describes the relentless pressure from his enemies that lasts "all day long." But even though he is afraid, he chooses to trust God and his word, and this act itself begins to dissolve his fear: if God is for me, what can a mere mortal do to me? See how tenderly God takes notice of our sufferings (verse 8). Once delivered, David worships God with gratitude and renews his determination to "walk before God in the light of life."

In the first passage from **1 Kings**, we meet Elijah and see who he is up against. In the second passage, we skip ahead to an account of Elijah collapsing under the threat against his life, even though he has witnessed extraordinary acts of God in the passages in between (which we will take up over the next few weeks). In chapter 16 we get a succinct preview of Ahab and his wife Jezebel and their evil reign. Then we meet Elijah, who immediately announces judgment from God in the form of famine. Observe how God cares for Elijah. Now skip to chapter 19. Unfazed by Elijah's triumph over the prophets of Baal, Jezebel vows to kill him. Elijah flees in fear and collapses into depression. Note the symptoms. Now watch as God cares for him with compassion, speaks to him on the mountain and then gives him a new task. What can we learn from these stories about facing persecution?

In **Luke 4**, we watch as Jesus experiences the highs and lows of acclamation and persecution. Jesus returns from his battle with Satan in the wilderness (not unlike Elijah's contest against the prophets of Baal) filled with power and garnering praise. But then he preaches a controversial sermon in his hometown. He makes some startling claims about himself and upsets the people by highlighting stories from the time of Elijah and Elisha when God showed mercy to non-Jews. Suddenly they want to kill him, but he manages to escape unharmed. This early incident foreshadows the persecution and eventual death of Jesus, experiences from which we ourselves are not exempt. Put yourself in his shoes as you dwell in this story.

Acts 5 conveys the people's growing fascination with the new Jesus-followers in Jerusalem: the amazing miracles, the open meetings, the many healings and the increasing number of believers. But the Jewish authorities are not pleased. Why might they be so opposed? Picture the sequence of scenes: arrest, jail break, re-arrest, hearing. Note the humorous aspects and the serious. Some want the apostles killed, but in the end they are merely flogged—but "merely" belies the severity of the reprimand. What about the apostles' stance and response inspires you? They are determined to be faithful witnesses to Jesus, their risen leader and Savior who offers forgiveness to the repentant and his Spirit to the obedient (verses 31-32).

Like Elijah, like Jesus, like the other apostles, Paul too faces severe persecution as he engages in the ministry of proclamation. He reveals to the **Corinthians** his remarkable perspective on what he does and what it costs him. Take time to meditate on this profound passage. Dwell on the treasure ("light of the glory of God in the face of Jesus Christ") and the clay jar (our bodies, our psyches). Ponder the power of God and the promise of resurrection. Renew your own resolve to speak in light of what you believe.

RESPONDING TO GOD

Do you face persecution of any sort? Let the examples from these Scriptures strengthen your resolve to speak of Christ even at the risk of ridicule or derision or discrimination. Let them also boost your willingness to trust God in the face of such difficulties.

Closing Prayer. While I live, Lord Jesus, I am always being given up to death for your sake so that your life may be made visible in my mortal flesh and your grace may extend to more and more people, thus increasing thanksgiving to you and glory to God. Amen.

The Serving and Suffering Community

Last week the story in Acts concluded on a strong note: the persecuted apostles escape with a beating and rejoice in the face of their trials. This week we focus on another episode of persecution, only this one ends in martyrdom. We must press into the mystery that God does not always exercise his power to deliver us from persecution. Some of us will undergo great suffering and even death. Also this week we examine an internal controversy of the early church and how the leaders solved it. This will call our attention to the various ways of serving within the community, each of which draws on the gifts given to us by the Holy Spirit.

Approaching God. O Lord, you are present in your holy temple—let all the earth keep silence—and you are enthroned in your heaven—let all people bow their knees; for your eyes behold all humankind and your gaze examines each one of us. Glory to you, Lord God, and to your Son Jesus, who stands at your right hand. Amen.

Presenting Myself. As a steward of your manifold grace, O Lord, I offer myself to serve others with the gifts I have received from you so that you may be glorified in all things through Jesus Christ. Amen.

Inviting God's Presence. For speaking with truth and grace, O Lord, I need your Word; for serving with equity and love, I need your strength; for enduring any sufferings that may come, I need your Spirit. Amen.

LISTENING TO GOD

Psalm 11; **1 Kings 17:8-16;** Luke 21:12-19;
Acts 6:1—8:3; 1 Peter 4:7-19

In **Psalm 11,** David counters those who advise him to flee to the mountains in order to avoid those trying to kill him. David declines their advice, no matter how dire things seem (verse 3), and vows instead to take refuge in the Lord. He trusts God to protect him. He asserts that God dwells in holiness and rules with power. God scrutinizes all persons and his testing purifies some and burns up others. The Lord is good and loves for us to do good; thus the upright will behold his face. This is exactly what happens for Stephen at the point of his martyrdom in Acts 7. In your meditation on this psalm, contrast the threat that lurks in the darkness with the grace that shines in the light of God's countenance.

We return to the Elijah story in **1 Kings 17.** The famine drags on and the wadi dries up. So God steers Elijah to the Phoenician region south of Sidon, enemy territory. Elijah asks a widow there for water and bread, but she is down to her final ration of flour and oil. Yet trusting in his prophetic word, she supplies Elijah's need; in turn, God miraculously supplies what she and her son need to live. She serves Elijah, he serves her.

In an apocalyptic section of **Luke 21,** Jesus foresees a time in the future when his followers will face arrest and persecution, betrayal and death. What does he assure his followers will be true under such terrible conditions? How can we square the prospect of death (verse 16) with the promise of not a hair harmed (verse 18)? If the martyr Stephen (Acts 7) could comment on this passage, what might he say?

In **Acts 6** a controversy arises within the young Jerusalem church. Apparently the program of daily distribution of food to widows and others is set up according to preexisting cultural and linguistic social groupings. The Hebraic Jews who speak Aramaic are meeting in their groups and the Hellenistic Jews of the Diaspora who speak Greek are meeting in theirs. The food allocations have come to reflect built-in biases. Analyze the solution they institute and its results. By the names of the seven, we see that they have empowered leaders from the slighted group. What in this account underscores the importance of serving each other in the community of believers? Luke goes on to highlight Stephen and how he gets into trouble. Study Stephen's defense before the Sanhedrin. What does he emphasize in his review of Old Testament history? How does he drive home the dangers of underestimating the voice of God-appointed leader-liberators and of overestimating the importance of the temple with its ritual practices? Meditate on the way Stephen dies. In the middle of this trauma, how does he receive grace and how does he show it? Take note of Saul's involvement and how he takes up the persecution with vehemence.

The text of **1 Peter** divides into two sections, the first highlighting service in the Christian community and the second discussing suffering. What marks of the church does Peter call for in verses 7-11? Take time to unpack his succinct treatment of spiritual gifts. The basic point is to serve one another in light of the grace and gift that comes from God, whether that gift relates primarily to speaking or teaching (as with "the twelve" in Acts 6) or serving in practical ways (as with "the seven" in Acts 6). In either case, God empowers the service and God gets the glory. Now focus on Peter's teaching about "sharing Christ's sufferings" in verses 12-19. How can blessing be imbedded in suffering? How does Peter encourage us to endure such ordeals?

RESPONDING TO GOD

In what ways has God gifted you for service to your fellow believers within your church community? Have you found a fitting place to use those gifts? If not, perhaps you should talk to someone in leadership this week about where you might be needed.

Closing Prayer. O righteous and gracious Lord, let me behold your face this week. Amen.

Setting People Free

The third dimension of the church's mission in the world arising from Acts (after proclaiming good news and facing persecution) concerns setting people free from those things that threaten, entrap, harm or oppress them. In following the examples of Jesus and the apostles, we seek to help people through the love of Christ and the power of the Spirit. In the biblical episodes for this week God prevents one death and reverses another, casts out evil spirits and pours out the Holy Spirit, tracks down an African seeker and stops an enemy in his tracks, frees a crippled woman and releases a paralyzed man. We too are called to care for others in their situations of need and by compassion, prayer and action to set them free in the name of Christ.

Approaching God. I love you, Lord, because you hear my voice and my supplications, you pay attention to my situation and my needs; therefore I will call on you as long as I live. Praise to you, merciful and gracious God.

Presenting Myself. What shall I return to you, O Lord, for all your bounty to me? I will lift up the cup of salvation with thanksgiving and call on your holy name.

Inviting God's Presence. Fill me with your Spirit this week, O Lord, so that free from the grip of sin and the fear of death I may speak readily to my friends of your goodness and pray boldly for them in their needs. Amen.

LISTENING TO GOD
Psalm 116; 1 Kings 17:17-24;
Luke 13:14-17; Acts 8:4—9:43; Acts 28:1-10

The speaker of **Psalm 116** has been set free from the snare of death and now rehearses his salvation with joyful gratitude. He opens with a declaration of love for God who in his grace and mercy hears our prayers. With the psalmist, recount the ways he has dealt bountifully with you. Where has he kept you from stumbling, from tears, from death itself? Also, reflect on the multidimensioned salvation God has provided us in Christ. Join the psalmist in a posture of humility ("I am your servant") and gratitude ("I will offer a thanksgiving sacrifice") and eagerness to acknowledge publicly all that God has done for you.

The prophet Elijah, in **1 Kings 17,** finds himself in a painful situation. While he is staying with the widow in Zarephath, who is taking care of him (and God her) during the drought, the woman's small boy falls ill and dies. She is distraught and all but blames him. Elijah pleads earnestly and repeatedly for God to give life back to the child. And God does, just as he will do later when Elisha prays (2 Kings 4:8-37) and Jesus prays (Mk 5:21-43) and Peter prays (Acts 9). These rare miracles point to the power of God to give each of us life after death through the risen Christ.

In **Luke 13,** Jesus sets a woman free from a spirit that had crippled her for eighteen years. He pronounces her liberation and lays his hands on her. Immediately she is healed and begins to praise God. Not so the synagogue leaders. What is their problem? How does Jesus answer them?

In **Acts 8 and 9,** we find five stories of healing and liberation. First, in 8:4-25, Philip—one of the seven chosen in Acts 6:5, a Hellenist—proclaims Jesus as the Messiah in the region of Samaria. Note the general results and then study the particular story of Simon the magician in verses 9-24. Scholars debate why in this case the Holy Spirit is not given until the laying on of hands by Peter and John, who come to check on the situation. What do you make of this? Perhaps, as the gospel crosses the dividing line between Jews and Samaritans (regarded as heretical half-

breeds), it is important for the Hebrew leaders of Jerusalem to play a vali-
dating role—important, I suspect, for both groups. Second, in 8:26-40,
Philip is led into an encounter with a high-ranking Ethiopian who is certainly a God-fearer, if not a proselyte to Judaism. Examine how this fascinating story unfolds. How is this African official set free? The third
story (9:1-30) features Saul's conversion (for comments, see week five of
Easter). Fourth, Peter heals Aeneas, who has lain paralyzed for eight
years (9:32-35). Fifth, Peter raises a woman, Tabitha, from the dead in
the coastal town of Joppa. Amazing! Consider how this overall sequence
of stories dramatizes the mission of Christians in the world: opposing
demonic powers and occult practices, explaining God's revelation across
cultural divides, turning enemies of the gospel into allies, releasing the
paralyzed and bringing life to the dead.

In **Acts 28,** Luke recounts the intriguing story of a shipwreck in which
the vessel and crew carrying Paul to Rome runs aground on the island of
Malta. You can read chapter 27 for the story of the tumultuous sea journey and Paul's several interventions to help save the whole enterprise.
But once on shore, Paul experiences God's power to protect from danger
(vipers!) and to bring healing to the father of Publius. Adversity leads to
new opportunity for helping and healing in the name of Christ. Paul
never loses sight of his mission.

RESPONDING TO GOD

Think of one person you know who is in need, perhaps a neighbor or
coworker or friend. What could you do this week to help that person
experience freedom or relief from whatever presses down on him or her?
Pray for? Pray with? Phone or e-mail? Go visit? Help out? Give money?
Go to bat for? Choose one thing that you can do that will embody Christ's
liberating love.

Closing Prayer. Return, O my soul, to your rest, for the Lord has dealt
bountifully with you. Amen.

The Embracing and Reconciling Community

In the renewal that Jesus brings, "there is no longer Greek and Jew, circumcised and uncircumcised, barbarian, Scythian, slave and free; but Christ is all and in all" (Col 3:11). No social hierarchy, no racial superiority, no spiritual privilege. We may absorb such distorted perspectives and attitudes from the wider society, but once we are in Christ and part of his church, they must be stripped off like soiled clothes. Instead we clothe ourselves with Christ and therefore strive to be an embracing and reconciling community. We mirror the love of God, which, as our texts this week demonstrate, shows no partiality.

Approaching God. I truly understand, O Lord, that you show no partiality, that in every nation and people group anyone who fears you and does what is right is acceptable to you—everyone who believes in you, Lord Jesus, receives forgiveness of sins through your name. Hallelujah!

Presenting Myself. Search me, O God, and know my heart; test me and know my thoughts; see if there be any prejudicial way in me and lead me in the way all-embracing. Amen.

Inviting God's Presence. As your chosen one, O God, holy and beloved by you, clothe me with compassion, kindness, humility, meekness and patience; above all, clothe me with love, which binds everything together in perfect harmony. Amen.

LISTENING TO GOD
Psalm 133; Jonah 1—4; Luke 7:1-10;
Acts 10:1—11:18; Colossians 3:1-17; Philemon

Psalm 133, a short but vivid evocation of unified community, was sung as people ascended to Jerusalem for the annual festivals. We nod our heads at the words "how good and pleasant" because we know how lousy and ugly it can get between kindred. What do the metaphors of oil and dew suggest? The precious, fragrant oil, a sign of God's presence, was poured liberally to anoint Aaron as a priest (Ex 29:7-9; 30:25). The morning dew on Mount Hermon (the tallest mountain in Israel) and Mount Zion (the most sacred height) conveys renewal and fresh expectancy. God intends to pour out his renewing presence in our community and bestow the life-giving blessing of unity. So let us joyfully embrace one another!

Jonah tells a dramatic story of God's determination to bring his message to the Assyrian capital of Nineveh in the eighth century B.C.E. Read the whole book and trace the various "turnings" in the story: Jonah's running away, God's turning him back by the storm, Jonah's repentance in the belly of the fish, Nineveh's turn to God and God's change of mind, Jonah's turning away in anger and God's attempt to turn his heart toward a repugnant people. Jonah simply cannot abide that God would show mercy to the enemies of Israel. But God is indeed gracious and merciful, abounding in steadfast love and eager to forgive (4:2). Are we?

In **Luke 7,** Jesus heals a Gentile centurion's slave in an incident that foreshadows the story of Peter and Cornelius. The centurion is a God-fearer, one who respects the Jewish nation and perhaps worships Yahweh in some fashion. The focus here is the faith of the centurion, but we also see the blessings of the kingdom extended by Jesus to non-Jews.

Acts 10 gives the remarkable story of Peter's encounter with Cornelius. This is the decisive breakthrough of the gospel to the Gentiles and also a breakthrough in the thinking of the Jewish believers. Read carefully for the broad strokes and telling details (for example, Joppa is where Jonah went when fleeing his call; a tanner would be ceremonially unclean due to his profession). Be delighted by the divine orchestration (angels, visions) and the human reactions (terror, puzzlement, amazement). God goes to extremes because the divide is entrenched and the prejudice visceral. But Peter's vision erodes his external categories of clean and unclean, and the Spirit's descent on Gentiles shatters his ethnocentric hierarchy of spiritual privilege. Peter will not let Cornelius treat him like a "god" (verse 25), and God will no longer let Peter treat a Gentile like a "dog" (as some Jews derogatorily called them).

Paul paints for the **Colossians** a picture of transformed life in the community of Christ. He emphasizes our radical union with Jesus—our true life is hidden in Christ. We let Christ's truths shape our lives, not the secular practices around us. We shed certain moral "clothes" and don others. We receive a new self that continues to be renewed in Christ's image. Then a kicker of an implication: in this renewal, there are no racial or social distinctions and thus no room for any kind of prejudice (verse 11). Paul calls us to embody the virtues of holiness (verse 12), practice the gestures of love (verses 13-14) and enjoy the blessings of the Spirit (verses 15-16), all in the name of Christ.

Paul's letter to **Philemon,** his brother in Christ and partner in the faith, illustrates the practical implications of our unity and equality in Christ. Read the short letter and see if you can piece together the story. Onesimus is Philemon's slave who, for an unspecified reason, has fled his master. Somehow he finds his way to Paul who leads him to faith in Christ. This makes Paul his spiritual father and Philemon his spiritual brother. Paul sends Onesimus back with this letter urging his friend to do the right thing: embrace him and be reconciled.

RESPONDING TO GOD

Is there any group of persons different from you—in race, culture, social background, sexual orientation, politics, education—that you find difficult to fully accept and freely love? Ask God's help to show some simple gesture of embrace toward just one person from that group this week.

Closing Prayer. So that we may be an embracing and reconciling community, Lord Christ, let your peace rule in our hearts, let your word dwell in us richly, and let your name govern all that we say or do. Amen.

Confronting the Powers

Luke's narrative of the early church alternates between significant breakthroughs (Pentecost, Samaria, the Ethiopian, Saul's conversion, Cornelius) and sobering setbacks (arrests, floggings, Stephen's stoning, Saul's rant). This week we reflect further on the church's role of speaking truth to those in power, a prophetic task that can bring dire consequences. Consider this succession of political rulers: Herod the Great who seeks to kill the infant Jesus, Herod the tetrarch who beheads John the Baptist, Herod Agrippa who orders James killed, and his son, Agrippa, who questions Paul. These stories of confronting the powers remind us that God's authority is greater than that of any human we may face.

Approaching God. O God, when your people were few in number and of little account, wandering as strangers from nation to nation, from one kingdom to another, you allowed no one to oppress them, you rebuked kings on their account, saying, "Do not touch my anointed ones or do my people any harm"; for you are greater than any earthly power, O Lord, you are king forever.

Presenting Myself. I give thanks to you, O Lord, and glory in your holy name; I sing your praises and remember the wonderful works you have done for me.

Inviting God's Presence. I am seeking your presence today, O Lord, and asking for your strength so that I may tell about your deeds to those around me. Amen.

LISTENING TO GOD

Psalm 105; **1 Kings 18; Luke 9:7-9;**
Luke 22:66—23:25; **Acts 12;** Acts 21:22—26:32

Psalm 105 exhorts the people to remember God's wonderful works and to praise him (verses 1-6). The psalmist recalls the covenant with the patriarchs (verses 7-11) and rehearses God's faithfulness to the nation: how the Jews ended up in Egypt (verses 12-26), how they got out (verses 27-38), and how God cared for them in the wilderness and brought them into the Promised Land (verses 39-45). Two figures faced political powers: Joseph found favor with a king and joined a government, and Moses plagued a pharaoh and secured an exodus. In each confrontation, trace God's hand. Take time to remember God's hand in your own history and sing his praises.

We return to the Elijah story in **1 Kings 18.** This is one of Scripture's great confrontations between the power of God and the idolatrous forces of evil (others include Moses against Pharaoh, David against Goliath, Esther against Haman and Daniel against the satraps—and lions). Read it for its inherent drama: Elijah's bold risk, his daring ridicule, his profound faith and his great victory. Elijah unmasks the false power of the idols and exposes the corruption and exploitation of Ahab. Even so, as we saw in week four, Jezebel is unfazed and Elijah is undone.

Luke 9 mentions Herod the tetrarch who had capriciously executed John the Baptist and is now curious about Jesus. For the story of John's arrest and beheading, see Mark 6:14-29. John ran afoul of Herod and Herodias because he condemned their marriage. Follow the awful story of Herod's rash vow, his wife's cunning manipulation, his daughter's complicity and his cruel capitulation to save face. Do we have the courage to confront powerful people with the demands of truth and justice?

Revisit in **Luke 22 and 23** Jesus' own encounter with religious and political powers. After his arrest, grilling and beating, Jesus appears formally before the Jewish Council and then publicly before the Roman procurator. Pilate sends Jesus over to King Herod for more questioning and abuse. Jesus offers no resistance or defense. Pilate discerns his innocence but, yielding to rabid lobbying and political expediency, condemns him anyway—

another unjust exercise of state power with apparent impunity.

Acts 12 tells of a blow to the early church at the hand of King Herod Agrippa. He has James, the brother of John, executed by sword. This pleases many Jews who oppose the Way of Jesus, so Herod decides to kill Peter as well. Read the account of his arrest and miraculous escape. Enjoy the humorous touches. Think about the role of prayer in this outcome and what this teaches us. Luke reports Herod's later death and offers an interpretation (verses 20-23). Notice the political machinations in this passage but also the danger of posturing before the power of God himself.

Acts 21—26 is an extended narrative of a Christian (Paul) contending with political powers. The tale reads like a plot for a television miniseries: false accusations by jealous opponents, instigation of hostile crowds, an attempted lynching, a hasty police intervention, a case of mistaken identity, an evangelistic testimony, the playing of the citizenship card, a courtroom ploy to sow dissension, an assassination plot, a nephew acting as an informant, a secret prisoner transfer, an attempt at political flattery, dialogue with a local governor, an official fishing for bribes, a languishing stint in prison, another trial before a new governor, an appeal to the highest authority (the emperor), and finally an extended defense before the king of the region, who ironically could have freed Paul but for the appeal already set into motion. Through it all, pay attention to the way Paul confronts and communicates to those in power.

RESPONDING TO GOD

Do you need to communicate your conviction about some matter of truth or justice to anyone in a position of authority over you, whether immediate (as in your boss) or distant (as in your senator)? If so, ask God for the courage and grace to do so this week or when the time seems right.

Closing Prayer. As you encouraged your servant Paul in prison, likewise help me keep up my courage so that I may bear witness for you wherever you may send me. Amen.

The Giving and Sending Community

The story of the church at Antioch, the third great city of the empire after Rome and Alexandria, is briefly told but full of import. God directs this multiethnic, Spirit-filled, socially concerned community to set apart two of its five leaders for a mission to Gentile cities. Thus, as Jesus instructed, the witness now spreads toward the ends of the earth. But God has always sent his people to bring blessing to others, as when he told Abraham to head west or when Jesus dispatched six dozen disciples to various villages. When we send, we also support; as we go, we also give. These then are the final characteristics of the Christian community as portrayed in Acts: giving and sending.

Approaching God. Let the peoples praise you, O God, let all the peoples praise you; let the nations be glad and sing for joy, for you judge the peoples with equity and guide the nations upon the earth. Amen.

Presenting Myself. Generous Lord, I desire to glorify you by my obedience to the confession of the gospel of Christ and by my generosity in sharing with others. Amen.

Inviting God's Presence. Lord God, be gracious to me and bless me; make your face to shine upon me so that I can make your way known upon the earth and your saving power among all nations. Amen.

LISTENING TO GOD

Psalm 67; Genesis 12:1-9; **Luke 10:1-20; Acts 11:19-30;
13:1-3;** 2 Corinthians 8—9; Galatians 1:11—2:10

Psalm 67 grows out of two ancient seeds—God's promise through Abraham: I will bless you and through you bless all nations (Gen 12:2), and God's blessing through Aaron: the Lord make his face to shine upon you (Num 6:25). In short, the psalmist seeks God's blessing on his people so that the peoples everywhere on earth would also be blessed by his saving power. It is a missionary prayer and its ultimate fulfillment comes through Jesus, the king who judges with equity and the shepherd who guides with love. The shepherd-king sends us to the nations with news to make them sing for joy.

In **Genesis 12** we read about the seminal call of God to Abraham—or Abram, as he was then called. Abram is sent to another land with peoples and cultures different from his own. For Abram, the call embodied great risk and sacrifice, but it held the prospect of a great blessing and legacy. By his faith and obedience all the families, all the ethnic groups, all the nations of the earth in all the ages to come would be blessed. What a vision! But still he must actually pack everything up and set out. And so he does. As a result, we are blessed today.

Earlier in **Luke**, Jesus sends out the twelve on a mission (see Luke 9 in week two), but now he sends out some thirty-five pairs of disciples on a similar assignment with similar instructions. Examine these again, including the need to depend on others for material support. This time Jesus begins on a different note: the call to pray for more "harvesters." Even as they embark on their mission, Jesus wants them to think about multiplying the number of missionaries. Jesus emphasizes that we represent him (verse 16). How does that make you feel? Notice the eschatological horizon: exclusion for some, inclusion for others. Finally, think again about the power and authority Jesus delegates to us (verses 17-20).

Carefully read the Antioch passages in **Acts 11 and 13** and let the details yield insights. Luke picks up with the diaspora of the Jewish believers mentioned in 8:1. They proclaim the good news wherever they find refuge, mostly to Jews; but some break the pattern and evangelize among

Hellenists, who are most likely Gentile Greeks. The resulting mixed community is distinctive enough that (a) the Jerusalem leaders send Barnabas to check it out and (b) the locals come up with a new name for them: *Christians* (Christ's people). What is life like in this dynamic new community? Why do you suppose the Holy Spirit chooses this church as the launching point for missionaries? How does this happen?

2 Corinthians. After the initial offering taken at Antioch for the Judean Christians, Paul mounts a decade-long project of soliciting relief funds from the Gentile churches for the impoverished church in Jerusalem. The Corinthians early on pledged to participate (see 1 Cor 16:1-4) but along the way, their collection effort faltered. Now Paul writes to motivate them to follow through on their initial intentions. Paul includes a wealth of teaching on the matter of stewardship. Study the two chapters to learn his principles. Giving is in response to God's great generosity. Also note that people are sent as well as money. How does this text speak to your own pattern of stewardship and giving?

Paul opens his **Galatians** letter by explaining his conversion and commission. He also recounts (probably) the trip to Jerusalem with Barnabas to deliver the famine offering taken in Antioch in response to prophecy. Paul's wants to validate his call to take the gospel to the Gentiles, even as Peter was called to reach the Jews. The letter goes on to assert that Gentile converts need not become circumcised, ceremonial law–keeping Jews; they are under grace and free in Christ. Note how both preaching the gospel and caring for the poor are seen as critical.

RESPONDING TO GOD

Does your church support missionaries? Do you pray for any of them or give money in support of them? Do you give money toward relief efforts at times of disaster or in response to human suffering in parts of the world? Have you considered going on a short-term mission experience?

Closing Prayer. May God continue to bless us; let all the ends of the earth revere him. Amen.

Hospitality

Think of your experience of God's grace in terms of hospitality: at a point of great need and alienation, he takes you into his family, provides a cleansing bath and gives you new clothes; he invites you to his nourishing table and blesses you with his presence. And he extends this welcome indefinitely. This is what God is like and what he wants us to be like. Hospitality means welcoming others and offering provision, protection and blessing. It doesn't happen only at our dining tables. Our texts this week reveal the shape of hospitality. In serving others, we actually serve God, as the Abraham story and Jesus' teaching about judgment make clear. In fact, our hospitality communicates the gospel and embodies God's grace, especially when we offer it to those with the greatest need and the least ability to pay us back.

Approaching God. O Lord, you are the God of all gods and the Ruler of all rulers, the great God, mighty and awesome; you do not play favorites and you cannot be bribed; you execute justice for orphans and widows and provide food and clothing for strangers. You are my praise! You are my God!

Presenting Myself. Today I set myself apart for you, O Lord, I dedicate myself to you in response to your choosing and blessing of me; today I mark my heart as wholly yours and will try to walk in your ways, especially your way of hospitality.

Inviting God's Presence. Fill me with your loving Spirit, O Lord, so that I will readily see you in the strangers I meet this day and gladly show them the respect and kindness that honors you. Amen.

LISTENING TO GOD

Genesis 18:1-17; Deuteronomy 10:12-22;
Psalm 23; Ruth 2; 4:13-22; **Matthew 25:31-46;**
Luke 14:1-14; 3 John

In **Genesis 18,** we witness a vivid scene of bedouin hospitality. Notice the lengths to which Abraham goes to care for these sudden visitors. What impresses you? We learn in verse 1 that these are divine guests—the Lord and two angels—but apparently Abraham, at least at first, entertains these angels unawares (see Heb 13:2). In the course of offering hospitality, Sarah receives her own iteration of the divine promise that she will bear a son in her old age (see 17:15-19), even though she finds this laughable on its face. Not so the Lord!

In **Deuteronomy 10,** Moses comes off the mountain, God's law in hand, and articulates to the people what God wants from them (and us). Carefully delineate what God desires and requires. Essentially, he says, love me with all your being and love your neighbor as I have loved you. Where does grace come into the picture? What is meant by circumcising the heart? (See Gen 17 for more on this "sign of the covenant.") Why does God especially protect and provide for orphans, widows and strangers (e.g., foreigners or immigrants)? Why are we to do the same? We show grace to the needy because God has been gracious to us.

Read **Psalm 23** as a picture of God's provision of hospitality. (See comments in week four of Easter.)

The story of **Ruth** takes only four chapters; it's worth reading the whole book. With her husband and two sons, Naomi leaves Judah for Moab due to a famine. While there the two sons marry Moabite women. Then Naomi's husband and sons die. Naomi decides to return to Judah, and one of her daughters-in-law, Ruth, insists on going with her, a gracious act in itself. Chapter 2 portrays Ruth gleaning, or picking up leftover grain (see Lev 19:9-10), in the field of Naomi's kinsman Boaz. Pick out all the gestures of hospitality Boaz extends to Ruth, a foreigner. Boaz protects, provides and blesses! See how Boaz himself embodies God's "wings of refuge" (verse 12). Enjoy the end of the story and how important Ruth is in Israel's history.

In **Matthew 25** Jesus concludes a lengthy discourse with a depiction of the Son of Man as king, implementing the final judgment of humanity. The basis of the judgment is startling: the provision of hospitality—food and drink, welcome and embrace, clothing and shelter, health care and prison visitation—to those in great need. Christ identifies himself with such people (Christian or not) and expects us to open our hearts and homes in compassionate hospitality.

In **Luke 14,** we have one of the many banquet scenes in Luke's Gospel—which shows the importance of hospitality and table fellowship. First, Jesus extends care to the man with dropsy, a hospitable act of sorts. Second, he tells a parable to make a point about humility. And third, he challenges his host to a truer type of hospitality, one that responds to the physically weakest and socially lowest, rather than only those from whom we can expect something in return. Christian hospitality is not self-serving. Do we ever do what Jesus suggests?

Third John is the New Testament's shortest and most private letter. An elder (or elderly leader) writes to his friend Gaius to commend him for his faith and his hospitality to traveling missionaries. He expresses frustration with Diotrephes, the self-serving leader of the house church who evidently refused to extend such hospitality. How does providing care to "strangers" make us "coworkers with the truth"?

RESPONDING TO GOD

Who do you know that could benefit from the kind of hospitality that reflects the character of God? What plans could you make this week to show such hospitality to someone in the coming days or weeks?

Closing Prayer. O Lord, I have come under your wings and found refuge; let me now be the means of extending your refuge to others, for the sake of your gracious name. Amen.

Our Bodies

Hospitality means looking out for bodily needs: food, drink, clothing, shelter, medicine. We care for others as we would want to be cared for, indeed, in the way that we care for ourselves. "No one ever hates his own body, but he nourishes and tenderly cares for it," wrote Paul in teaching that husbands should love their wives as they do their own bodies (Eph 5:29-30). God wants us to attend to bodily needs and enjoy bodily pleasures. As with every good gift, however, dangers come with the package. Our sensual pleasures in cuisine, wine, cosmetics, clothes, exercise and sex can easily morph into idolatrous and indulgent desires and even self-destructive addictions. The Scriptures for this week celebrate the goodness of our bodies—by which we love God and neighbor—and also warn of the inherent temptations.

Approaching God. Father God, you made us in your image as embodied creatures, male and female; Son of God, you became incarnate and lived as one of us; Son of Man, for us you gave your body to be broken and your blood to be poured out; Holy Spirit, you have made our bodies your home and assured us of resurrection and life in the world to come. All praise to you, Lord God. Amen.

Presenting Myself. Creator and Father, I am your creature, I am your child: today I trust in you for all my bodily needs and focus my attention on your loving rule; I am your creature, I am your child. Amen.

Inviting God's Presence. Spirit of God, help me to live this day in light of your holy and indwelling presence. Amen.

LISTENING TO GOD

Psalm 128; Song of Solomon; **Ecclesiastes 9:7-10;** **Matthew 6:25-33; 1 Corinthians 6:12-20**

Psalm 128 announces a beatitude: blessed are those who take God seriously and conform their lives to his ways. The blessing is epitomized by fruitfulness in two senses: good work that yields plenty of food and a good marriage that yields plenty of kids around the table. Echoing the cultural mandate given to the first humans (Gen 1), this psalm celebrates both cultivation and procreation—and the fruit that comes from both kinds of labor.

The **Song of Solomon** is a sensuous, poetic celebration of human love and sexuality as two young lovers anticipate their wedding. Read the opening verse cycle (1:1—2:7) and you quickly get the idea: erotic attraction, admiration of beauty, rapturous words, longing for consummation and passionate joy—all the marks of romantic love. Read the whole book and enjoy the cycles of anticipation and encounter, the luxuriant imagery and metaphor, and the sheer intoxication with life and love. Christians over the centuries have squirmed at the inclusion of this book in holy Scripture and felt compelled to interpret it as an allegory of God's love for his people. The most straightforward reading, however, affirms our human sexuality and the beautiful gift of marital intimacy.

The preacher of **Ecclesiastes** wrestles with the philosophical conundrums of our earthly existence. In 9:1-6 he bemoans two apparent truths, that death comes to all humans and that it matters not whether one is good or bad. But in the face of such vanity or futility, he offers an interlude of life-affirming counsel in 9:7-10: enjoy good food and wine, dress well and care for your appearance, treasure intimacy with your spouse, tackle your work with energy and be glad for each day you are alive. In other words, be grateful for your body and all the things it enables you to do.

Jesus addresses the matter of bodies and their needs in his Sermon on the Mount in **Matthew 6.** The issue is not food and clothes themselves—

there's nothing wrong with having and enjoying such things—but the way we go about getting them. What does it mean to "worry" about them and to "strive" after them? What is the danger here? (Hint: glance at verses 19-24.) Conversely, what does it mean to strive for the kingdom of God and his righteousness? Jesus calls us to a posture of trust for our physical needs, even when we are able to work and earn and purchase. The problem comes when we idolize these provisions and pleasures and make their acquisition a consuming passion. God will supply what we need so we can have the without-a-care freedom of birds.

In **1 Corinthians** Paul challenges the perspective and practice of those who justified sexual intercourse outside of marriage (including prostitution) on the grounds that, like eating, sexual activity was merely bodily and therefore spiritually inconsequential. Paul quotes some common sayings (verses 12, 13 and probably 18) and then augments or counters them. Study his argument. Rather than downplay the body, he actually elevates its importance: by our bodies we are united to Christ, we are "members" of his body, the church, and we are dwelling places for his Spirit. Furthermore, we find here the sacred importance of sex: it expresses a spiritual intimacy between two participants. (In 7:1-7 he affirms sexual equality and enjoyment in marriage.) Our sexuality, then, is a good gift, but not something we carelessly indulge in or let ourselves be dominated by or regard as merely physical; with our bodies and sexuality we can glorify God.

RESPONDING TO GOD

What is your attitude toward your own body with its needs and pleasures? Do you need to hear God's permission to care for and enjoy your body? Or do you need to rein in the time, energy and money that you are anxiously and indulgently spending on your body?

Closing Prayer. Lord God, I acknowledge that I am not my own, that I belong to you, body and soul, for you have bought me with the price of your Son's life; therefore, let me glorify you in my body, this day and every day. Amen.

WEEK TWELVE OF ORDINARY TIME
Beginning the twelfth Sunday after Pentecost

Generosity

God is generous. He gives us his image in our very being. He gives us the bounty of creation to sustain our lives. He gives us himself in the incarnation of the Word. He gives us redemption through the sacrifice of his Son. He gives us his very Spirit to indwell us. He gives us the promise of resurrection and life forever in his presence. What is our response to such incalculable grace? One response, simply put, is generosity toward our neighbors.

Approaching God. O the depth of your riches and wisdom and knowledge, O God! Your judgments are unsearchable, your ways inscrutable! Who has known your mind? Who has offered you counsel? Who has given you anything that would obligate a gift in return? For from you and through you and to you are all things. To you be the glory forever. Amen.

Presenting Myself. In response to your mercies, O Lord, I present myself to you as a living sacrifice; may my whole life be an expression of worship pleasing to you. Amen.

Inviting God's Presence. Renew my mind, Holy Spirit; free me from the distorted ways of thinking common in the culture around me; reshape my perspectives and guide my decisions so that my life increasingly conforms to your will. Amen.

LISTENING TO GOD
Psalm 112; Genesis 13; Matthew 20:1-16;
Luke 21:1-4; Romans 12:1-13

Psalm 112 pronounces blessing on those who revere God and happily adhere to his ways. These blessings include strong descendents, good reputation and great wealth. How does the psalmist go on to describe the character of such commendable persons? Take note of the prominence given to generosity as an attribute. Blessed to be a blessing! Notice also how the hearts of these right-living persons are centered in God and therefore not prone to anxiety at bad news or intimidation before dishonest opponents. To what extent could this psalm be a fair description of your reputation?

We return to Abram's story in **Genesis 13,** an episode that precedes the divine visitation in chapter 18 (see week ten). Abram and his nephew Lot have both grown wealthy and tensions have arisen. What are the issues? How does Abram, the elder of the two, choose to handle the situation? Why is this an instance of generosity? See how God responds to Abram's unselfish gesture. Are you in any kind of situation that calls for you perhaps to follow Abram's example?

Jesus tells a parable in **Matthew 20** to stress the grace at the heart of God's kingdom. The Lord blesses us according to his generosity, not according to our merit. Read and digest the parable. Let the surprise at the end fully register with you. In fact, imagine a scene like this between an employer and a group of day laborers playing out in our own day. In addition to the lesson about spiritual grace, what does the parable suggest about our opportunities to be generous with material resources? Shouldn't our pattern of giving reflect the generosity that characterizes God?

In **Luke 21,** Jesus calls his followers' attention (and ours) to the striking contrast in giving patterns between the rich and the poor. His observation becomes a teachable moment: what does he want us to understand and therefore do? Let his words sink in as you think about the resources you have and the pattern of giving that you practice. By the way, year after year in the United States, poor people give a higher per-

centage of their annual income in charitable contributions than those
who are rich.

The hinge of Paul's letter to the **Romans** comes with the soaring doxology of 11:33-36 and the sobering "therefore" of 12:1. Having exposed
the gospel as the power of God for salvation through faith, Paul begins to
spell out the implications for living in light of this great mercy of God.
Two of the marks of faithful life in Christ are generosity and hospitality
(verse 13). But study verses 1-7 for the deeper underpinnings of these and
the ten or so other marks in verses 9-13. Paul speaks of what we give to
God and what God gives to us. We present ourselves wholly to God—
our bodies, our minds—with the goal of being transformed and doing
what pleases him. He distributes to us grace in the form of spiritual gifts
or special capacities to serve one another in the "body of Christ." List out
the seven such gifts mentioned here and the particular way each should
be exercised (for example, in the case of "giving," do so generously).
What gift has God given you? In what way are you giving yourself to
God? Which aspects of faithful living need to mark your life more?

RESPONDING TO GOD

Where do you have an opportunity to be generous this week with your
money or time or God-given abilities?

Closing Prayer. In light of your great generosity toward me, O Lord,
give me the grace to be generous myself, this week and always. Amen.

Our Minds

God has created each of us with a mind with which to learn and think and make decisions. Our cognitive, rational and volitional capacities reflect his image as Creator; when we exercise them, we glorify him. Scientific discovery, philosophical inquiry, psychological theorizing, technological invention, creative expression—all such endeavors of the human mind can bring honor to God and satisfaction to us. But they can also dishonor God and damage us. Knowledge is not enough; we also need wisdom. "In [Christ] are hidden all the treasures of wisdom and knowledge" (Col 2:3). We must feed and exercise our minds from a posture of intellectual humility and spiritual openness.

Approaching God. Who has known your mind, O Lord, so as to instruct you? Who has directed your spirit or served as your counselor? With whom did you need to consult for enlightenment or to learn the path of justice? No one, O Lord, for no one is like you in wisdom and power.

Presenting Myself. O Lord, I desire to trust in you with all my heart and not rely on my own insight; I want to acknowledge you in all of my ways and walk in the straight paths that you lay out; I don't want to be wise in my own eyes, but rather to properly fear you and turn away from all evil. To these ends, O Lord, have mercy on me. Amen.

Inviting God's Presence. O Father, Lord of heaven and earth, reveal to me your wisdom and your ways so that, with childlike openness of mind, I may know you more deeply and love you more truly. Amen.

LISTENING TO GOD

1 Kings 3:1-12; 4:29-34; Psalm 19; Proverbs 1;
Matthew 11:25-27; 1 Corinthians 2

1 Kings 3 tells how Solomon, successor to his father David, gained his famous wisdom. An interchange with God occurs in a dream. As you study it, what impresses you? Notice Solomon's humility as he contemplates the weight of his new role. God promises to give him a wise and discerning mind. Read in **1 Kings 4** the summary of his wisdom and its various dimensions. Solomon systematically studied nature, he discoursed with learned peers, he absorbed traditional bodies of knowledge, he published his thinking, he expressed his creativity in songs and he acquired acumen through governing. What does the figure of Solomon, even if idealized, tell us about God's desire for us to fully use our minds and thereby bring him praise? Furthermore, we too may ask for wisdom from God who gives it generously and ungrudgingly (Jas 1:5).

Psalm 19 points to two ways God speaks: creation and Scripture. Both engage our minds. What do the "heavens" convey with their voiceless praise in verses 1-4? (Compare this to Paul's assertion in Rom 1:18-23.) In particular, what does the image of the sun suggest (verses 5-6)? In verse 7, the focus shifts to the "law of the Lord," and David extols it in a series of nuanced verses. God's law reveals his character and his general will for us; it benefits our whole being: soul, mind, heart and eyes. Such wisdom exceeds financial wealth and sensuous pleasure in value. How, according to verses 11-13, does the law practically (and sometimes painfully) help us? Conclude your reflections with the prayer of verse 14.

Proverbs presents the collected wisdom of Solomon and others. A "proverb" (root meaning: "a comparison") can be any kind of wise pronouncement, from a straightforward maxim to a witty wisecrack. Tease out from verses 2-6 the purposes of this book; think about how it engages both our minds and our hearts. Two foundational ideas jump out from verse 7: wisdom spreads its roots in the soil of awe before God, and wisdom bears its fruit as we take what God says seriously. Consider how the next section (verses 8-19) portrays the voices vying for our allegiance. Do you feel any pressures like this? The rest of the chapter (and also chapter 8) personifies Wisdom as one offering her counsel freely in the public sphere. Two suggestions for further study: first, think about the oft-quoted admonition of 3:5-8 and, second, read several times the chapter of Proverbs that corresponds to your birthday (for example, chapter 19 if you were born on, say, April 19) and reflect on its wisdom.

Matthew 11 records a startling prayer by Jesus that contains a profound and paradoxical truth. It says something important about God and something sobering about us. Two clarifications: "these things" refers to the words and acts of Jesus (and his disciples—see Lk 10:21-24); "infants" stands here for those who are humble, unlearned and open-hearted as children. Contemplate the two insights here, that learning depends on more than mere study and that knowing means more than mere knowledge. It is by God's gracious revelation that we understand spiritual truth and by Jesus' gracious choice that we know spiritual intimacy with his Father.

In **1 Corinthians 2,** Paul without apology defends the wisdom and power of the gospel that holds up the crucified Jesus as God's Christ and humanity's Savior. To the educated, this seems foolish and to the powerful, it looks weak. In chapter 2 Paul describes his own approach in proclaiming this upside-down message. What lessons can we learn from him? What is the role of the Spirit in shaping our minds? Paul does not condemn intellect and influence in themselves, but he stresses the limitation of our human minds, which are prone to arrogance even as they are susceptible to deception. (See also Is 40:12-31, which verse 16 quotes.)

RESPONDING TO GOD

What are you doing these days to feed your mind? What are you doing to stay humble in mind?

Closing Prayer. Let the words of my mouth and the meditations of my heart be acceptable to you this day, O Lord, my rock and my redeemer. Amen.

Justice

Loving our neighbor requires more than responding to need; we must also address the cause of the need. It's one thing when a person is poor due to famine but another when it's due to economic exploitation. This week, we hear Amos warning the powerful against "trampling the poor" and watch Nathan confront his king's unjust actions. We listen as Jesus stands up for people oppressed by their religious leaders. And we look at two psalms that disclose God's heart for justice. We must repent of our own participation in injustice and stand ready to speak out and take action.

Approaching God. Blessed be your name, O Lord, from this time on and forevermore; from the rising of the sun this morning to its setting this evening, praise be to your name! You sit high above the nations of the earth and your glory exceeds the heavens, yet you lift the poor from the dust and the needy from the ashes. Praise to you, O Lord.

Presenting Myself. God, be merciful to me, a sinner.

Inviting God's Presence. Strengthen my heart, O Lord, and incline your ear to do justice for the vulnerable and the oppressed so that those who strike terror will do so no more. Amen.

LISTENING TO GOD

2 Samuel 11:1—12:25; **Psalm 10;** Psalm 113;
Amos 5:10-24; Matthew 23:1-36; **Luke 18:1-17**

Read the story in **2 Samuel 11 and 12.** David may be king, but he is not above the requirements of God's justice. David abuses his power and violates his neighbor. Consider Nathan's courage and his cleverness in confronting the king. He exposes not only David's lust, greed and murderous scheming but the injustice of his actions. David repents and receives forgiveness, but he also faces consequences. How tempting to use whatever power we possess to our own advantage and at the expense of others—and then to rationalize it. Furthermore, how difficult to confront a powerful person who has acted unjustly. But love of neighbor means always treating her justly and defending him against injustice.

The first half of **Psalm 10** laments the arrogance and audacity of the wicked and questions why God allows them to continue unchecked in their violent exploitation of the vulnerable. Read verses 1-11 a couple times and let the feelings of the psalmist sink in. Glancing through the morning newspaper might help you contemporize the lament. Next, examine the prayer in verses 12-18. What does the psalmist ask of God, and what does he believe about God? Let this psalm free you to express your own lament and your own plea for God to enact justice.

Psalm 113 opens and closes with "Praise the Lord!" Read carefully to find out why. The first stanza (verses 1-3) declares the praiseworthiness of God's name: blessed to the end of time and to the ends of the earth. The second (verses 4-6) recognizes the transcendence of God: exalted so high that he must stoop to even see our earth. But the third (verses 7-8) celebrates the immanence of God: that one so high cares about ones so humble. In fact, he will lift the poor and needy and seat them in places of honor. Does verse 8 seem like an anticlimax? The psalmist quotes here from the song of Hannah (see 1 Sam 2, especially verse 8), the barren woman who was heard by God and gave birth to Samuel. Think also of Sarah of old and Mary to come.

In **Amos 5,** the prophet confronts Israel over its economic injustice and hypocritical worship. Analyze this passage. What kinds of injustice have angered God? The "gate" in this passage is the location of the village court, where the elders settle disputes and adjudicate wrongs. Thus justice is perverted in the courts as well as the marketplace. What does Amos say God will do (verses 16-20)? We need to think hard about God's displeasure at our worship when it is not accompanied by emphatic ("rolling down") and enduring ("everflowing") justice and righteousness (verses 21-24).

Matthew probably compiled into one discourse Jesus' various pronouncements against the scribes (copiers and teachers of the law) and Pharisees (enforcers of a strict adherence to the law). Jesus calls his followers to a contrasting way of pleasing God—integrity, modesty, humility—and then launches into a series of prophetic denunciations. For each "Woe . . . ," identify the hypocrisy that Jesus decries. Why do you think he is so exercised over these matters? Could it be his concern for the common people? The pharisaical approach amounts to spiritual oppression. The weightier matters—justice, mercy, faith—are eclipsed by legalistic zeal. Do we preach and practice a piety that in effect elevates us but weighs down others?

Luke 18 gives two parables and a brief scene; each touches on justice. The first (verses 1-8) focuses on persistence and faith in prayer but also reveals God's predisposition to grant justice to those who cry out for it. The second parable (verses 9-14) features a self-righteous Pharisee and a despised tax collector—probably someone who overtaxed the people to line his own pockets. This account underscores God's mercy toward humble penitence and his disregard for proud piety. The third section (verses 15-17) shows Jesus making room for children and mothers with infants; Jesus valued them for what they epitomized. What do we learn from these three texts about seeking justice and loving our neighbor?

RESPONDING TO GOD

What person or group of people do you know that suffers some form of injustice? How can you pray for them this week? What perhaps could you do for them this week?

Closing Prayer. Rise up, O Lord; O God, lift up your hand; do not forget the oppressed. Amen.

Our Hearts

I give you thanks, O Lord, with my whole heart," exults the psalmist (Ps 138:1). From the heart flow our emotions, passions, desires and loyalties. From the heart comes our inward character and outward behavior. From the heart springs our love, whether for God or lover or neighbor. So we must attend to our hearts and to the things on which they feed and to which they attach. As our passages for this week suggest, a healthy heart will be marked by loyalty, integrity, light, receptivity and, above all else, love.

Approaching God. You sent your only Son into the world, O God, that we might live through him; in this is love, not that we loved you, O God, but that you loved us and sent your Son to be the atoning sacrifice for our sins.

Presenting Myself. I will sing of your love and your justice, O Lord, I will sing gratefully to you; and I will study the way that is blameless, O Lord, that I might walk with integrity of heart. Amen.

Inviting God's Presence. Abide in me, Holy Spirit, so that I may abide in you and your love. Amen.

LISTENING TO GOD
1 Samuel 18:1-9; 20:1-42; **Psalm 101;**
Matthew 6:19-24; Matthew 13:1-23;
1 Corinthians 13; 1 John 4:7-21

1 Samuel tells the story of the extraordinary, but complicated, friendship between Jonathan, the son of King Saul, and David, the young hero of Israel. Jonathan is drawn to David after the Goliath showdown (18:1-5). Discovering a soul mate, he pledges his love and symbolizes his loyalty; he even implies an intuitive openness to David taking the throne instead of him. We learn the root of Saul's murderous jealousy toward David in 18:6-9. Read chapter 20 for the heartbreaking turn in the story. Jonathan's naiveté is shattered, his relationship with his father damaged and his friendship with David made difficult. Jonathan's love for David, epitomized in the final scene, mirrors God's covenantal love for us and depicts our capacity for deep, open-hearted relationships with one another.

David outlines in **Psalm 101** the kind of king he aspires to be. He intends to be loyal to his Lord and to ensure justice for his people; he promises to study God's ways and walk in them. This means integrity of heart over against those who are perverse in heart (acting evilly) and proud in heart (acting arrogantly). David knows that he needs to guard his heart from any influences that will debase it and, by implication, to feed his heart with those things that will nourish it (see Phil 4:8). David pledges to surround himself with honest advisers and to deliver justice in his daily judicial hearings.

We return to Jesus' Sermon on the Mount in **Matthew 6** (see week eleven) to examine three teachings that pertain to the loyalty of our hearts. In each case, Jesus presents a choice between two options. In the first, we must choose which treasure gets priority in our lives: earthly goods (material wealth) or heavenly "goods" (moral wealth). In the second, we must choose what kind of eye we will have. The meaning of this enigmatic metaphor is debated, but it relates to health or soundness of vision; depending on what we set our hearts on, we will walk in either light or darkness. In the third teaching, we must choose who or what will get our allegiance. If we devote ourselves to mammon (Aramaic for "possessions," "wealth") we cannot also serve God. Our hearts cannot be divided; we must decide. In what way do these stark words strike you today?

Jesus' parable of the sower in **Matthew 13** might more aptly be titled the parable of the soils. It is about the condition of our hearts. When we hear teaching about the kingdom of God, how do we respond? Is the soil of our heart soft and fertile? Or is it hard (no comprehension) or shallow (no commitment) or weedy (no contentment)? The disciples puzzle over the nature of parables, how they both illuminate and obscure at the same time, and Jesus quotes Isaiah 6:9-10 in response. But notice that when they ask, he reveals more. So it is for us: if our hearts are hungry to understand and eager to obey, we'll be given insight and fruitfulness.

Paul's famous chapter on love, **1 Corinthians 13,** fits into his extended discussion of the use (and abuse) of spiritual gifts in the Christian community (1 Cor 12; 14). This lyrical passage is often quoted, especially at weddings, but seldom studied. Read it carefully today as a meditation on the importance, character and enduring nature of *agapê*, or selfless, love. No matter how powerful our exercise of spiritual gifts or how sacrificial our giving, without love we amount to nothing. Study Paul's exposition: how love acts and how it does not act. How do you stack up against this description? Think of those who love you in these ways. To grow in love is to enlarge our hearts with the presence of Love himself.

The epistle of **1 John** weaves a tapestry of themes, love being chief among them. Trace the threads in chapter 4 of God's love for us, our love for God and our love for one another. How do they interweave? What do these truths have to do with our hearts? If our hearts are free of fear, they are free to love. To abide in God (and he in us) is to abide in love.

RESPONDING TO GOD

In meditating on the shape of love from 1 Corinthians 13, choose one person in your life that you want to love in this way this week.

Closing Prayer. Create in me a clean heart, O God, and renew a right spirit within me. Amen.

Forgiveness

This week, to hospitality, generosity and justice we add a fourth imperative to the cycles of love for neighbor: forgiveness. How hard to forgive someone who has wronged us, who has hurt us, who obviously hates us! At the same time, how unbelievably good to be forgiven by someone we have deeply wronged. Of course, our motivation and ability to forgive others derives from the great forgiveness we have received from God through Christ. His grace to us is so great that we can even choose to love our enemies—as he did.

Approaching God. Yahweh, Yahweh, you are a merciful and gracious God, slow to anger and abounding in steadfast love and faithfulness, keeping steadfast love for the thousandth generation, forgiving iniquity and transgression and sin, yet by no means clearing the guilty, visiting the iniquity of the parents upon the children to the third and fourth generation.

Presenting Myself. I bow my head toward the earth, O Lord, and worship you; pardon my iniquity and sin that I might be part of that great throng of people whom you will take to yourself as a rightful inheritance. Amen.

Inviting God's Presence. If I have found favor in your sight, O Lord, I pray let your presence go with me this day and bless me in all that I say and do, for your name's sake. Amen.

LISTENING TO GOD

Genesis 32—33; **Exodus 33:12—34:9;**
Psalm 103; **Matthew 5:38-48;**
Matthew 18:21-35; Romans 12:14-21

Genesis 32—33 is a story of forgiveness. Years earlier, Jacob had cheated his brother Esau out of his rightful blessing from their aged father (see Gen 27). Jacob then fled into exile to escape Esau's fury. Now Jacob is returning home and about to face his brother. Graciously, Esau forgives his brother (compare the scene in 33:4 with Jesus' parable of the prodigal son in Luke 15). From Jacob's point of view, Esau has acted like God (verse 10). In fact, does not Jacob, after praying with a contrite heart (32:9-12), encounter God in a grace-filled, identity-changing way? The gifts previously offered in fear to appease Esau are now extended in joyful gratitude. Likewise, we give ourselves to God not out of fear of his punishment but in response to his grace.

The situation in **Exodus 33** is this: in his displeasure over the golden calf debacle (see Ex 32), God has announced that he will no longer accompany the people to the Promised Land. Moses effectively intercedes for the people and also seeks for himself a deeper encounter with God. God agrees to give him a glimpse his glory (literally "weight") and greater knowledge of his name, Yahweh ("I AM WHO I AM"—Ex 3:14), and thereby his character. Exodus 34:5-9 portrays the encounter itself. What does God proclaim about himself? God's character predisposes him to mercy and steadfast love, although in his holiness he will not forestall all consequences of evil and sin. Moses rightly responds with awe and worship; God pardons the people and renews his covenant love.

Psalm 103 reminds us this week of God's great mercy that moves us to also show mercy. For comments, see week four of Epiphany.

Jesus' teachings about nonretaliation and love for enemies in **Matthew 5** may strike us as the two most unsettling portions of his Sermon on the Mount. As seen in Leviticus 24:19-20, the law allowed (and at the same time limited) punishments to the point of equivalence. But Jesus forbids us (at the personal level, not the judicial) from taking vengeance

into our own hands: we must not respond to evil—insult, theft, abuse—
with evil. And this goes even for our enemies. We cannot limit our love
to "neighbors," or those like us in nationality, ethnicity, faith and so on
(see Lev 19:17-18); we must also actively love "strangers" and even those
who are against us. How would Jesus have us do this? Why would he? In
what way does love for enemies make us like God? As you grapple with
these teachings, does a particular "enemy" come to mind? How should
you apply Jesus' teachings in relation to that person?

Peter asks Jesus a question in **Matthew 18** about how many times we
should forgive the same person. Surely there is a limit. But Jesus' answer
means unlimited forgiveness. (For an interesting contrast, see Gen 4:24.)
How does the parable reinforce Jesus' point? Of course, we are like the
servant who has been forgiven a tremendous, impossible-to-pay debt. Will
we forgive those who owe us? Clearly Jesus means business on this matter
of forgiveness, as emphasized by the phrase he taught us to say every time
we ask God to forgive us: "as we forgive those who sin against us."

In week twelve, we identified marks of a Christian such as hospitality
and generosity by looking at **Romans 12**. This week we look at the conclusion of this chapter for further instructions on relating to others, especially those outside the community of Christ. In four cases where Paul
prohibits a negative behavior against our enemies, he also enjoins a positive one. Identify and think about each of these pairings. We are not at
liberty to curse or retaliate or take revenge; rather we are called to bless
and do good and show kindness. Our hearts must not become poisoned
but remain compassionate and humble. In this way, radical to be sure,
we embody the love of God who sent his Son to suffer and die for us,
even while we were enemies (Rom 5:6-11).

RESPONDING TO GOD

Is there anyone in your life right now that you need to forgive for some
wrong against you?

Closing Prayer. As you have forgiven me an enormous debt, O merciful Father, enable me by your Spirit to forgive those who owe me in any
way. Amen.

Our Souls

We reflect this week on our souls, that part of ourselves that pertains most directly to spirit and indeed to God's Spirit. In the Bible, the concepts of soul *(psyche)* and spirit *(pneuma)* each carry a range of meanings, which at points overlap, as do the concepts of heart and soul. I've made no attempt here to sort out these distinctions, but rather have chosen Scriptures that encourage us to take care of our souls, that interior aspect of our being where the Holy Spirit dwells and we experience intimacy with God and even mystical encounters with his presence. If we do not tend to our souls, how can we love God fully?

Approaching God. As a deer longs for flowing streams, O God, so my soul longs for you; my soul thirsts for you, the living God. When shall I come and behold your face?

Presenting Myself. Here I am, gentle Lord: you know the state of my soul this day, whether disconsolate or weary or calm as a weaned child with its mother; let me come to you now for hope and rest and quiet joy, for you are a refuge for my soul. Amen.

Inviting God's Presence. O Lord Jesus, enlighten the eyes of my heart to comprehend the breadth and length and height and depth of your love, which surpasses knowledge, so that I may be filled with all the fullness of God. Amen.

LISTENING TO GOD

Psalm 42—43; Psalm 131; **Matthew 11:28-30;**
2 Corinthians 12; **Ephesians 1:15-23; 3:14-21**

Psalms 42 and 43 belong together—note the one title, the repeated refrains and the common theme. This remarkable psalm affords us a window into the soul of someone who feels far from God's presence—perhaps a worship leader stranded in the north near the source of the Jordan, far from the temple where the great festivals of worship take place. Read the psalm several times and let yourself identify with the speaker. Meditate on the themes of spiritual desolation: thirst for God, doubt-raising taunts, oppressive adversaries, God's seeming absence, discouragement. Then dwell on the notes of spiritual consolation: memories of exuberant worship and hope of such again, God's steadfast love and listening ear, the light and truth that lead to God. As a river's head-waters thunder toward the roaring ocean, let yourself cry from the depths of your soul to the one whose deep love is your eternal home.

Psalm 131 is disarmingly short. Three verses: the first on what we don't want to be like, the second on what we do what to be like and the third a declaration of faith. What dangers to the soul are implied in verse 1? David seems to be rehearsing a posture of humility in relation to others and contentment in relation to his situation—over against pride and presumption. He aspires to have a calm and quiet soul. What does his surprising analogy to a weaned child with its mother suggest? He pictures a soul that is contented and trusting, not needy and grasping, a childlike security rather than an infantile dependency. Such a soul, even in disquieting circumstances, will choose to hope in the Lord.

Jesus invites all who are soul-weary to come to him for rest. His call in **Matthew 11** echoes the description of God in Psalm 23: the good shepherd who leads us to restful places and restores our souls. Most immediately, Jesus speaks to those burdened by the demands of keeping the law as prescribed by the scribes and Pharisees (recall Mt 23 in week fourteen). To learn from Jesus and follow him—the definition of a "disciple"—yields a different effect: his expectations rest on us lightly because they come with loving grace. Although he is our Lord, Jesus does not "lord it over us." With gentleness he takes care of us, body and soul, even as he leads us. Respond to his invitation today.

In **2 Corinthians 12,** Paul obtusely speaks of "visions and revelations." He reluctantly "boasts" of this experience as part of a deliberate strategy to defend his credentials and credibility to the Corinthians, who are being swayed by other unreliable teachers. I include this passage as an example of a mystical or ecstatic spiritual experience. Paul is purposely vague about what he saw and heard. We are immediately reminded of similar experiences by other biblical figures: Moses (Ex 33), Elijah (1 Kings 19), Isaiah (Is 6), Ezekiel (Ezek 1), Jesus and three disciples (Mt 17), Stephen (Acts 7) and of course John (Revelation). Give thought to Paul's "thorn in the flesh" that is given to prevent him from being too "elated" (proud? conceited?) and to teach him the sufficiency of God's grace.

We return to **Ephesians 1 and 3** (see weeks two and four of Easter) to meditate on Paul's prayers for the church as they relate to our souls. Consider again the gift of "a spirit of wisdom and revelation" by which the eyes of our hearts are enlightened (1:17-18). Or ponder how we are strengthened in our inner being with power through his Spirit, know the love that surpasses knowledge and are filled with all the fullness of God (3:16-19). To pray for and pursue these blessings for our souls pleases God. In what ways have you experienced such things in your soul? In what ways do you desire to do so?

RESPONDING TO GOD

This week, do your best to set aside some extended time alone for quiet contemplation; give attention to the state of your soul, and open yourself to God's loving and healing presence.

Closing Prayer. Send out your light and your truth, O Lord; let them lead me into your holy presence, that I may worship you with exceeding joy and praise you with beautiful music, O Lord my God. Amen.

Vocation

The word *vocation* derives from Latin *vocatio*, which means "calling." Simply put, a calling requires a caller and implies a purpose. Nowadays we tend to use *vocation* to refer to a career. Fair enough, but the idea goes much deeper. First, Genesis 1 and 2 reveal the essence of our common calling: to care for and cultivate the earth and to develop human community—creation and procreation, work and family, culture and society. Second, the New Testament describes our shared calling as Christians: to believe in Christ, to live worthy of the gospel, to walk in love, to bear witness and so on. Third, we find examples of individuals called to specific paths or tasks by God: Abraham, Moses, Esther, Jeremiah, Mary and Paul, to cite a smattering. Each of us, then, has a multilayered vocation.

Approaching God. O Lord, you have been our dwelling place in all generations. Before the mountains were brought forth or ever you had formed the earth and the world, from everlasting to everlasting, you are God.

Presenting Myself. Before you, Eternal God, I am like a dream that evaporates upon waking, I am like the grass that flourishes in the morning but withers by evening; you see my iniquities and your light exposes my sins; my years are numbered and will come to an end like a sigh. Have compassion on me, O Lord, have compassion on your servant. Amen.

Inviting God's Presence. Satisfy me with your steadfast love so that I may rejoice and be glad this day and all my days; let me see your work in my life and the world, O Lord, let me see your power at work. Amen.

LISTENING TO GOD
Genesis 1:24-31; 2:1-25; Psalm 90;
Luke 5:1-11; Acts 16; Romans 8:28-39;
Colossians 3:22-41

Review from **Genesis 1 and 2** the spare but pregnant description of God's intentions for human creatures made in his image. What does he want us to do? What large and long-term implications unfold from these simple mandates: have dominion, be fruitful, fill the earth, till the ground, keep the garden, name the animals? Since God works, we work; since he creates, we create; since he cultivates, we cultivate; and since he loves, we love. What dignity and responsibility he affords us! The tragedy of Genesis 3 does not obviate these dimensions of our human vocation; it only makes them more difficult and dangerous.

Psalm 90, attributed to Moses, ends with a double prayer for God to prosper our work. Everything that leads up to this request serves to set the conditions for understanding human work: God's eternal being, God as source of our being, our finitude as creatures in a fallen world, our limited wisdom, our moral culpability and our need for God's compassion and patient guidance. Acknowledging all of this, we ask for eyes to see what God is doing in the world—his work—and then we request God's favor on our work, which by implication should align with his. This psalm affirms our vocations but insists on a posture of humble dependence; let its wisdom sink in.

Luke 5:1-11 is a study in how Jesus shrewdly calls Simon (Peter) and his fishing buddies to leave the family business and join him in his mission. First, how do you read Simon's response to Jesus' request to put out into deep water and let down the newly cleaned nets? Humbly compliant? Slightly sarcastic? The clue comes in verse 8, where Simon is on his knees among the flopping fish. Simon—and the others—are caught in Jesus' net! Put yourself in the same boat. Do you believe that Jesus has authority and power in your area of vocational expertise? Do you ever pray and "consult" him concerning your work? Furthermore, do you believe he can make you effective in "catching people"—his line of work, so to speak?

Acts 16 records Paul's travels in Asia (modern Turkey) and Macedonia and yields subtle insights on how God calls and guides us. First, observe the instructive variety of ways by which things come about: recruitment (v. 3), simple initiative (vv. 6, 8) veto by the Spirit (vv. 6-7), a night vision (v. 9), a serendipitous encounter (vv. 13-14), annoyance (v. 18), manipulation of the judicial system (vv. 19-24), divine intervention by earthquake (v. 26) and political maneuvering (v. 37). What do you make of this variety of means? In addition, reflect on how two people, by virtue of their vocations (textile merchant and prison guard), are each in a position to help advance the gospel.

Chew on the theological meat of **Romans 8:28-39.** First, Paul assures us of the profound promise of God to bring some redemptive good out of even our worst sufferings. Do you need to trust in this promise just now in your life? Paul further assures us of the powerful implications of being called by God: this chain of divine intentions is anchored in God's gracious love and ends in our transformation. Finally, let yourself revel in the soaring exposition and celebration of God's love for us in Christ. This is the destiny to which we're irreversibly called!

Setting aside for a moment our rightful revulsion to slavery, read in **Colossians 3** Paul's words to slaves and masters in the context of Roman society and transpose them into principles for the workplace of today. What does this say to us as employees? As employers or supervisors? Where does God come into the picture with regard to your work responsibilities?

RESPONDING TO GOD

What is one thing you have learned about vocation that has a direct bearing on how you should think or go about your work, whether in your paid job or in your home or in your community?

Closing Prayer. Let your favor be upon me, O Lord my God, and prosper for me the work of my hands—O prosper the work of my hands!

Daily Bread

God cares about our bodies. He knows we require rest and replenishment each day. As creatures, we are made to need daily bread and nightly sleep. Indeed, Jesus teaches us to ask the Father for our daily needs. For our part, of course, we must actually turn in at a reasonable hour and sit down for healthy meals. We look to God not only for daily sustenance for our bodies and minds but also for food and rest for our souls, as this week's passages remind us. In both respects, his mercies are new every morning (Lam 3:22).

Approaching God. I remember, O Lord, that you have rescued me from my enslavement to sin and death, just as you once delivered your people from Egypt; I remember, O Lord, how during difficult times you have protected me and provided, just as you once fed your people in the wilderness; and I remember, O Lord, that you have brought me into good situations and blessed me, just as you once led your people into a land of abundance; today I remember, O Lord.

Presenting Myself. I will not say that my own abilities and hard work have gotten me to where I am; rather, O Lord, it is you who gives the power to succeed and the wherewithal to gain wealth; therefore I will live by your Word and walk in your ways, ever in awe of you, O Lord.

Inviting God's Presence. Unless you are working, O Lord, I work in vain; unless you are watching, O Lord, I watch in vain; so let me trust in you as I work and rest in you as I sleep. Amen.

LISTENING TO GOD
Exodus 16; **Deuteronomy 8;** Psalm 3;
Psalm 127; Mark 1:29-39; Mark 8:1-21

Exodus 16 gives the fascinating account of God providing food for the Israelites during their desert sojourn after the exodus from Egypt. While there are speculations about the natural phenomena that may be in view here (migratory quail, honeylike excretions of Sinai insects), the clear emphasis falls on God's miraculous provision. What spiritual lessons do we learn? Mull over the emphasis here on daily sufficiency rather than accumulated surplus. What do you make of God's insistence on the "solemn day of rest"? Why does God have them preserve a jar of manna for display to posterity? Does this passage connect with your own life?

Moses puts the experience of receiving daily manna in perspective in **Deuteronomy 8.** He warns the people of the great danger of forgetting God in the midst of prosperity. Pay attention to God's intention for his people: to enjoy an abundant, self-sustaining existence in a fertile land where they can "eat bread without scarcity." So what is the danger? Can you identify with the tendency to believe that what we have comes from our own hands? Think again about the point of these wilderness experiences. It was not just about bread (or water or clothes or health) but about a vital trust in the living God and his life-sustaining Word. How does this passage relate to you?

The context for **Psalm 3** is David's grievous flight from Jerusalem into the wilderness to escape the forces led by his son Absalom, who seeks to usurp the throne (2 Sam 15). As in many of his psalms, David voices here both an urgent cry for God's protection and a confident affirmation of God's faithfulness. The image of lying down to sleep and waking the next morning secure in the sustenance of the Lord is striking. He seems able to release the one day in peace and receive the next one in hope (see also Ps 4:8).

Psalm 127 also commends an anxiety-free life, but here the focus is on how we approach work rather than how we contend with adversaries. Ponder the point in verses 1-2. There seem to be two ways of working:

anxious, self-reliant striving or confident, God-dependent effort. God warns us against the vanity—both the pride and the futility—of driving ourselves in our work. He wants us to have a healthy rhythm of work and rest, a wise balance of responsibility and trust. In the second half of the psalm, we find the contrasting picture: fruitfulness that comes not from anxious labor but the pleasurable intercourse of lovers and the effortless process of gestation.

Read in **Mark 1** about an extraordinary day of "work" for Jesus, especially after the sabbath sun sets. Why do you think Jesus gets up so early to pray the next morning? When his new disciples, who have apparently slept in, track him down, they are abuzz with the excitement and openness in the village; they want to seize the moment. But Jesus calmly ignores their anxious lobbying and announces plans to move on. Is there a connection between Jesus' discipline of morning prayer and his discernment of what he should do next? His "daily bread" includes alertness to the Spirit and attention to the words of the Father. Likewise for us.

In **Mark 8** we read of a second miraculous mass-feeding by Jesus, this time satisfying four thousand people (perhaps in Gentile territory) in a manner much like the episode with five thousand in Mark 6. We scratch our heads at the sign-hungry Pharisees—what else do they need to see? But then, apparently, there is something the disciples do not yet "see," as evidenced in their exchange with Jesus in the boat. What do they fail to understand about Jesus? What about you? How deep does your confidence in his compassion and power go?

RESPONDING TO GOD

First, very simply, are you eating well and getting your rest? Second, are you letting God feed you each day from his Word and refresh you by his Spirit?

Closing Prayer. O God, I look to you to fully satisfy my every need according to your riches and glory in Christ Jesus. Amen.

Stewardship

One way to fruitfully understand our work is through the lens of stewardship. A steward exercises responsibility for something that belongs to another. An owner delegates someone to take care of or manage her property or affairs or personnel. Whether a parent secures a babysitter or a restaurateur hires a manager or an investor relies on a financial adviser, something valuable is being entrusted to the other person. Rightfully, the steward is held accountable for his or her diligence and effectiveness. Ultimately, of course, God is owner of all things and assigns responsibilities to us: to care for (his) creation, to look after (his) people, to make good use of abilities and resources (given by him), and to exercise spiritual capacities (empowered by his Spirit). In these ways, we join him in his work and share in his joy.

Approaching God. The heavens are your heavens, O Lord, and from them you do whatever you please, but the earth you have given to human beings as your stewards; therefore I bless you, O Lord, from this time on and forevermore. Amen.

Presenting Myself. Not to me, O Lord, not to me, but to your name give glory, for the sake of your steadfast love and your faithfulness; I stand in awe of you, O Lord, and in you I put my trust.

Inviting God's Presence. Be mindful of me, O Lord, for you bless those who fear you, both small and great. Amen.

LISTENING TO GOD

Psalm 115; Ezekiel 34:1-16; Matthew 25:14-30;
Luke 12:35-48; 1 Peter 4:7-11

Psalm 115 contains the remarkable statement, "The heavens are the LORD's heavens, but the earth he has given to human beings." Putting it simply—and also grandly—we've been entrusted with this planet and all of its cultural potential, from tools to tapestries to telecommunications. God gives us the freedom and the responsibility of stewardship. How does this psalm set our stewardship in its proper frame? We need to think carefully about our susceptibility to the two great dangers exposed here: to go about our business for our own glory and to become subject to the things we produce. As stewards, we must remember who first made the world and then asked us to make something of it; only by trusting in him can we do this well.

The stewardship in view in **Ezekiel 34** is responsible servant-leadership by those in positions of power, whether political or spiritual. Exiled in Babylon, the prophet writes this indictment after hearing news of the fall of Jerusalem (Ezek 33:21). The shepherds of Israel represent the long line of unfaithful and self-serving kings. Mull over the shepherd metaphor for what it says about good (and bad) leadership. Note especially the language emphasizing that the people belong to God and that the leaders are delegated responsibility by God. So when they fail, God steps in and acts as the true shepherd; he gathers, he heals, he feeds and he brings justice. Meditate on Jesus' claim to be the good shepherd (Jn 10) in light of this passage. See also Peter's exhortation to spiritual shepherds (1 Pet 5). Whom has God entrusted to your care or leadership? Are you a good shepherd?

Jesus tells a parable in **Matthew 25** about stewardship. The context concerns readiness for the end days and the certain (though unannounced) coming of the Son of Man. We don't wait passively or watch pensively but rather get busy making the most of whatever God has entrusted to us for the sake of his kingdom. In the parable, a talent refers not to an ability (although the English meaning derives from this parable) but to a very large sum of money, about fifteen years' worth of income. Reflect on the serious responsibility that comes with stewardship but also the grace and generosity that God shows.

We turn to **Luke 12** for three more parables about readiness and faithfulness. The first (verses 35-38) calls for us to be alert and ready to receive our master. Note the striking reward: the servants are served by the master—reverse hospitality! The second short parable (verses 39-40) makes the obvious point that since we do not know when Jesus will come; we should always be prepared. The third (verses 41-48) uses the stewardship motif, combining the two types of responsibility discussed above: using resources and caring for people. How does verse 48 sum up the idea of stewardship?

We revisit here a short passage from **1 Peter 4** (see week five) because it underscores the notion of stewardship—in this case, the stewardship of God's manifold grace. God has distributed gifts to us, whether natural or supernatural, to be used in serving others. God not only gives an ability, he empowers its use. Notice the familiar emphases in the first few verses: readiness for the end (self-discipline and prayer), love (the greatest gift, given to all) and hospitality (caring for others with resources given to us). Good stewardship of what God entrusts brings God glory.

RESPONDING TO GOD

Take time this week to make an inventory of the various ways in which you are a steward on behalf of God. Think about your resources, your opportunities, your influence, your family, your leadership roles, your talents, your spiritual gifts, your home and your environment. Do you need to renew a sense of responsibility and accountability before God in any of these areas?

Closing Prayer. Help me, O Lord, to be a faithful steward so that on the last day I might hear you say, "Well done, trustworthy servant; you have been trustworthy in a few things, I will put you in charge of many things; enter into the joy of your master." Amen.

Sabbath

To keep the sabbath is to both obey a command and receive a gift. God provided for a weekly day of rest—a special day, a holy day—so that we would have space to focus our attention on him (gratitude, worship, reflection) and be renewed as whole persons (body, mind, heart, soul). Sabbath-keeping puts us in touch with the Story of God. We remember God's work of creation and how he rested and took delight in its goodness. We remember God's work of redemption, how he set his people free from bondage and despair. We remember God's work of resurrection, how he exercises the power to remake all things and give us eternal life. God gave us the sabbath as a weekly blessing, a foretaste of the eternal rest to come.

Approaching God. In six days, O Lord, you made the heavens, the earth and the sea—and all that is in them—and on the seventh day, you rested. Furthermore, with a mighty hand you brought your people out of the land of Egypt where they had been enslaved. Therefore you have blessed the sabbath day and made it holy.

Presenting Myself. This week, O Lord, I will not trample the sabbath by pursuing my own interests or going my own way; rather, I will call the day a delight and honor it by taking delight in you.

Inviting God's Presence. By your gracious mercy, O Lord, cause me to ride on the heights of the earth and let me feast on the promise of your steadfast love. Amen.

LISTENING TO GOD

Exodus 20:8-11; Deuteronomy 5:12-15;
Leviticus 25:1-24; Psalm 92; Isaiah 58:13-14;
Mark 2:23-3:6; Hebrews 4:1-11

Compare the stating of the fourth commandment in **Exodus 20** and **Deuteronomy 5**. What differences do you notice? God gives two great reasons for keeping the sabbath as a distinctive day of rest and worship: in remembrance of God's rest after his work of creation and in remembrance of Israel's deliverance from slavery in Egypt. Exodus emphasizes God's creational blessing in the rhythm of work and rest; Deuteronomy stresses God's redemptive blessing in the relief from oppression and abuse. Meditate on the grace embedded in this command.

The sabbath principle is extended in **Leviticus 25** to encompass a sabbath year of rest for the land and a Year of Jubilee for the whole society. First, consider the sabbatical year (verses 1-7). How is this akin to the weekly sabbath observance? What would be the spiritual and practical implications of such a practice in an agrarian society? Second, study the hallowing of every fiftieth year with a proclamation of liberty (verses 8-24). What truths about God and his expectations for his people are conveyed by such a radical practice? Recall these Ordinary Time themes: ultimate ownership and temporary stewardship, economic justice and social equality, care for creation and trust in the Creator. We find no evidence that Israel ever practiced the Jubilee, but the spiritual and social principles remain valid, as taught by Jesus.

Psalm 92 is designated a "Song for the Sabbath Day." Meditate on it in that light: the call to give continuous praise, the delight in God's creation, the remembrance of God's saving acts, the gratitude for strength (horn) and renewed blessing (oil), and the promise of flourishing in God's presence. Sabbath-keeping keeps us "green and full of sap."

Focus in **Isaiah 58** on the final if-then pronouncement about taking the sabbath seriously. Skim the full chapter for context: God spurns ritual worship practices that are not accompanied by right social practices. What do we learn about sabbath-keeping here? It is not a day to do whatever we please, but neither is it so restrictive as to bring no delight. The blessing of keeping sabbath is twofold: an elevated perspective on life and a feasting on the covenantal provisions of God.

Mark reports back-to-back incidents in which Jesus speaks or acts controversially with regard to the sabbath. In the first, his disciples casually glean a snack. When accused of countenancing a disregard for sabbath laws, by this time highly detailed and restrictive, Jesus cites an episode from David's life where human need trumped religious rules (see 1 Sam 21:1-6; consider also the parallel between Jesus and David as an anointed but not yet recognized king). Absorb the significance of Jesus' teaching about the basic purpose of the sabbath, which he demonstrates in the healing of the withered hand. Contrast Jesus' sabbath instinct—to heal—with that of the Pharisees—to kill.

The writer of **Hebrews** enlarges the idea of sabbath rest to mean a permanent state of settledness, security and peace. First he (or she) highlights in chapter 3 the experience of those Israelites who for reasons of disbelief and disobedience failed to enter "God's rest," or the Promised Land. By analogy, there is a state of spiritual rest available to us now and an eternal rest promised to us later. Study the argument. Could it be that this rest aligns with the ideas we've been examining: working in concert with God's work (Ps 127), taking the easy yoke of Christ (Mt 11) or doing the good works already prepared for us (Eph 2)? And could not the future rest include the joy of working in the new heaven and earth where the burdensome effects of the Fall have been removed? Today, if you are hearing his voice about these matters, do not harden your heart.

RESPONDING TO GOD

This week, give thought to your sabbath practices. Are you satisfied with the way you guard a day each week for rest and renewal? Do you need to make any adjustments in light of hearing God's voice this week?

Closing Prayer. Today, O Lord, I embrace by faith the good news of your promised rest, now and forever. Amen.

Society

From the beginning God designed us to live in relationships: families, tribes, communities, cities, nations. Each level of human society carries great cultural complexity: beliefs, values, mores, rules, structures and, of course, history. Although our fallen state distorts and damages us at each level, part of our work as creatures and as Christians is to seek and shape a society marked by God's shalom—a state of peace, justice, wholeness and human flourishing. In obedience and hope, we invest ourselves in this vision for human society.

Approaching God. O Lord, who may abide in your presence? Who may dwell on your holy hill? Lord God, who is holy as you are holy?

Presenting Myself. I am not holy, O God, but in response to your grace and with the help of your Spirit, I will seek to walk with integrity and do what is right, to speak the truth from my heart, to treat others as I would have them treat me, to love my neighbors as myself. Amen.

Inviting God's Presence. O Lord, make your home in me and let me find my home in you, so that I may freely seek the welfare of the community where you have sent me to live. Amen.

LISTENING TO GOD

Leviticus 19:1-18; Psalm 15; Isaiah 65:17-25; **Jeremiah 29:1-14;**
Matthew 7:1-5, 12; Romans 13:1-10; **Revelation 21:1-8**

Leviticus 19:1-18 elaborates on the Ten Commandments (Ex 20:1-17). See if you can trace them. At the heart of these laws is the call to be holy, given that God is holy (verse 2). Holiness has to do with our moral standing before God and our moral behavior toward others. Holiness is social. Study this passage for the principles of community that reflect God's character. Notice the refrain "I am the LORD," and consider its effect here. Reflect on the closing imperative ("Love your neighbor as yourself") as a summation. If one of these standards convicts you today, respond appropriately.

Psalm 15, perhaps a liturgy for the beginning of worship, stresses the holiness that God looks for in those who worship him, namely social relations of integrity and justice. God's "tent" can be read as the early tabernacle and his "holy hill" as the site of the later temple on Mount Zion, suggesting Israel's formal worship; but "tent" can also invoke the hospitality tradition, suggesting welcome into God's presence and acceptance into his family. Take time to think about each of the "ten commandments" listed. When we live with our neighbors in these ways, we will never be moved, never expelled from our home with God.

In **Isaiah 65,** the prophet paints a picture of the new creation. The city of God will be joyful and its society a delight. Read this vision of the future as a prescription for how to pray and act now ("Your will be done on earth as it is in heaven"). What kind of society should we all be working toward? For starters, in the delightful society, infant mortality is rare and elder care extensive, the economy is just and labor practices are fair, work is meaningful and families are protected, violence is low and collaboration is high. This social justice and peace is God's shalom.

Jeremiah, writing from depopulated Jerusalem to the first wave of exiles in Babylon, warns against a naive confidence in the false prophecies about imminent collapse of the empire and speedy return to Judah. Instead, he counsels them to settle into an engaged life even in the midst of a foreign culture. Think about the profound implications of seeking the welfare of whatever community or city in which we find ourselves, however unhappy our sojourn. For you, what positive investment might this mean in your own community? How can we interpret God's promise of "a future with hope" when trapped in oppressive situations?

We have from Jesus in **Matthew 7** a sharply stated caution and a revolutionary command; if followed, both will deeply affect how we relate to others. The first (verses 1-5) warns against presumptuously judging others—we may be setting the criteria for our own treatment. Don't overlook the reverse idea tucked in here: generosity begets generosity. Jesus' humorous parable makes a serious point. The so-called golden rule in verse 12 is without precedent—all previous formulations were in the negative: "don't do to others . . ." How would widespread adherence to this injunction change society, from neighborhood to nation?

In **Romans 13,** Paul discusses the role of the state and our obligations to it. He outlines the ideal, the state as the instrument of God (but see Rev 13 for the state as the ally of the devil). God delegates civil authority in order to promote good and restrain evil; the state is meant to serve God's purposes. Note the repetition of "God's servant," the same word used for "ministers." What are the implications here for citizens? For government officials? When is it right and necessary to show civil disobedience? Verses 8-10 return to our obligation to love neighbors.

Read with joyful longing the vision of the New Jerusalem in **Revelation 21.** What will life be like in the holy city?

RESPONDING TO GOD

Spend some time this week praying in specific ways for the welfare of your community. What is one tangible action you could do to make your corner of society a bit more the way God intends it to be?

Closing Prayer. Lord God, Alpha and Omega, let your kingdom—your shalom, your new society—come on earth as it is in heaven, as it will be in the New Jerusalem when you make your home among us. Amen.

Beauty

Beauty invites contemplation. After each episode of creation, God appraises his work and finds it good. The trees in the first garden are not only good for food, they are pleasing to the eye. God created us with aesthetic sensibilities. We are drawn to the beautiful because the beautiful points us to God and moves us to worship. Of course, we can also idolize beauty, as Ezekiel 16 dramatizes. So in addition to daily bread and sabbath rest, God invites us to contemplate the beautiful—and, we could add, the good and the true. Our texts for this week highlight beauty in several ways: the artistic craftsmanship of the temple, the loveliness of a royal wedding, the impressive skyline of a city and the luminous glory of God's face.

Approaching God. Great are you, O Lord, and greatly to be praised; your holy mountain, beautiful in elevation, is the joy of all the earth and your royal city is the citadel for all of the people; your throne endures forever and your name, O God, like your praise, reaches to the ends of the earth. Amen.

Presenting Myself. Come, my heart says, and seek his face! Your face, O Lord, do I seek.

Inviting God's Presence. One thing I ask of you, O Lord, one thing I will seek after: to live in your presence all the days of my life so that I may behold your beauty and learn your ways. Amen.

LISTENING TO GOD

2 Chronicles 2—4; **Psalm 27;** Psalm 45; Psalm 48;
Mark 9:2-8; **Revelation 21:9-21**

The opening chapters of **2 Chronicles** describe in exquisite detail the building of the first temple under Solomon. Chapter 2 tells of the preparations, chapter 3 of the construction and chapter 4 of the interior furnishings. As you read, pay attention to the elements of beauty: the design, the materials, the artisanship, the intricacy and the extravagance. Why such expensive beauty? What does this say about our God? What does this say about us?

David pens **Psalm 27** in the midst of a stressful situation. He is highly conscious of his many adversaries, but he proclaims his confidence in God as his source of protection and salvation; he vows to wait in faith. Yet deliverance is not his deepest desire. What does he seek? To see the face of God is to behold beauty. In God's presence, we glimpse the glory of his being, we see the goodness of his character and we learn the truth of his ways. Make this psalm your prayer today.

Psalm 45 is a royal wedding song written for the king and the woman he is set to marry. It reads like the Song of Songs. Look for all the elements of beauty, from the handsome groom to the radiant bride, from the colorful (and fragrant!) robes to the music in the ivory palace. A literary tribute for an extravagant celebration. But even more is implied here. The poet startlingly addresses the king "O God" in verses 6-9—verses quoted in Hebrews 1:8-9 in reference to Christ. This and other messianic hints fit with the portrayal of God as bridegroom to his people; it is we who ultimately are presented as his beautiful bride (see Ezek 16; Eph 5; Rev 21).

Psalm 48 combines the beauty of Zion and the glory of the Lord in one celebratory poem. The psalm invites readers to ponder the steadfast love of God even as they marvel at the city of his temple. But on closer reading, this psalm slips into a vision that goes beyond Jerusalem at a given historical moment and begins to anticipate the eternal city in which God is enthroned and from which the praise of his name goes out to all the earth. With the psalmist, ponder this beautiful "sight."

Mark 9. Jesus too feels strongly about Jerusalem, but he laments the city's rejection of his message and foretells the destruction of its magnificent temple. As a counterweight to these dire perspectives, perhaps we do well to review the extraordinary transfiguration of Jesus in Mark 9. I cannot imagine what this experience is like for Jesus, but for the three disciples it is an encounter with luminous beauty. They stand—or rather fall down—terrified and overwhelmed with awe! Think about it—they are eyewitnesses to the majestic glory. (See 2 Pet 1:16-18.)

We return for a second helping of **Revelation 21.** In verses 9-21, the seer is shown the "bride of the Lamb," which turns out to be the holy city coming down out of heaven (talk about mixed metaphors!). Read the description of the New Jerusalem with your imagination fully engaged. What does the imagery convey to you? If nothing else, does it not pulse with beauty? God destines us for a home of exquisite beauty that reflects his own glorious being. Take time to contemplate this vision.

RESPONDING TO GOD

Do you make room in your life for beauty? Do you take time to see it and contemplate it? This week, choose one way to encounter beauty—creation, art, architecture, music, poetry, a person, an idea, an icon—and let that experience stir in you both love and longing for God, the source of all that is good, true and beautiful.

Closing Prayer. O Lord, after Solomon ended his prayer of dedication for the beautiful temple he had built for you, fire came down from heaven and consumed the offerings and sacrifices and your glory filled the temple; when all the people saw this, they bowed down and worshiped you and gave thanks, saying, as I say this day: You, O Lord, are good, for your steadfast love endures forever. Amen.

Culture

Put simply, culture is what we make of the world. The concept of culture is incredibly complex, encompassing all human endeavors and social structures and material artifacts. It certainly means more than "the arts." We are all inescapably embedded in culture. And culture-making is part of what God intended us to do from the start. How we create and shape culture—and how it shapes us—matters to God. We are either using our cultural capacities to honor or dishonor him: we can build tabernacles or craft golden calves, erect Babels or rebuild walls, make war or make music. And the best of what we make of this world will be redeemed and find its place in the world to come.

Approaching God. O Lord, you are the Savior of the world; your victory over sin and death is known to all nations.

O Lord, you are the king of all the earth; your authority is everywhere celebrated with joyful praise. O Lord, you are the judge of all the peoples; your coming will bring about equity and righteousness.

Presenting Myself. O Lord, I desire to contribute to the culture around me, to be like salt, stopping things from going bad and adding flavor to what is good, to be like light, dispelling darkness and enhancing vision; I want my offering to be used in building a place for your presence and glory. Amen.

Inviting God's Presence. Fill me with your Spirit, O Lord, and give me a measure of skill, intelligence, knowledge and creative vision so that I can make something of the world that would be pleasing and honoring to you. Amen.

LISTENING TO GOD

Psalm 98; Genesis 4; **Exodus 35:30—36:7;** Nehemiah 2; Isaiah 60;
Matthew 5:13-16; Revelation 21:22-27

Culture arises in **Psalm 98** with its call to sing to God a new song and praise him with a joyful orchestra. All worship wears cultural clothing. We can read this call to praise in the context of Israel's history—the exodus, the return from exile—but we can also rehearse it in light of Christ—the resurrection, the second coming. Notice which aspect of God receives emphasis in each of the three stanzas (in the first, "victory" includes the idea of salvation). Notice the progression of praise: Israel, all people of the earth, creation itself.

Before reading **Genesis 4,** give thought to God's action in Genesis 3:21. He makes a cultural artifact—clothing—for the man and woman (actually, an improvement on their flimsy fig leaves) in a gesture of protection from the rugged landscape and mercy for their newfound shame. Study chapter 4 for its clues to the beginnings of culture.

The first mention of spiritual gifts in the Bible comes in **Exodus 35.** Examine verses 30-35 for the different ways that God "fills" and "inspires" Bezalel and Oholiab. They're not only gifted with artistic skills and aesthetic intelligence, they're also equipped for teaching and management. In fact, all the artisans receive their skill and understanding from God. The people play their part by freely contributing material resources and treasured possessions. You can read in Exodus 36—40 about the construction of the tabernacle and the making of the ark and other sacred objects. How striking that the biblical narrative includes such an extensive and detailed account of this cultural project.

The story of **Nehemiah** centers on a massive cultural undertaking: rebuilding Jerusalem's wall and revitalizing a city after destruction and decades of desolation. The broken wall symbolizes the defenseless and dispirited remnant of a population. When Nehemiah, a Jew serving in the Persian court, hears of these conditions (chapter 1), he weeps and laments the sins of his people. But chapter 2 tells of his courageous initiative and galvanizing leadership that leads to the rebuilding project. If you read on, you will see Nehemiah addressing additional cultural challenges: external threats, internal dissensions, economic oppression, food distribution, urban repopulation and national spiritual renewal.

Isaiah 60 envisions the gathering of God's people into his holy city in the age to come, a place of light and beauty and glory, the place where God dwells. But read this prophecy especially for its cultural dimension. Who will come to the city and what will they bring? It seems that the cultural wealth of the nations, that is, the best of what humans have designed and created—after a process of purification, no doubt—will be given a place in the new order. Our cultural achievements will somehow make it into the culture of the kingdom to come!

Jesus declares in **Matthew 5** that we are the salt of the earth and the light of the world. Reflect on these metaphors: what is salt good for, and what does light do? No doubt the main meaning of "good works" here pertains to love of neighbor, but it also suggests that our good work in shaping society and making culture benefits others and glorifies God. How can we be salt—preventing decay, adding flavor—and light—dispelling darkness, bringing illumination—in our own culture?

How does the final section of **Revelation 21** echo Isaiah 60? In this city of light and life, how will the cultures of the world be included? Use your imagination: what might be part of the city's cultural glory? What will it be like to live there?

RESPONDING TO GOD

Think about the myriad of ways you play a part in preserving, changing or making culture, whether in your home or your community, whether by your work or your creative expressions. What is one opportunity this week to affect culture so that it is more pleasing or honoring to God?

Closing Prayer. Father in heaven, let my life so shine that others will see my good works—and my good work—and give glory to you. Amen.

Thanksgiving

Our texts this week call us to thanksgiving. We give thanks for the bounty of the earth: common grace. We give thanks for the blessings of Christ: spiritual grace. We give thanks for the promises of God: eschatological grace. We remind ourselves that all we have comes from God, not our own hands (Deut 8:7). We express our gratitude by giving a portion back to God and sharing generously with others. We also celebrate God's generosity by feasting with gratitude in anticipation of the great feast in the age to come.

Approaching God. You, O Lord, are gracious and merciful, slow to anger and abounding in steadfast love; you are good to all, O Lord, and your compassion is over all that you have made; all your works shall give thanks to you, O Lord, and all your faithful shall bless you. Amen.

Presenting Myself. I joyfully give thanks to you, Father, for you have enabled me to share in the inheritance of the saints in the light; you have rescued me from the power of darkness and transferred me into the kingdom of your beloved Son, in whom I have redemption and the forgiveness of my sins; praise and thanks to you, Heavenly Father.

Inviting God's Presence. Fill me this day with a spirit of gratitude, that I may properly bless your name, gracious Lord.

LISTENING TO GOD

Deuteronomy 26:1-11 (C); Psalm 100 (C);
Psalm 145; Luke 17:11-19 (A);
Colossians 1:1-14; Revelation 22:1-7

In **Deuteronomy 26,** Moses gives instructions to the people in anticipation of the future time when they will enjoy prosperity in the land God
had promised. This liturgy of sorts calls for a presentation of agricultural
produce at the place of worship in remembrance and thanksgiving. Study
the creed (verses 5-10) that Moses gives them to say. What would be the
point of rehearsing this history? For us, what would be a comparable set
of affirmations? Finally, notice the joyful fellowship in the celebratory
feast that follows the act of thanksgiving and worship.

The well-known and much beloved **Psalm 100** is a hymn of thanksgiving, as its title indicates. It opens on a note of jubilation, inviting all
the earth into joyful worship. Unpack the good news of verse 3—we can
read it from the viewpoint of ancient Israel and from our vantage point as
Christians. Let this compact but potent psalm reinforce what you know
about the Lord your God, and let it move you to give thanks and bless his
name.

In contrast to Psalm 100, **Psalm 145** is expansive and extravagant
with praise. This final composition of David in the Psalter opens with a
burst of praise for God and his greatness and goes on to speak of his
wondrous works, his gracious character, his glorious rule, his faithful
words, his care for all creatures and his responsiveness to all who call on
him. Examine this psalm as you might a large jewel, turning it slowly so
that the light strikes its many facets and reflects the radiant beauty of the
Lord God. Let the psalm generate gratitude within you and appropriate
its words to bless the Lord, your God and King.

Luke 17 records an incident of healing that highlights the exemplary
behavior of a Samaritan. The man is one of a band of lepers ostracized
from society because of their disease. Jesus heals all of them, but only
this one returns to express gratitude. Why do you suppose this is the
case? Are there blessings from God in your life that you are simply taking

for granted? Take time to give thanks today.

Paul opens his letter to the **Colossians** with a prayer of thanksgiving for them based on the report he has heard. Implicitly, he commends and encourages them. Are any of these true of your experience—faith, love, hope, fruitfulness, grace? If so, be thankful! Then Paul spells out just how he prays for the Colossians. What does Paul desire for them? Again, have you experienced such things in your own life—a fuller understanding of God's will, a greater fruitfulness in your service, a growing strength to endure difficulties, a deeper gratitude for your redemption in Christ and the promise of sharing in the kingdom of light? If so, be thankful!

Return to the end of **Revelation** for this final installment of the vision of the heavenly Jerusalem. Bask in the powerful pull of these images and metaphors. The river of life. The healing of the nations. The goodness of the culture. The justice of the government. The beauty of the face of God. The prospect of reigning with God forever. Let the vision evoke in you waves of longing and prayers of thanksgiving. You can trust these words.

RESPONDING TO GOD

Simply put, this is a week to reflect on God's blessings, physical and spiritual, past, present and future, and express our thanksgiving with joy.

Closing Prayer. Almighty and gracious Father, we give you thanks for the fruits of the earth in their season and for the labors of those who harvest them. Make us, we pray, faithful stewards of your great bounty, for the provision of our necessities and the relief of all who are in need, to the glory of your Name; through Jesus Christ our Lord, who lives and reigns with you and the Holy Spirit, one God, now and for ever. Amen. (Book of Common Prayer)

Christ the King

The kingdom of the world has become the kingdom of our Lord and of his Messiah, and he will reign forever and ever." So declares the angel in John's Revelation (Rev 11:15). And by faith so declare we. While we Americans don't relate easily to the idea of a monarchy, the theme of God's kingly rule pervades the Scriptures, as our texts this week illustrate. This kingdom is not solely a matter of authority, power and majesty but also of justice, righteousness and compassion. The kingdom of God and the rule of Christ stretch from the creation of all things to the consummation of all things. This is a week to contemplate his sovereign glory, pledge afresh our loyalty and renew our longing for the fullness of his reign. Come, Lord Jesus!

Approaching God. O Lord, you reign as king; you are robed in majesty and girded with strength; you have established the world—it shall never be moved—and you have established your throne from of old—you are everlasting!

Presenting Myself. Once I was estranged from you and hostile in mind, acting in evil ways, but then, holy Father, you rescued me from the power of darkness and transferred me into the kingdom of your beloved Son, in whom I now have redemption, the forgiveness of my sins.

Inviting God's Presence. Help me, Lord Jesus, to continue in this faith, established and steadfast, without shifting from this hope that is promised by the gospel and secured by your death. Amen.

LISTENING TO GOD

Psalm 93 (B); **Ezekiel 34:23-31 (A)**;
Daniel 7 (B); John 18:28-37 (B);
Colossians 1:13-23 (C); Revelation 1:1-8 (B)

Psalm 93 starts a sequence of royal psalms (93—99, excluding 94) that declare, "The Lord reigns!" Study this compact psalm, which conveys deep truths in brief words. Notice the use of double and triple expressions (for example, "He is robed . . . the LORD is robed" in verse 1). The psalmist declares God's majesty and strength. God's rule goes back to the very creation of the world and will extend to the very end of time— it is unshakable. What do floodwaters and pounding waves represent? God is stronger, more majestic than any thundering tumult we can imagine. Why the abrupt shift of focus in verse 5? Is not God's glory more than sheer power? Does it not flow also from the rightness of his words and holiness of his character?

We return to **Ezekiel 34** (see week twenty) to read the eschatological conclusion of the prophet's shepherding analogy. Ezekiel envisions God setting up a shepherd-king akin to the ideal of David. Then he speaks of a covenant of peace. Based on these images, what will characterize this future era? Jesus is even now our righteous king and good shepherd, and he will return one day to establish his reign and bring about a universal shalom of safety and security, bounty and blessing, justice and peace.

The vision in **Daniel 7** is couched in apocalyptic language full of mysterious symbolism and fantastical images. Not surprisingly, scholarly interpretations vary widely. As with many prophecies, there is a historical and an eschatological horizon. Read the full chapter to take in the vision, but focus on the "Ancient One" (literally "Ancient of Days") and "one like a human being" (literally "son of man"). Jesus referred to himself as the Son of Man and spoke of coming with the clouds of heaven.

June 18. In a calculating ploy, the Jewish authorities bring Jesus to Pilate's headquarters (note the irony in their concern for ritual purity). John records the terse, inconclusive exchange, built around Pilate's four questions. What do you make of Jesus' answers—or non-answers?

First, Jesus probes Pilate's motive: genuine curiosity or perfunctory prosecution? Then he speaks of his kingdom, but enigmatically, so as to disregard Pilate's categories and assert his own. Reflect afresh on the paradox of God's rule in the midst of this world. Lastly, Jesus points to truth as the heart of his kingdom, not power; by his statement, Jesus turns the tables and interrogates Pilate, who condemns himself by not listening. How about us? Do we belong to the truth?

We return to **Colossians 1** to meditate on its great christological declaration. Give attention in verses 13-14 to the way Paul describes salvation: a rescue from a dark power, a transfer of allegiance, a gift of redemption, a pardon from sin. Study the theologically rich doxology of verses 15-20. Paul proclaims Jesus' preeminence by virtue of his role in creation and his role in redemption; he is the "firstborn" (the unique, privileged one) in both the physical universe through incarnation and the spiritual realm through resurrection; he is Lord of the cosmos and leader of the church; he images God's being and embodies God's fullness. He transforms our own finite, futile lives (verses 21-23).

Read the opening of **Revelation.** They present a vision of Jesus in his kingly glory. Ponder the threefold designation for Jesus in verse 5. Reflect on the threefold work of Jesus in verse 6. Muse on the threefold temporal dimension of the Lord God in verse 8. Let your imagination engage with this stunning vision of "one like the Son of Man," even at the risk of being overwhelmed. Feel the touch of Jesus and hear his words of reassurance as the living one who has power over death, the eternal King!

RESPONDING TO GOD

This week, joyfully worship Jesus as your king and renew your allegiance to him in all things.

Closing Prayer. Lord Jesus Christ, you are the faithful witness, the firstborn from the dead, and the ruler of the kings and queens of the earth; you have loved us and freed us from our sins by your blood and have made us to be a kingdom, priests serving you as our God: to you be glory and dominion forever and ever. Amen.

Epilogue
Full Circle Once Again

Liturgy gathers the holy community as it reads the Holy Scriptures
into the sweeping tidal rhythms of the church year
in which the story of Jesus and the Christian makes its rounds
century after century, the large and easy interior rhythms
of a year that moves from birth, life, death,
resurrection, on to spirit, obedience, faith, and blessing.

EUGENE PETERSON

There is an immense variety of ritual in the official worship of the church.
The Liturgical year is the most comprehensive and profound of them all.
[It] focuses on the three great theological ideas that form the
heart of Christian revelation: divine light, life, and love.

THOMAS KEATING

If you sit with a four-year-old in your lap and read aloud a good story, chances are, when you've finished the last page and closed the book, she will blurt out, "Again!" Children's imagination and delight are inexhaustible. We, however, are prone to boredom and cynicism, always craving the new. "Been there, done that," we chant dismissively. "Same old story," we wearily sigh. And we may be tempted to feel this way about the Christian year. Sure, the first time through may have been interesting, but do we really want to repeat the exercise every year, especially if the church we attend pays it little attention? Like inscribing the same circle over and over on a surface, won't it soon become a rut?

The answer is no. The ancient circle of seasons does not get old and the familiar narrative does not grow dull. Nor will the "recurring patterns of longing and fulfillment, of repentance and grace" become tiresome. With each circuit through the sacred calendar, we enter more deeply into the drama of God's redemption of the world and of us. The Christian year helps us to live inside the Story that grounds us in our truest identity and gives our lives their deepest meaning. We absorb its liberating truth, we embrace its transforming goodness and we revel in its luminous beauty.

The annual seasons stay the same, but our experience of them is different each year since our world is always changing and we ourselves change. And our experience of God is anything but static. While his character never alters, in his infinite creativity he indwells us dynamically and we know his love, holiness, authority, provision, mercy and protection (to echo the Lord's Prayer) in ever fresh ways. So when it comes to living the Christian year, we do well to adopt a childlike eagerness: Again!

At the time of this writing, one liturgical year is ending and a new one beginning. Once again I've come full circle. With the long stretch of Ordinary Time nearing its end, I paused at the start of November to think about the saints who have finished their races and inspired mine. Over the next weeks, the Scripture readings heightened my eschatological longings even as the days grew shorter. Both Reign of Christ Sunday and Thanksgiving Day fell in the final week, yielding a happy combination of praise and gratitude. As these themes carried me over the first Sunday threshold into Advent, I found myself lamenting anew the brokenness of the world and looking for fresh signs of God's shalom. As always, Advent is giving me a timely vantage point for reflecting on the world, my life and God. I am thankful to be reentering the familiar yet full-of-fresh-promise Cycle of Light.

LIGHT. LIFE. LOVE.

I am often struck and at times overwhelmed by the depth and richness of the liturgical tradition—its historical development over the centuries, its diverse expression across the church, its theological underpinnings, its integral relation to congregational worship and its formative influence on so many lives. There is even a term for its study: *heortology*, from Greek *heorte* ("feast") and *logos* ("discourse"). I've learned much in my own investigations, which I have sought to include judiciously in these pages.

I wonder now about you. Perhaps you have used this book to live devotionally through an entire year, including the months of Ordinary Time. Or maybe you have mined the book to better understand the seasons but skipped the devotions or used them selectively. If your church largely ignores the Christian year, observing its rhythms may have felt to you like struggling upstream. Or you may have been swimming with the strong current of your liturgical congregation. But whether all of this seems brand new or old hat, feels liberating or overwhelming, I encourage you to stick with it. Continue to avail yourself of this means of grace. Enjoy the freedom to experiment and find the patterns of observance that work for you. And be patient. Like any new habit, the doing gets easier over time and the dividends grow more rewarding.

The Christian year gives us a panoramic view of the triune God and his Story. But we don't just survey the landscape; we inhabit it. We cling in hope to his promises when our world is falling apart. We welcome his every arrival into our impoverished lives. We marvel at his ongoing revelations of grace and truth. Facing our temptations, we seek to emulate his submission to the Father's will. We lose ourselves at the foot of his cross. At his triumph over evil and death, we cannot contain our joy! We overflow with his living presence, which moves us to love our neighbors as ourselves. Finally, we look for his return in glory and the resurrection of our bodies in the world to come.

In devoting ourselves to Jesus, over time, our stories conform to his Story, our lives to his Life. From him we learn the waiting that enlarges, the giving that enriches and the telling that enlightens. With him we experience the turning that blessedly humbles us, the dying to self that leads to healing and the rising that heartens our whole being. And in pouring out ourselves like him, we receive his transforming power. This is the Christ-centered choreography of the Christian year.

The good news can be summed up in a trinity of declarations: Jesus is the light that darkness cannot overcome. Jesus is the life that death cannot hold. Jesus is the self-sacrificing love that evil cannot fathom. We divide the sacred calendar into cycles, but these great themes flow through every season; they saturate the Story of God from beginning to end: Creation. Covenant. Promise. Incarnation. Kingdom. Golgotha. Resurrection. Ascension. Pentecost. Return. New Creation. A full circle.

Light. Life. Love. To live the Christian year is to be immersed in the oceans represented by these words. May it be so for you, year after year. Amen.

Appendix
Dates for the Christian Year Through 2025

Year	First Sunday of Advent	Year	Sundays in Epiphany	Ash Wednesday	Easter Sunday	Orthodox Easter	Pentecost Sunday
2009	Nov 29	2010	Six	Feb 17	Apr 4	Apr 4	May 23
2010	Nov 28	2011*	Nine	Mar 9	Apr 24	Apr 24	Jun 12
2011	Nov 27	2012	Seven	Feb 22	Apr 8	Apr 15	May 27
2012	Dec 2	2013	Five	Feb 13	Mar 31	May 5	May 19
2013	Ded 1	2014	Eight	Mar 5	Apr 20	Apr 20	Jun 8
2014	Nov 30	2015	Eight	Feb 18	Apr 5	Apr 12	May 24
2015	Nov 29	2016	Five	Feb 10	Mar 27	May 1	May 15
2016	Nov 27	2017	Eight	Mar 1	Apr 16	Apr 16	Jun 4
2017	Dec 3	2018	Six	Feb 14	Apr 1	Apr 8	May 20
2018	Dec 2	2019	Eight	Mar 6	Apr 21	Apr 28	Jun 9
2019	Dec 1	2020	Seven	Feb 26	Apr 12	Apr 19	May 31
2020	Nov 29	2021	Six	Feb 17	Apr 4	May 2	May 23
2021	Nov 28	2022	Eight	Mar 2	Apr 17	Apr 24	Jun 5
2022	Nov 27	2023	Seven	Feb 22	Apr 9	Apr 16	May 28
2023	Dec 1	2024	Six	Feb 14	Mar 31	May 5	May 19
2024	Dec 2	2025	Eight	Mar 5	Apr 20	Apr 24	Jun 8
2025	Nov 30	2026	Six	Feb 18	Apr 5	Apr 12	May 24

*In 2011, use the devotional for Transfiguration Sunday over the last ten days of Epiphany.

Acknowledgments

This book, of course, represents the loving and wise influence of so many people in my life: family, friends, colleagues, teachers, fellow parishioners and countless authors, both ancient and contemporary. I am grateful to God for the riches of such grace.

My first words of gratitude go to my wife, Charlene, for her unwavering support and encouragement in this project. For nearly thirty years her love and loyalty have sustained me. I'm also thankful to Evan for cheering his dad on during more than two years of writing.

I am deeply indebted to my parents, Bubber and Beverly Gross, for laying the foundations for my faith when I was a child, for giving so sacrificially in support of me all my years, for believing in me, praying for me and, above all else, loving me.

Doug and Marilyn Stewart have been friends and spiritual mentors for three decades, and this book reflects much of their spiritual wisdom. Steve and Sharol Hayner have likewise invested in me, offering their care and encouragement from just down the block here in Decatur.

Lauren Winner, friend and fellow traveler in the faith, urged me to write this book. Along the way I have leaned on her for counsel and inspiration. I am grateful to her for writing an insightful and kind foreword.

Cindy Bunch, my editor at IVP, planted the original seed for this book and then patiently tended every stage of its growth, including the necessary pruning. It would not have come to fruition without her.

The enthusiastic encouragement on the book from two experienced writers kept me going along the way: Luci Shaw and Phyllis Tickle, thank you.

Lastly, I wish to thank for their support the people from three important spheres of my life: fellow worshipers at All Angels' Church, especially Nancy, Albert, Carolyn and all from our old "house church"; friends from North Avenue Presbyterian Church, especially Scott, Courtney, Steve and Anne; and current colleagues in InterVarsity, especially Jim, Janet, Dan, Cam, Jimmy, Jason, Andrea, Bruce and Tom.

Additional Resources

Books About the Liturgical Year

Conway Ireton, Kimberlee. *The Circle of Seasons: Meeting God in the Church Year*. Downers Grove, Ill.: IVP Books, 2008. An accessible and appealing introduction to the Christian year through the eyes and experiences of a young mother.

Mathewes-Green, Frederica. *Facing East: A Pilgrim's Journey into the Mysteries of Orthodoxy*. New York: HarperSanFrancisco, 1997. An engaging memoir of entering with her family into Eastern Orthodoxy as told through the lens of one liturgical year in that tradition.

Stookey, Laurence Hull. *Calendar: Christ's Time for the Church*. Nashville: Abingdon, 1996. A theologically robust treatment of the liturgical year with mainline churches primarily in view.

Webber, Robert E. *Ancient-Future Time: Forming Spirituality Through the Christian Year*. Grand Rapids: Baker, 2004. A thorough overview of the Christian year and how it can become formative for our spiritual lives.

Webber, Robert E., ed. *The Services of the Christian Year*. Complete Library of Christian Worship, vol. 5. Nashville: Star Song, 1994. A comprehensive resource for church leaders of all denominations for understanding and using the Christian year in congregational worship.

Books to Enrich Devotional Reflection

Imaging the Word: An Arts and Lectionary Resource. 3 vols. Cleveland, Ohio: United Church Press, 1994-1996. A set of beautiful coffee-table-sized books, corresponding to the three lectionary cycles, combining Scripture texts, quotations, poetry and art for each week of the year.

L'Engle, Madeleine, and Luci Shaw. *Winter Song: Christmas Readings*. Wheaton, Ill.: Harold Shaw, 1996. A compilation of excerpts and poems from the writings of these two well-known Christian literary figures.

Pennoyer, Greg, and Gregory Wolfe, eds. *God with Us: Rediscovering the*

Meaning of Christmas. Brewster, Mass.: Paraclete, 2007. A glossy volume for Advent and Christmas combining art and scriptural meditations from Scott Cairns, Emilie Griffin, Richard John Neuhaus, Kathleen Norris, Eugene Peterson, Beth Bevis and Luci Shaw.

Purcell, Steven D. *Even Among These Rocks: A Spiritual Journey.* Brewster, Mass.: Paraclete, 2000. A poetic sharing of one man's personal Lenten journey, presented in his own calligraphy with generous helpings of art, music and literature. A treasure of a book.

Sourcebook series from Liturgy Training Publications in Chicago. Multiple volumes covering the seasons of the year, providing a wealth of liturgical texts from Scripture, hymns, and the works of church leaders ancient and contemporary.

Watch for the Light and *Bread and Wine.* Farmington, Penn.: Plough, 2001, 2003. Two volumes of readings from a range of literary and theological writers for the Cycles of Light and Life, respectively.

Wright, Wendy. *The Vigil, The Rising* and *The Time Between.* Nashville: Upper Room, 1992, 1994, 1999. Three volumes to cover the cycles of the year with an insightful weave of personal story and spiritual reflection, drawing from a variety of literary, artistic and theological resources.

For a full list of suggested resources, visit the page for *Living the Christian Year* on www.ivpress.com.

Notes

Chapter 1: Discovering Sacred Time

Page 14   *The Downfall of the Lord of the Rings*: J. R. R. Tolkien, *The Return of the King* (Boston: Houghton Mifflin, 1965), p. 307.

Page 15   "God is the larger context": *Eat This Book: Conversations in the Art of Spiritual Reading* (Grand Rapids: Eerdmans, 2006), p. 44.

Page 16   "Holy and gracious Father": The Book of Common Prayer (New York: Church Publishing, 1979), p. 362.

Pages 18-19   "Every service": C. S. Lewis, *Letters to Malcolm, Chiefly on Prayer* (New York: Harcourt, Brace and World, 1963), p. 4.

Page 19   "calendar of celebration": Daniel T. Benedict Jr., *Patterned by Grace: How Liturgy Shapes Us* (Nashville: Upper Room, 2007), p. 15.

Page 25   "Within each [liturgical] season": Dorothy C. Bass, *Receiving the Day: Christian Practices for Opening the Gift of Time* (San Francisco: Jossey-Bass, 2000), p. 86.

Page 28   Add in the dizzying: For a broad survey of how some fifty denominations and church movements regard and practice the Christian year, see Robert E. Webber, ed., *The Services of the Christian Year*, Complete Library of Christian Worship, vol. 5 (Nashville: New Song, 1994).

Page 30   In fact there are many: Laurence Hull Stookey makes this same point in *Calendar: Christ's Time for the Church* (Nashville: Abingdon, 1996), p. 141.

Page 30   *Anamnesis* means the opposite: Stookey, *Calendar*, p. 29.

Page 30   "An active kind of remembrance": Ibid.

Page 31   "I finally got it": Eugene Peterson, *Christ Plays in Ten Thousand Places: A Conversation in Spiritual Theology* (Grand Rapids: Eerdmans, 2005), p. 67.

Page 31   "The great festivals": Stookey, *Calendar*, p. 33.

Pages 31-32   "Beren now, he never thought he was going to get that Silmaril": J. R. R. Tolkien, *The Two Towers* (New York: Houghton Mifflin, 2004), p. 886.

Page 32   "to hear you somehow makes me as merry": Ibid., p. 887.

Page 32   Keeping the Christian year: I'm indebted to Laurence Hull Stookey for this metaphor; see chapter 1 in *Calendar*.

Chapter 2: Advent

Page 37   "Of all types of waiting": Wendy M. Wright, *The Vigil: Keeping Watch in the Season of Christ's Coming* (Nashville: Upper Room, 1992), p. 32.

Page 38   "During the waiting times": Luci Shaw, *Breath for the Bones: Art, Imagination, and Spirit* (Nashville: Thomas Nelson, 2007), p. 119

Page 39   "warm Latin joy": Christopher Hill, *Holidays and Holy Nights: Celebrating the Twelve Seasonal Festivals of the Christian Year* (Wheaton, Ill.: Quest, 2003), p. 67.

Page 39   "The pull between": Ibid.

Page 40   "The strange survival": Ibid., p. 68.

Page 40   Gregory the Great: Ibid.

Page 41   The custom is: For suggestions on celebrating St. Lucy's Day, see Martha Zimmerman, *Celebrating the Christian Year* (Minneapolis: Bethany, 1994), pp. 65-70.

Page 41   Since the seventh century: Thomas J. Talley, *The Origins of the Liturgical Year* (New York: Pueblo Press, 1986), p. 151.

Pages 41-42   Here are the traditional texts: These renderings of the "O" Antiphons can be found in Thomas J. O'Gorman, ed., *The Advent Sourcebook* (Chicago: Liturgy Training Publications, 1988), pp. 102-52.

Page 43   "It declares the promise": Christopher J. H. Wright, *Knowing Jesus Through the Old Testament* (Downers Grove, Ill.: InterVarsity Press, 1992), p. 56.

Page 47   "But we are told": Denise Levertov, *The Stream and the Sapphire* (New York: New Directions, 1997), p. 59.

Page 48   "By patient watchful attendance": Hill, *Holidays and Holy Nights,* p. 65.

Chapter 3: Christmas

Page 62   "Break the confines": David Impastato, ed., *Upholding Mystery: An Anthology of Contemporary Christian Poetry* (New York: Oxford University Press, 1997), p. xxiii.

Page 62   "Him who dwells": A. Jean Lesher, ed., *O Holy Night! Timeless Meditations on Christmas* (Winona, Minn.: Saint Mary's Press, 1998), p. 60.

Page 62   "Blessed mother": *The Prymer: The Prayer Book of the Medieval Era Adapted for Contemporary Use*, trans. Robert E. Webber (Brewster, Mass.: Paraclete, 2000), p. 9.

Pages 62-63   "Today you see": Lesher, *O Holy Night!* pp. 41-42.

Page 63   "This air . . . ": Gerard Manley Hopkins, *Gerald Manley Hopkins: The Major Works*, ed. Catherine Phillips (Oxford: Oxford University Press, 1986), p. 158.

Pages 63-64   "After / The white-hot": Luci Shaw, *Accompanied by Angels: Poems of the Incarnation* (Grand Rapids: Eerdmans, 2006), p. 26.

Page 65   "We take our Christmas": Mary Ann Simcoe, ed., *A Christmas Sourcebook* (Chicago: Liturgy Training Publications, 1984), p. 79.

Page 66   "Christmas is the enfleshment": Laurence Hull Stookey, *Calendar: Christ's Time for the Church* (Nashville: Abingdon, 1996), pp. 106-7.

Page 67   beginning with Louisiana: Penne L. Restad, *Christmas in America: A*

History (New York: Oxford University Press, 1995), p. 96.

Page 69   "the still point": T. S. Eliot, *Four Quartets* (New York: Harcourt, Brace and World, 1943), p. 5.

Page 70   "Brightness radiating": Eugene H. Peterson, *Christ Plays in Ten Thousand Places* (Grand Rapids: Eerdmans, 2005), p. 103

Page 74   "Without poverty": In William Willimon, "The God We Hardly Knew," in *Watch for the Light: Readings for Advent and Christmas* (Farmington, Penn.: Plough, 2001), pp. 141-42.

Page 74   "Our words rush out": Dietrich Bonhoeffer, *The Mystery of the Holy Night* (New York: Crossroad, 1997), p. 43.

Chapter 4: Epiphany

Page 85   In the eighth century: See Adolf Adam, *The Liturgical Year* (New York: Pueblo, 1981), pp. 144-46, and Joseph F. Kelly, *The Origins of Christmas* (Collegeville, Minn.: Liturgical, 2004), pp. 99-101.

Page 85   The initials stand for: Ibid., p. 146.

Page 85   "The holy water": Frederica Mathewes-Green, *Facing East: A Pilgrim's Journey into the Mysteries of Orthodoxy* (New York: HarperCollins, 1997), p. 202.

Page 87   She sets an example: For a detailed commentary on the Magi episode in Matthew and the presentation account in Luke, see Raymond E. Brown, *The Birth of the Messiah* (New York: Doubleday, 1977), pp. 165-201, 435-70.

Pages 89-90 "Before the beautiful": Hans Urs von Balthasar, *Seeing the Form*, vol. 1 of *The Glory of the Lord: A Theological Aesthetics*, trans. Erasmo Leiva-Merikakis (San Francisco: Ignatius, 1998), p. 247.

Page 91   Finally, a teacher: For more on the communal discovery method, see Bob Grahmann, *Transforming Bible Study* (Downers Grove, Ill.: InterVarsity Press, 2003).

Chapter 5: Lent

Page 128   "Bright sadness": Alexander Schmemann, *The Great Lent: Journey to Pascha* (New York: St. Vladimir's Seminary Press, 2001), p. 32.

Page 129   These six weeks: Ibid., p. 33.

Page 129   Nothing but water: Neil Alexander, "An Introduction to Lent," in *The Services of the Christian Year*, Complete Library of Christian Worship, vol. 5, ed. Robert E. Webber (Nashville: New Song, 1994), p. 226.

Page 130   "Christians also saw": Adolf Adam, *The Liturgical Year* (New York: Pueblo, 1981), p. 93.

Page 130   Each of five preceding Sundays: For a brief treatment of these pre-Lenten Sundays, see Schmemann, *Great Lent,* pp. 17-30.

Page 131   This note of joy: For an anecdotal account of Orthodox Lent, see Frederica Mathewes-Green, *Facing East: A Pilgrim's Journey into the Mysteries of Orthodoxy* (New York: HarperSanFrancisco, 1997).

Page 133   Think of Jesus praying: For most churches, Lent ends on Maundy Thurs-
                day evening, thus the Gethsemane scene properly belongs to the Paschal
                Triduum; however, the Lenten theme of temptation and testing comes to
                a powerful climax here.
Page 134   "There is no Lent": Schmemann, *Great Lent,* p. 93.
Page 134   "Christian fasting": Lynne M. Baab, *Fasting: Spiritual Freedom Beyond
                Our Appetites* (Downers Grove, Ill.: InterVarsity Press, 2006), p. 16.
Page 135   After two or three days: For an introductory explanation of the physiol-
                ogy of fasting, see ibid., pp. 97-99.
Page 136   "In a more tangible": Marjorie J. Holmes, *Soul Feast: An Invitation to the
                Christian Spiritual Life* (Louisville: Westminster John Knox, 1995), p.
                71.
Page 138   "Penetrating gaze": Ibid., p. 83.

Chapter 6: The Paschal Triduum
Page 167   "Every Sunday": Laurence Hull Stookey, *Calendar: Christ's Time for the
                Church* (Nashville: Abingdon, 1996), p. 54.
Page 167   "the most holy triduum": Adolf Adam, *The Liturgical Year* (New York:
                Pueblo, 1981), p. 64. See also John D. Grabner, "The Great Triduum," in
                The Services of the Christian Year, Complete Library of Christian Wor-
                ship, vol. 5, ed. Robert E. Webber (Nashville: New Song, 1994), p. 278.
Page 168   "The fast of the eyes": Adam, *Liturgical Year,* p. 66.
Page 168   In recent decades: Stookey, *Calendar,* p. 93.
Page 170   "When an 'official' atheist": Sue Lane Talley, "Holy Week in the Eastern
                Orthodox Tradition," in *Services of the Christian Year,* p. 284.
Page 172   "It symbolized neither": John R. W. Stott, *The Cross of Christ* (Downers
                Grove, Ill.: InterVarsity Press, 1986), p. 76.
Page 172   "This suffering from God": Jürgen Moltmann, "The Feast of Freedom,"
                in *Bread and Wine: Readings for Lent and Easter* (Farmington, Penn.:
                Plough, 2003), p. 148.
Page 174   "He identifies the first": Eugene Peterson, *Christ Plays in Ten Thousand
                Places* (Grand Rapids: Eerdmans, 2005), pp. 195-98.
Page 175   "On the road": Ibid., p. 198.

Chapter 7: Easter
Page 187   "Now as myth transcends": C. S. Lewis, "Myth Became Fact," in *God in
                the Dock: Essays on Theology and Ethics,* ed. Walter Hooper (Grand Rap-
                ids: Eerdmans, 1970), p. 66.
Page 187   "pierces you with a joy": Humphrey Carter, ed., *The Letters of J. R. R.
                Tolkien* (Boston: Houghton Mifflin, 1981), p. 100.
Page 187   "The Birth of Christ is the eucatastrophe": J. R. R. Tolkien, *Tree and Leaf*
                (Boston: Houghton Mifflin, 1965), p. 72.
Page 191   "Extends its beams": Marjorie Proctor-Smith, "How to Celebrate the
                Fifty Days," in *The Services of the Christian Year,* Complete Library of

Christian Worship, vol. 5, ed. Robert E. Webber (Nashville: New Song, 1994), p. 376.

Page 191   The origin of the word *Easter*: Adolf Adam, *The Liturgical Year* (New York: Pueblo, 1981), pp. 62-63.

Page 191   "In other tongues": Laurence Hull Stookey, *Calendar: Christ's Time for the Church* (Nashville: Abingdon, 1996), pp. 53-54

Page 194   "One has the picture": C. S. Lewis, "The Grand Miracle," in *God in the Dock: Essays on Theology and Ethics*, ed. Walter Hooper (Grand Rapids: Eerdmans, 1970), p. 82.

Page 195   This is unfortunate: Stookey, *Calendar*, p. 53.

Page 195   "It is almost too brilliant": Madeleine L'Engle, *The Irrational Season* (New York: Farrar Straus Giroux, 1977), p. 99.

Pages 196-97   "The earth shakes": Wendell Berry, *A Timbered Choir* (Washington, D.C.: Counterpoint, 1998), p. 25.

Page 198   "[I] see my ancient carcass": Malcolm Muggeridge, "Impending Resurrection," in *Bread and Wine: Readings for Lent and Easter* (Farmington, Penn.: Plough, 2003), pp. 284-85.

Page 198   "All in our lives": Wendy M. Wright, *The Rising: Living the Mysteries of Lent, Easter, and Pentecost* (Nashville: Upper Room, 1994), p. 162.

Chapter 8: Ordinary Time

Page 224   "to become attentive": Wendy M. Wright, *The Time Between: Cycles and Rhythms in Ordinary Time* (Nashville: Upper Room, 1999), p. 15.

Page 224   She was born Agnes: Most of this biographical information is taken from Mother Teresa, *No Greater Love*, ed. Becky Benenate and Joseph Durepos (Novato, Calif.: New World Library, 1997), pp. 189-206.

Page 224   "I was quietly praying": Ibid., p. 195.

Page 225   "When we handle": Ibid., p. 31.

Page 226   "Do not think": Ibid., pp. 22-23, 27, 30, 71.

Page 226   "You must not be afraid": Ibid., p. 83.

Page 227   "Tension is a creative": Kathleen Norris, *Amazing Grace: A Vocabulary of Faith* (New York: Riverhead, 1998), p. 290.

Page 228   "When worship is our response": Mark Labberton, *The Dangerous Act of Worship* (Downers Grove, Ill.: IVP Books, 2007), p. 14.

Page 231   As theologian Miroslav Volf asserts: Miroslav Volf, *Work in the Spirit: Toward a Theology of Work* (Eugene, Ore.: Wipf & Stock, 2001), p. 91.

Page 232   The color green: Christopher Hill, *Holidays and Holy Nights* (Wheaton, Ill.: Quest Books, 2003), p. 147.

Page 232   For over a thousand years: Adolf Adam, *The Liturgical Year* (New York: Pueblo, 1981), pp. 167-68.

Page 232   This feast day: Laurence Hull Stookey, *Calendar: Christ's Time for the Church* (Nashville: Abingdon, 1996), p. 137.

Page 235   "Those who can": Dorothy C. Bass, *Receiving the Day: Christian Practices for Opening the Gift of Time* (San Francisco: Jossey-Bass, 2000), p.

43. I have borrowed the phrase "receiving the day" from Bass, who discusses this practice in chapters 3 and 4 of her book.

Epilogue

Page 320   "recurring patterns of longing": Dorothy C. Bass, *Receiving the Day: Christian Practices for Opening the Gift of Time* (San Francisco: Jossey-Bass, 2000), p. 82.

Additional resources for this book
can be found online on the book's page
at www.ivpress.com including

- a Scripture index
- an expanded list of resources
- more on the lectionary
- brief devotions for selected holy days

formatio
TRADITION. EXPERIENCE.
TRANSFORMATION.

Formatio books from InterVarsity Press follow the rich tradition of the church in the journey of spiritual formation. These books are not merely about being informed, but about being transformed by Christ and conformed to his image. Formatio stands in InterVarsity Press's evangelical publishing tradition by integrating God's Word with spiritual practice and by prompting readers to move from inward change to outward witness. InterVarsity Press uses the chambered nautilus for Formatio, a symbol of spiritual formation because of its continual spiral journey outward as it moves from its center. We believe that each of us is made with a deep desire to be in God's presence. Formatio books help us to fulfill our deepest desires and to become our true selves in light of God's grace.